Praise for
PEACERUNNER

"This gripping and wonderful story is personal for me. I was born and raised in Northern Ireland, and as I started my professional acting career in Belfast, the violence of the Troubles was raging. Bruce Morrison and the other heroes (unsung to my mind) of this terrific book accomplished the seemingly impossible and ultimately miraculous! The world needs more stories like this and more men like this. This is a must-read."

—*Liam Neeson*

"*Peacerunner* is a riveting account of the nonviolent tactics used to bring peace to Northern Ireland. Bruce Morrison is a true humanitarian devoted to reconciliation. His commitment to justice and the highest use of political service is an inspiration to us all."

—*John Lewis, US Representative*

"This important and wonderfully human story revolves around one extraordinary American's determination to help end an ancient bloody conflict that people thought would never stop. The light it casts on the intricacies of the Irish Peace Process, especially the American role, is a genuine revelation. Penn Rhodeen's fast-paced account is a joy, like a novel you'd devour for pure pleasure. His deep understanding of the politics and the astute strategies, dogged persistence and interactions grand and subtle between unforgettable characters—from leaders of nations and Nobel Prize winners to political activists and guerrilla fighters—make *Peacerunner* an exceptionally rewarding read. Fascinating and inspirational."

—*J. J. Lee, historian and director of Glucksman Ireland House, New York University, author of* Ireland 1912–1985 Politics & Society *and* The Modernisation of Irish Society, 1848–1928, *and coeditor of* Making the Irish American

"With clarity and insight, Penn Rhodeen's *Peacerunner* illuminates Bruce Morrison's largely unsung role on the arduous path to peace in Northern Ireland. In a sequence of novelistic revelations, the book depicts the true heroes of the story, among them Morrison, Bill Clinton, and George Mitchell, as well as offering dispassionate portraits of the many recalcitrants, from Ian Paisley to John Major, while Sinn Féin's Gerry Adams, despite his links to the IRA, emerges as a pragmatic politician more interested in the future than the past. The historic Good Friday Agreement in 1998 was not the end of the Troubles, but a critical turning point. How and why peace broke out in Northern Ireland, an important story most Americans don't understand, is elucidated cogently and gracefully in Rhodeen's *Peacerunner.* Terrific work."

—*Katharine Weber, author of* The Music Lesson,
The Memory of All That, True Confections, *and*
Triangle *and editor at large of* Kenyon Review

"*Peacerunner* is a terrific new addition to the story of Irish America and the literature of the Irish Peace Process. The story of how Bruce Morrison and other brave and stalwart Irish Americans helped bring peace to Ireland has been told by Penn Rhodeen with remarkable insight and a marvelous cast of characters. And he has written it with such style and momentum that it's great fun to read. All Irish Americans, no matter which side of the conflict our families were on, should read and remember this story—and pass it on with great pride to our children and grandchildren."

—*Loretta Brennan Glucksman, chairman emeritus of*
American Ireland Fund

"Here is an enthralling story of redemption, how one man, our former congressman, picked himself up after a crushing defeat and helped create an international triumph of peacemaking. What Bruce Morrison did in Northern Ireland should stand as a model for helping resolve conflicts all over the globe. You don't have to be Irish to love reading *Peacerunner*."

—*Rabbi Herbert N. Brockman, Congregation Mishkan Israel,*
Hamden, Connecticut

"This is a great and important story, thrilling and beautifully written, about how the world gets better."

—*Rebecca Moore, director of Google Earth*

PEACERUNNER

PEACERUNNER

THE TRUE STORY OF HOW AN EX-CONGRESSMAN HELPED END THE CENTURIES OF WAR IN IRELAND

PENN RHODEEN

BenBella Books, Inc.
Dallas, Texas

BenBella Books, Inc.
10300 N. Central Expressway
Suite #530
Dallas, TX 75231
www.benbellabooks.com
Send feedback to feedback@benbellabooks.com

Printed in the United States of America
10 9 8 7 6 5 4 3 2 1

Library of Congress Cataloging-in-Publication Data
Names: Rhodeen, Penn, author.
Title: Peacerunner : the true story of how an ex-Congressman helped end the centuries of war in Ireland / Penn Rhodeen ; foreword by President Bill Clinton.
Other titles: Peace runner
Description: Dallas, Texas : BenBella Books, Inc., 2016.
Identifiers: LCCN 2015030747| ISBN 9781941631713 (trade cloth) | ISBN 9781941631720 (electronic)
Subjects: LCSH: Morrison, Bruce A.—Travel—Northern Ireland. | Northern Ireland—Politics and government—1969-1994. | Peace-building—Northern Ireland—History—20th century. | Conflict management—Northern Ireland—History—20th century. | Politicians—United States—Biography. | Ex-legislators—United States—Biography. | Clinton, Bill, 1946- | United States—Relations—Northern Ireland. | Northern Ireland—Relations—United States. | BISAC: HISTORY / Europe / Ireland. | HISTORY / Europe / Great Britain. | BIOGRAPHY & AUTOBIOGRAPHY / Political. | POLITICAL SCIENCE / Peace.
Classification: LCC DA990.U46 R49 2016 | DDC 941.60824—dc23 LC record available at http://lccn.loc.gov/2015030747

Editing by Oriana Leckert
Copyediting by Eric Wechter
Proofreading by James Fraleigh and Amy Zarkos
Indexing by WordCo Indexing Services, Inc.
Cover design by Sarah Dombrowsky

Text design by Publishers' Design and Production Services, Inc.
Text composition by Integra Software Services Pvt. Ltd.
Printed by Lake Book Manufacturing

Distributed by Perseus Distribution
www.perseusdistribution.com

To place orders through Perseus Distribution:
Tel: (800) 343-4499
Fax: (800) 351-5073
E-mail: orderentry@perseusbooks.com

Significant discounts for bulk sales are available.
Please contact Aida Herrera at aida@benbellabooks.com.

Dedicated with love and gratitude to my wife

Maria Hodermarska

and to my sons and daughters

Aaron Rhodeen
Alexander Rhodeen
Lily Rhodeen
Annabel Rhodeen
Gabriella Rhodeen

and to Maria's sons

Ethan Jones
Andrézj Jones

CONTENTS

Foreword by President Bill Clinton   xiii

CHAPTER ONE
First Journey to Ireland   1

CHAPTER TWO
Catastrophe: One Averted, One Total   11

CHAPTER THREE
Longshot   21

CHAPTER FOUR
The Troubles: 800 Years in the Making   29

CHAPTER FIVE
Getting the Candidate On Board   41

CHAPTER SIX
When Clinton Wins, the Real Work Begins   57

CHAPTER SEVEN
The Unofficial Peacemakers in Northern Ireland   69

CHAPTER EIGHT
An American Nobody Meets the Elite in Cambridge   111

CHAPTER NINE
Helping the President Go First for Peace   121

CHAPTER TEN

The Road to Ceasefire: It Took Forever
and Happened in a Flash   145

CHAPTER ELEVEN

The British Respond to the Ceasefire: Words, Words, Words   157

CHAPTER TWELVE

Stalemate   171

CHAPTER THIRTEEN

Bill Clinton Comes to the North   179

CHAPTER FOURTEEN

George Mitchell Offers a Way   189

CHAPTER FIFTEEN

After a Year and a Half, the IRA Loses Patience   193

CHAPTER SIXTEEN

All-Party Talks at Last, Good Friday Ahead   209

CHAPTER SEVENTEEN

Finishing Up, Holding It Together, and Starting Out   223

Epilogue   235

Cast of Characters   249

Glossary   261

Index   265

Author's Note and Acknowledgments   279

About the Author   287

FOREWORD

During my campaign for president in 1992, I was invited to attend an Irish issues forum at the Sheraton Hotel in New York City convened by Assemblyman John Dearie to discuss a number of issues important to the Irish American community. The conflict in Northern Ireland wasn't a big part of my foreign policy agenda at the time. But, I knew that I needed to demonstrate knowledge of the issues and to have a credible policy because of Northern Ireland's importance to the Irish American community, especially in New York, where they would comprise a significant part of the electorate in New York's Democratic primary.

I had been interested in Irish politics since the start of the Troubles in 1968, when I was a graduate student at Oxford University. Since then, I had followed the ongoing struggle between nationalists and unionists with more than a passing degree of interest, but, as a long line of American policymakers before me had concluded, it wasn't entirely clear how the United States, with its large and diverse Irish population, could get involved in Northern Ireland without jeopardizing our important relationship with Great Britain. However, the Irish Americans were playing an increasingly well-organized and vital role in our politics, thanks in part to legislation authored in 1990 by Representative Bruce Morrison, a friend of Hillary's and mine from law school, that increased the number of visas available to Irish citizens.

Bruce and other advocates of American involvement helped me prepare for the forum. By 1992 Bruce had accumulated considerable knowledge and experience as a member of Congress from Connecticut, through his membership in the Friends of Ireland and on the Ad Hoc Committee for Irish Affairs and from his trips to Ireland and regular contacts with the people there.

From the beginning of the meeting, it was clear that those who came wanted the United States to play a more active role in brokering a solution to the ongoing conflict in Northern Ireland. In particular, the group pressed me, if elected, to become personally involved in the search, too, and to agree to appoint a special envoy to Northern Ireland. As I said, I was well aware that doing so would present challenges in the relationship with the United Kingdom, which remained of fundamental importance to so much of what I hoped to accomplish in the world, but I thought it was a problem that could be managed.

Over the next several months, Bruce and a few other supporters formed Irish-Americans for Clinton-Gore, a group that would do a great deal to help me win and to ensure that I stuck to my promise to help advance the new Irish agenda. The success of his Morrison visa program and the high regard in which he was held by Irish activists because of it made Bruce the natural leader of this group, and over the next six years, he would put the faith of the Irish to good use, becoming a valuable intermediary in the quest to achieve peace in Northern Ireland.

Peacerunner is the remarkable story of how this came to be and how a private citizen became a trusted interlocutor on both sides of the Atlantic, constantly pushing all the parties to resolve their complicated differences.

As I read Penn Rhodeen's skillful account of Bruce's role in the successful march toward the Good Friday Agreement, it wasn't the ending—an historic peace accord that moved Northern Ireland from warfare to politics—but the remarkable efforts by all parties to secure it that kept me reading from start to finish.

Thanks in no small measure to Bruce's dogged commitment to peace and his willingness to devote years of his life to working with so many others to achieve it, what began as a hope became a central focus of my administration and one of my proudest achievements as president.

I'll always be grateful that after leaving Congress, Bruce found yet another way to serve as a private citizen and that he did it with such tremendous skill, sensitivity, and inspiration. I confess that when I read the book, I learned about a few things he did even I didn't know about! But it was all to the good. I hope you enjoy the story of that remarkable journey by a remarkable man who helped to start it and pushed it along to the very end.

—PRESIDENT BILL CLINTON

CHAPTER ONE

First Journey to Ireland

Derry/Londonderry, Northern Ireland
August 1987

One policeman studied the passport while two of the others aimed their assault rifles straight at the American standing no more than six feet away, facing them. His passport was the special type issued to members of Congress, but in this moment, there didn't seem to be anything special about it. The congressman, Bruce Morrison of Connecticut, made matters worse when he pulled out his notepad and started writing down the identification number of the cop holding his passport. But Morrison couldn't help himself: He'd been a legal aid lawyer, and collecting identification information was instinctive. The cop grabbed the pad and shouted, "What are you doing?"

"I'm taking down your number."

"That's an offense, collecting information about the security forces!"

"I thought that's what the numbers are for."

For Gerry O'Hara, Morrison's host in Derry, being held at gunpoint wasn't a new experience. He watched the exchange, guns on him, too, with a mixture of amusement and alarm that he knew to keep to himself. O'Hara was an official of the Irish political party Sinn Féin, invariably described as the political arm of the outlawed Irish Republican Army (IRA). Because the IRA had been waging a violent campaign for Irish unification since the early twentieth century,

Sinn Féin had been classified as a terrorist organization by the United Kingdom, Ireland, and the United States.

O'Hara, whose insistence that the police use his Irish name, Gearóid O hEára, annoyed them to no end, knew that his Sinn Féin involvement was the reason he and his guests were in this mess. He'd been through it hundreds of times, often facing several stops in a single day. Although he knew from past experience that the cops weren't likely to open fire, he was still concerned that Morrison, glaringly inexperienced with police in Northern Ireland, might inadvertently escalate the situation.

"I remember thinking, 'You don't know what you're dealing with,'" O'Hara later recalled, adding with a bit of wistfulness that Morrison was "only doing what you would do in a normal society."

But in 1987, Northern Ireland was anything but a normal society. The British army had occupied it since the early years of the Troubles, the tense and violent time that began in the late 1960s, when increasingly assertive Catholics began demanding an end to the pervasive discrimination against them in all realms of life, including abuses by the Northern Ireland police force, the Royal Ulster Constabulary (known as the RUC). For more than two decades, the IRA had been engaged in guerilla warfare with the British army, the RUC, and various loyalist paramilitary organizations, all of which reciprocated in full, violent kind. In the July before Morrison's arrival, there had been six killings. The toll for the year would reach nearly a hundred—thirty-nine of them civilians. In such a small country, the effect was profound and terrible: No one felt safe. Violent death could come at any moment.

The RUC, known for its rough treatment of Northern Ireland's Catholic minority, seemed more like an army than a local police force. Its men aggressively patrolled the streets in armored Land Rovers and British Saracen personnel carriers, wielding British army weapons and often decked out in full riot gear.

Morrison had never been to Ireland before, though he'd been in Chile on congressional human rights business and had witnessed how the notorious Pinochet dictatorship imposed its military and police presence on civilian life. In his travels through Northern Ireland, he found the military and police presence in everyday life to be even more oppressive than under Chile's military dictator.

Before the RUC stopped them, O'Hara was giving Morrison and Dennis Prebensen, an American supporter of Irish unification who had invited his congressman to Northern Ireland, a tour of his city.

Because it was his town, O'Hara was at the wheel. He knew that a car with plates from the Republic of Ireland, driven by a local Sinn Féin official and carrying two strangers, could well provoke a police stop. He'd warned his passengers of that possibility and told them that if they did get stopped, they'd follow the standard protocol Sinn Féin had devised to avoid being detained and maybe sent seventy-five miles away to the Castlereagh Holding Centre in East Belfast. "We'd realized," O'Hara later explained, "that the pretext for taking you off to some army barracks for three or four hours was that they needed to search the car. So we developed a tactic of saying, 'Well, if you want to search the car, there's the keys—let me know when you're finished,' and we would walk off."

For his part, Morrison assumed that O'Hara's warnings about getting stopped were exaggerated. He told himself, "It's Gerry's job to tell the American congressman how awful it is. This isn't going to happen." So he was genuinely shocked when things turned bad.

The men were driving on Queen's Quay, a major street running alongside the River Foyle. They were headed through the warehouse district toward Guild Hall, an ornate Victorian symbol of the British Empire and therefore a constant provocation to the Irish. Suddenly it happened, all in a blur: armored Land Rovers, a Saracen troop carrier, O'Hara jamming on the brakes. Memories differ on the precise sequence of the events leading to the stop, but what happened next remains clear to all three: About a dozen heavily armed police piled out, shouting and gesturing angrily as they surrounded the car and rousted the men out. Some were dressed like conventional police, but others looked ready for combat, with helmets, bulletproof vests, and fatigue pants tucked into their boots. Assault rifles were fixed on the captives.

O'Hara, who had been forced facedown over the front of the car, was the reason for the stop. "What are you doing with a terrorist scumbag like him?" one of the cops shouted at the Americans. As more questions came flying at Morrison, O'Hara assumed the role of his guest's lawyer, yelling, "You don't have to answer!" This, of course, made the cops even angrier.

The police searched the car, and when they found Prebensen's stash of books on Irish history and republican heroes, they didn't hold back their contempt. After they were done with the car, their activity and questions ebbed a bit, but their rifles remained high. It wasn't clear that they had any specific objective beyond harassing O'Hara and whoever had the bad judgment to ride with him.

O'Hara—who at seventeen had been in the midst of the 1972 Bloody Sunday Massacre, in which British paratroopers shot and killed fourteen unarmed demonstrators in Derry, including O'Hara's close friend Gerry Donaghy, also just seventeen—remained convinced that an actual shooting was unlikely. Morrison felt protected by his office, confident that the British government wasn't about to shoot a member of the US Congress. If he'd realized that the police holding him had no idea what a congressman was, he might have worried a little more.

As time passed, Morrison had the feeling that the police "didn't seem to have anywhere to go, and whether we had anywhere to go was of no interest to them." In truth, O'Hara and the Americans weren't on a tight schedule. Morrison and Prebensen had arrived in Derry a day or two earlier and were staying at O'Hara's home. This outing was supposed to be a relaxed tour of Derry from a Sinn Féin point of view. Morrison had already taken other tours; in order to get a full picture of the situation, he had asked the American consulate to recommended an itinerary. He'd also taken a tour with John Hume, leader of the Social Democratic Labour Party (SDLP), which was made up of moderate

Catholics who opposed violence and focused on economic development as a key to progress.

The differences in viewpoints were revealing and sometimes amusing. Hume, for example, had proudly shown the Americans a housing estate he'd helped get built. When O'Hara took them to the same estate, his message was quite different.

"See how they designed the streets?" O'Hara asked. "That's so the tanks can come in." Indeed, O'Hara never let up. When Morrison said the situation was complicated, O'Hara snapped, "It's not complicated: Brits out!"

———

Still at gunpoint, Morrison thought about how this situation would play out back home. He found it interesting that all three of them were being held so close together along the fence by the river. "It wasn't like Gerry was separated as the Sinn Féin guy—the presumptive terrorist—and Dennis and I were told to sit in the car, which would have been the American version. This had a very different flavor—like we were all in the company of a terrorist and we were all gonna to be investigated."

After ten or fifteen minutes passed, another officer, older and clearly of a higher rank, appeared on the scene. He spoke with the RUC men and examined the papers they'd collected. O'Hara watched him as he studied Morrison's passport; it was clear to O'Hara that this officer knew exactly who he was dealing with and that he understood that "he had an international incident on his hands." But the new arrival never spoke to the detainees.

There was still plenty of time for Morrison to take the strange situation in. That it wasn't happening on some blasted out street late at night, as was so often shown on television, but instead near the handsome center of the city on a bright summer morning, made it all the more bizarre. He noticed pedestrians on the river side of Queen's Quay crossing over to the other side as soon as they spotted the scene ahead and only crossing back when they were well clear of it. Three men were being held at gunpoint—maybe a new experience for them, maybe not—but everyday life was still going on, with a few minor adjustments.

———

There was nothing in Morrison's background that should have involved him in this centuries-old Irish mess. He had been adopted at birth and had no way of knowing how Irish he might be. His adoptive parents—a Con Ed executive and a librarian—were Lutherans. They'd raised him in Northport, a pleasant town on the north shore of Long Island. He went to MIT, graduated in three years, and then got a master's degree in chemistry from the University of Illinois. Along the way he realized that he was "more interested in working with people than molecules," so he entered Yale Law School in the class of 1973; Bill Clinton and Hillary Rodham were classmates. After graduation, he worked as a staff lawyer for New Haven Legal Assistance Association, which provided lawyers to the poor, and within a couple of years became director of the program.

After the first year of the Reagan presidency, Morrison felt there were more urgent things to do than head legal aid, so he decided to run for Congress. Since he was a political nobody, it would be uphill all the way. First he had to beat the president of the New Haven Board of Aldermen, who was widely seen as the prohibitive favorite, for the Democratic nomination. Then he had to beat the popular Republican incumbent. In a general election campaign marked by terrific energy, a clear position on protecting Social Security, edgy and inspired advertising, and the failure of the incumbent to recognize the strengths of his upstart challenger, Morrison won by less than one percent of the votes cast.

Morrison had an abiding interest in human rights issues, but no special focus on the Troubles in Northern Ireland. Soon after he was sworn in, however, he learned that all new members of Congress with significant Irish American constituencies had to decide whether to join Friends of Ireland, the established vehicle for expressing general support and affection for Ireland, or the less genteel Ad Hoc Committee for Irish Affairs, which wanted Irish unification—getting the six counties of Northern Ireland out of the United Kingdom and into a 32-county Republic of Ireland.

Friends of Ireland avoided controversy; its major concerns seemed to revolve around St. Patrick's Day. It was headed by Irishman Thomas Foley, the House Democratic whip. Foley was no friend of Sinn Féin; when it came to Northern Ireland, his sympathies lay with the British position. He abhorred the IRA and anyone who seemed to have the remotest sympathy for their cause. Even when the Irish Peace Process finally began to gather steam in the mid-1990s, Foley, by then Speaker of the House of Representatives, remained determined to keep Sinn Féin away from the negotiating table.

The Ad Hoc Committee was headed by Mario Biaggi of New York, who was decidedly not Irish but had a huge Irish American constituency in the Bronx and, as a former New York City police officer, strong support from the city's legions of Irish American cops. The Ad Hoc Committee didn't merely favor a united Ireland politically: Several of its members had close ties with supporters of Irish Northern Aid (Noraid), an American group that aggressively sought funds for the republican cause in Northern Ireland. While Noraid insisted the money was collected to help widows and orphans of fallen IRA heroes, the authorities claimed it was being used for IRA guns and bombs.

Morrison was advised by his staff to join Friends of Ireland, and he did so. But before long, he came to feel that it wasn't the group for him. He had a general awareness of the situation in Ireland and, although he didn't have fully formed views on it, he was more interested in substantive issues than Irish celebrations. He didn't favor the more extreme pro-IRA views of some members of the Ad Hoc Committee, but the group's willingness to engage with serious issues impressed him.

He hadn't yet committed to switching over when a man named Richard Lawlor asked to meet with him. Morrison's staff was alarmed: "You can't meet with this guy. He's a terrorist." Morrison met with him anyway. Lawlor, a Hartford lawyer and a former Connecticut state representative, was the national vice chairman of Noraid. He was willing to press the case for a united Ireland anytime, anywhere, and he did it well. Lawlor argued to the new congressman that the Catholics in Northern Ireland were being subjected to terrible discrimination in employment, housing, and all other major spheres of public life, as well as widespread deprivations of civil rights and unrelenting abuse by the RUC.

As they talked, Morrison didn't think he was dealing with a terrorist. He felt that many of Lawlor's points were worth exploring from a human rights perspective. Lawlor urged him to join the Ad Hoc Committee, and in time he did so. He was happier tackling serious questions instead of wondering which green tie to wear on St. Patrick's Day.

————

It had been a good twenty minutes since the higher ranking officer arrived at the Derry standoff. The car from the Republic sat empty in the roadway. Things seemed stalled. Morrison, O'Hara, and Prebensen stayed still, backs to the river, guns still pointed at them. Morrison remembers one of the rifles aimed directly at his knee, a visual echo of the IRA practice of kneecapping: crippling lesser targets with a bullet to the knee.

And then, like a sudden summer shower, it was over. Keys and papers were handed back. There was no explanation and, of course, no apology. The police piled back into their vehicles; as suddenly as they'd appeared, they vanished.

Life carried on as if none of it had ever happened. The wide River Foyle, glistening in the August light, rolled on in its stately way to the Atlantic Ocean. Pedestrians walked freely alongside Queen's Quay, the path ahead unimpeded by any unpleasantness. It was nearly lunchtime.

————

When Morrison got back to the United States a few days later, he called a press conference at the state capitol in Hartford. He told reporters: "Northern Ireland strikes you on first impression as a police state." He described himself as a strong supporter of a united Ireland, adding that he would push for relaxing visa restrictions on Irish republican leaders so that Americans could hear different viewpoints. "What we hear in the United States comes to us from a British perspective," he said. He denounced the discrimination and abuse and called for efforts to improve economic conditions in Northern Ireland.

Back in Congress, he got more involved in Irish issues and became co-chairman of the Ad Hoc Committee. He offered colleagues his impressions of Sinn Féin president Gerry Adams, whom he had met with in Belfast. Although many were certain that Adams was IRA to the core, Morrison's impression was different: "This is a politician. This isn't a general. This man—his skills, his focus, his way of thinking—is political. He's a political organizer. I recognize this person."

Morrison described his experience in Derry as "radicalizing," which at first took the form of support for the cause of a united Ireland. In time, that radicalization developed into something broader and deeper: an unwavering determination to do everything he could to help make peace. He would go on to dedicate untold hours, travel endless miles, and seek out support from anyone—American, Irish or British, Catholic or Protestant—who could help advance the prospects for peace. He brought to bear every aspect of his political know-how and intellectual firepower, and he did it with remarkably little ego. In short, he became a radical seeker of peace in Northern Ireland.

———

Morrison would return to Northern Ireland many times in the coming years and would play a crucial role in the long chain of events that would eventually lead to peace. But as the 1980s drew to a close, his focus was on two enormous projects at home. In Connecticut, instead of running for re-election to Congress in 1990, he would run for governor. And in Washington, he would lead a major overhaul of the immigration laws. Both projects would, in very different and sometimes surprising ways, help him make good on his determination to seek peace in Northern Ireland.

CHAPTER TWO

Catastrophe:
One Averted, One Total

Here it was, Friday evening, late October, 1990, on the floor of the House of Representatives. Congressman Morrison's immigration bill was, without warning, in terrible trouble, almost certainly at the end of a long road that had started so promisingly.

As chairman of the Immigration Subcommittee of the House Judiciary Committee, Morrison brought a point of view on immigration that went against the prevailing belief that the issue was nothing but an annoyance to deal with, a political loser. Whenever immigration issues came up, the typical response from most of his colleagues was a whiney, "Why do we have to do this?"

Morrison was sure that dealing with immigration didn't have to be like swallowing cod liver oil. He believed many issues had wide appeal: family reunification, protection for Soviet Jews, help for Chinese after Tiananmen Square and Salvadorans fleeing a brutal civil war. He also felt that a bill allowing more skilled workers into the country, limiting unskilled workers, and regulating temporary workers would win the support of a broad range of constituencies.

In 1990, he rolled it all together into a comprehensive House bill. Business liked the increase in skilled workers, and labor liked the limits on unskilled workers and the regulation of temporary workers. Provisions helping particular ethnic groups brought their own constituencies on board. Fifty thousand new visas for the Irish had the additional virtue of appealing to a large segment of the Reagan Democrats, which Morrison's party needed to win back if it hoped to take the White House in 1992. For each of these groups, Morrison's bill became *their* bill, especially the Irish: Whenever it came before the House, members would ask him, "Is this the Irish bill?"

―――――

The Senate passed its own comprehensive immigration bill in 1989, and the House passed Morrison's version in 1990. Then the joint conference committee hammered out a compromise bill from both versions. The Senate passed the compromise, and the House was voting on a House rule that had to pass before the bill itself could be taken up. Morrison had every reason to believe the votes were there.

Then it all went bad.

After all the horse-trading, adding in, taking out, adjusting, nipping and tucking necessary to line up an unprecedented coalition, this bill, the only immigration bill ever supported by both the AFL-CIO and the United States Chamber of Commerce, the bill a Republican president stood ready to sign, Morrison's grand goodbye to Congress after four terms, was going down—and his friends were the ones doing the damage.

The trouble started when California congressman Ed Roybal, a founder of the Hispanic Congressional Caucus, rose to argue that a pilot program buried in the bill that would add biometrics—a fingerprint, for example—to drivers' licenses, would be a precursor to a national identity card. This program was an experiment dear to the heart of Senate sponsor Alan Simpson, but the Hispanic caucus hated it. Roybal's argument persuaded enough representatives, mostly progressives who typically voted with Morrison, to vote *no* on the rule and effectively kill the bill.

The defeat was sudden and total. Because the joint conference committee had already issued its report in the form of the compromise bill and by House rules the committee was automatically dissolved upon issuing its report, it was no longer possible to go back and get rid of the fatal provision. Starting over in the Senate was no solution because so little time remained in the session. Besides, a filibuster by a single senator—and there were plenty waiting in line—would kill it there. And for Morrison there was no next year to try again, because he would be leaving Congress in January. It was now or never, and all of a sudden it looked like never.

Then a savior appeared: Joe Moakley, a veteran Massachusetts congressman and Chairman of the House Rules Committee, whose staff knew the House rules inside and out. There was a lot about the bill that Moakley liked, and one part he loved: protection for Salvadoran refugees. This was Moakley's special passion. For years he had fought for temporary status to protect those who had fled the Central American nation's civil war. Four years earlier, then-Chairman Roman Mazzoli had promised to include protections for Salvadorans in his 1986 bill. When Mazzoli failed to keep his promise, Moakley felt double-crossed. He never got over it, and he never stopped caring about the Salvadorans.

When Morrison defeated Mazzoli for the chairmanship in 1989 and began work on his bill, he approached Moakley with his own plan for the Salvadorans. Moakley was skeptical the new chairman could get it done, but Morrison said, "I'm going to deliver this for you." Watching him pull it off, Moakley had been impressed and grateful. So when disaster struck, he turned to Morrison right then and there on the House floor and said, "Let's go figure this out."

Morrison and Moakley, along with one of his aides, proceeded to put together a plan. It involved obscure legislative maneuvers and rules that Morrison, who was no slouch in this area, never even knew existed. Simply put, the plan was this: First, pass a House concurrent resolution—a housekeeping measure that isn't actual legislation—striking out Simpson's license project. Next, send the corrected resolution over to the Senate for passage. Finally, tell Ed Roybal that the committee bill was back before the House—this time with the license provision out—and bring it up for a new vote.

Getting the House to pass the concurrent resolution was no problem. After that was done, Moakley told Morrison what he had to do next, which Morrison wasn't looking forward to: "You gotta call Simpson."

Alan Simpson, a longtime senator from Wyoming—bright, coy, unpredictable, and often cranky—was a leading Republican who often went his own way, especially on immigration. Because it was Simpson's pet project that had to be dropped, Morrison could see trouble ahead. He remembered how exasperating it had been to deal with Simpson on earlier stages: He'd delayed sending the Senate bill to the conference committee, and when he finally did so, it was accompanied by a long list of things he wanted added. He constantly threatened to filibuster the entire thing, probably to get what he wanted, but maybe just to keep everyone else off balance. This would not be a fun call.

Morrison girded up, made the call, and got a pleasant surprise: Simpson readily agreed to deletion of the biometrics experiment provision, telling Morrison, "Aw, I didn't give a shit about that anyway." Simpson then quickly got the corrected version through the Senate. When it came back to the House, Ed Roybal's nays were back on board, and it passed easily and went to the president for his signature. When Simpson noticed Morrison at the edge of the group watching George H. W. Bush sign the bill, he pulled him into the center, between himself and Ted Kennedy and right behind the president, telling him, "You belong here."

Catastrophe was averted, both for the advocates of immigration reform and for Morrison personally: one of his two grand projects for the year succeeded after all, and, looking ahead, it gave him enormous stature in Ireland that would prove invaluable when he got himself involved with the quest for peace there.

But Morrison had no time to savor his victory, because the 1990 Connecticut gubernatorial election was just ten days away. He flew back to New Haven and embarked on a simple but brutal campaign schedule: He was going to campaign around the clock until it was over.

It was a plan he took literally: A TV clip showed him pumping gas late at night for a startled customer. It was a valiant effort in what many at this stage were sure was a lost cause. But it hadn't started out that way.

———

When Morrison had decided to heed the chants of "Run, Bruce, run!" echoing through the ballroom of New Haven's Park Plaza Hotel on election night 1988, after trouncing his opponent to win his fourth term in Congress, victory seemed entirely plausible, certainly much more so than when he first ran for Congress. The incumbent he would need to beat this time was Bill O'Neill, an old-style organization Democrat who had never been a favorite of liberals.

O'Neill became governor in 1980 when the popular Ella Grasso died, and as lieutenant governor, he succeeded her. He was seen by many as too conservative, essentially a caretaker who never would have been a strong candidate on his own. To his political pals, basically the Irish American establishment of the party, he was a great guy. He was also a tough political infighter, ruthless when he had to be. Both times he ran for re-election he faced intense opposition but managed, with the support of the old pols, to avoid primary elections. It was generally thought that he would be vulnerable in a head-to-head primary.

Morrison announced his challenge to O'Neill in early January of 1990. The venue was a New Haven nightclub called Toad's Place, which had recently been in the national news when the Rolling Stones turned up to do a short set before kicking off their next American tour. On this January night, Toad's was a place for politics. Morrison had spent the day touring the state on a bus filled with supporters, starting with the mill towns of the Naugatuck River Valley that John F. Kennedy had so memorably visited on the eve of the 1960 election that would make him president. During Morrison's tour, the campaign sported an up-to-the-minute technological innovation on loan from a local construction company: cell phones, huge and heavy, lugged around in sturdy canvas cases with stout shoulder straps.

When night came, Morrison's supporters jammed Toad's and cheered as their man promised victory and better days ahead. His likely opponent in the general election would be John Rowland, a politically astute conservative Republican congressman. Rowland's effort to get Congress to open its sessions with the Pledge of Allegiance had been ridiculed by liberals but, as Morrison always pointed out, it polled astonishingly well. Rowland had also made a splash by smashing a piece of Japanese electronic gear on the steps of the Capitol to express his support for products made in America.

For his part, Morrison looked forward to a clear-cut progressive-versus-conservative general election campaign. He was confident that he could take Rowland and smart enough not to underestimate him.

But first he had to get the Democratic nomination. There were mixed signals about whether or not Governor O'Neill would run again. Not only was he politically vulnerable, but he had a history of significant health problems. But he saw Morrison's challenge as a personal attack, once asking him why he was coming after him since, "I never went after you."

Finally in March, O'Neill decided to step aside. This was no graceful handing-off of the baton to a new generation while the old campaigner headed to a well-deserved retirement. It was clear that O'Neill was bitter and not about to do anything to make things easier for his upstart challenger. Although Morrison's path to the nomination now seemed clear, there was trouble ahead.

Even before O'Neill announced that he wasn't running, former senator Lowell Weicker entered the race as an independent, despite having told Morrison to his face that he wouldn't run and would support him. Weicker had been narrowly defeated just two years earlier by Joe Lieberman, who ran to the Republican's right, lambasting him for being soft on Cuba and other un-Americanisms. Weicker lost that election by just 10,000 votes, taking 49 percent of the statewide vote. He continued to have a lot of support from Democrats who fondly remembered him as a member of the Senate Watergate Committee, where his doubts about Nixon set him apart from almost all the Republicans on the committee. In his three terms in the Senate, Weicker had positioned himself as one of a vanishing breed: a somewhat liberal Republican.

Six and a half feet tall and burly, the wealthy Greenwich pharmaceutical heir was literally and figuratively a gigantic figure on the Connecticut political scene. By running for governor as an independent, he had set up the second major three-way race of his career. In his first, he had been elected to the Senate in a race against two Democrats; one a sitting senator who wasn't renominated, and the other the nominee of a badly split party.

This new three-way setup between Weicker, Rowland, and Morrison looked equally promising for Weicker—and dismal for Morrison. It seemed clear that Weicker would take a good many Democratic votes, the lion's share of the independents, and what was left of the moderate wing of the Republican Party; Morrison could count on committed progressives, diehard Democrats, and maybe not a whole lot more. Additionally, the kind of strategic voting often found in races with three major candidates was likely to make matters worse for Morrison. The argument in 1990 for Democrats went like this: Don't vote for the your party's nominee (Morrison) because that will take votes away from the candidate leading in the polls whom you are okay with (Weicker) and might get the one you really dislike (Rowland) elected. When Morrison's pollsters tested Weicker's popularity among Democrats, the results were devastating, but by that point Morrison was already committed to the race. There was no going back.

With O'Neill out, Morrison won the Democratic nomination at the state convention, but State Senator William Cibes, advocating a state income tax, got enough convention votes to mount a primary challenge in September. Morrison won the primary by a nearly two-to-one margin, but starting the fall campaign season mired in a battle with another Democrat over a state income tax, the most contentious issue in Connecticut politics, was no help to his already bleak general election prospects.

It was increasingly clear that many in the Democratic establishment who resented Morrison's challenge to O'Neill were sitting on their hands, if not actively supporting one of his opponents. Yet despite all that, he never let up, pushing relentlessly to the end. Recalls his campaign manager Ted Baldwin:

> Bruce had committed to the race and he never gave it less than his all. At the same time he did his work in Congress and served his constituents at an amazingly high level. His ability to do more than one major thing at a time was exceptional. He worked as hard as anybody could. There was never a moment when we needed him for the campaign that he wasn't there.

On election night, Morrison's worst fears were realized in spectacular fashion: The three-way race was a total disaster.

The *New York Times* told the sad tale in the morning:

> Mr. Morrison, who conceded defeat just after 9:30 P.M., 90 minutes after the polls closed, was rejected by about three-quarters of the members of his own party.
>
> He avoided, however, the ignominy of taking his party down to complete disintegration. Had he drawn less than 20 percent of the vote—an outcome that seemed possible based on polls conducted last week—the Democrats would have lost their status as a "major party" under state law and would have been forced to submit petitions to get new candidates on the ballot.

It was an unimaginable calamity for the party that had won eight of the last nine elections for governor. As silver linings go, receiving 20 percent of the vote was about as feeble as it gets. A three-way race with Weicker would have likely been impossible for any Democrat, but ultimately that didn't matter: Morrison lost horribly to Weicker and became a pariah in his own party. And he couldn't go back to

Congress: His successor Rosa DeLauro had just won her first of thirteen terms (and counting).

The writing on the wall was brutally clear: Morrison's political days in Connecticut were over.

Just how irredeemably over they were was driven home in mid-January when Morrison, now nothing more than an ex-congressman, went to the Jefferson-Jackson-Bailey dinner, the traditional mid-winter Democratic party fund-raiser, that year at a central Connecticut Radisson ballroom big enough to hold a thousand. The size of the room meant that, even with decent seating, the head table could be far, far away. But for Morrison and his fiancée, there was no decent seating: The organizers put them in a virtual Siberia, practically in the kitchen. It was an unmistakable message that the party's most recent candidate for governor was now a very dead duck. That this was no greatly exaggerated death was made painfully clear when Morrison greeted O'Neill and his wife, Nikki. It was bad enough when O'Neill's manner showed so clearly that he was still seething over Morrison's challenge. But it really hit bottom when Nikki O'Neill said quietly through clenched teeth as Morrison shook her hand, "This is really hard for me."

Morrison went home that night in a complete funk. It couldn't have been clearer that he was a political goner in Connecticut. The door wasn't just shut—it was triple locked, bolted, chained, and welded over with steel plating. Only one question dominated his thoughts: What do I do now?

It is no wonder, then, that at that moment Morrison had absolutely no inkling that a new door was opening on the horizon, one that would give him a chance to help make world history.

CHAPTER THREE

Longshot

M orrison's humiliation at the Democratic banquet perfectly captured his dreadful situation. Not only was he friendless in his own party, but he had no job, no income, and a massive campaign debt, including personal loans in six figures secured by his house. So he decided to start his own private legal practice in New Haven, with a special focus on immigration law.

By late winter 1991, as Morrison was getting his practice underway, he started thinking about something beyond making a living. Although he understood that his days as a political candidate were over, his activist impulses hadn't left him. So, like any good politician, he decided to look where he still had support: Ireland, now 50,000 new visas strong. Those visas had made him a revered figure throughout the island.

Though the violence and despair of the Troubles were still going strong, there had been some recent promising developments in Northern Ireland. For one, Sinn Féin leader Gerry Adams had been publicly advocating for a political path as an alternative to the IRA's efforts to unify Ireland by force of arms. Then in the late 1980's, moderate nationalist leader John Hume had begun confidential discussions with Adams, despite Sinn Féin's ties to the IRA, which offered Adams the prospect of wider political acceptability and contributed to the development of a real peace process.

Morrison hoped that with his newfound stature in Ireland he could do something in support of these hopeful developments.

"I thought I should spend my legacy on something," he says. He wasn't sure yet what that something should be, but he knew just the man to discuss it with.

Niall O'Dowd, a New Yorker through and through, was an Irish immigrant, once illegal, who became a successful publisher. His *Irish Voice* newspaper and *Irish America* magazine had considerable influence in the Irish American community. He had a vast array of contacts in the Republic and Northern Ireland—everyone from mainstream politicians to shadowy paramilitary men—and an equally large number throughout Irish America. Morrison had worked with him on immigration issues, and O'Dowd had been a strong supporter of his campaign for governor. He was the perfect person for Morrison to visit.

They met in the late winter in O'Dowd's Manhattan office, an unremarkable workaday place where he ran his publishing business. Its most distinctive feature was a view of the Empire State Building. It didn't take long for Morrison to realize that this wasn't just a meeting for him: It was also a meeting that the publisher had been waiting for.

O'Dowd's path to New York and to American citizenship had been a long and colorful one. He left Ireland in 1978 after graduating from university, ultimately making his way to San Francisco, where he sustained himself, like so many young Irishmen, as a house painter. He was also in demand for his talent at Gaelic football. When his visa ran out, he stayed anyway—also like so many others. Years later, his experience with illegal status made him determined to advocate for immigration reform, which was the issue that first brought him together with Morrison. O'Dowd had been enormously impressed with Morrison's determination and effectiveness in crafting the 1990 immigration bill and getting it passed. The *Irish Voice* mentioned him frequently during that time, although, Morrison says, "It wasn't always sweetness and light. One of his columnists regularly questioned whether I was actually going to deliver. She was constantly saying that I couldn't get it done—that no one had ever passed a bill in only one year and that because I was running for governor, I was going to be distracted and wasn't going to pay attention."

As the two men spoke in what Morrison later called "an easy meeting of the minds," it was clear that they shared many views and perceptions of the situation in Northern Ireland. They also had high regard for each other. O'Dowd respected Morrison's intellect, his political astuteness, and his reputation throughout Ireland as an American who practically walked on water. Morrison was impressed with O'Dowd's passion and vision, not to mention his amazing network of contacts. He had deeply appreciated O'Dowd's support in the governor's race, especially in marshaling financial backing from prominent Irish Americans.

As the publisher and the politician tossed ideas back and forth, it was clear that not only was O'Dowd the right man for Morrison, but Morrison was the right man for O'Dowd, who had long wanted to find a way to get the United States involved in helping to end the Troubles. The idea was not a new one—throughout much of the twentieth century, Irish republicans had sought to "internationalize" their struggle by getting the United States involved as a counterbalance to Great Britain—but an important difference now was that O'Dowd could drum up support for that vision through his publications and his contacts on both sides of the Atlantic. He had already seen how effective that could be: When the *Irish Voice* started referring to the new Irish visas as "Morrison Visas," Morrison's reputation throughout Ireland rose even higher.

Morrison knew that for O'Dowd's vision to succeed, influential Irish Americans would have to get behind it. He also knew that O'Dowd, a pioneer in elevating the status of what it meant to be an Irish American, was the right man to galvanize them. O'Dowd publicized and celebrated Irish American successes in business, politics, science, and other areas at the highest levels of American life, even establishing a hall of fame for Irish Americans. Morrison has a deep respect for O'Dowd's transformational accomplishments:

When I was growing up, the traditional image of Irish America would be the Irish cop, the firefighter, the carpenter, the electrician, the priest. But of course the truth is that with maybe 40 million Irish Americans in the country, they ran the full range of achievement. Niall recognized that the self-image of Irish America was kind of moored in a particular category of occupation and living style. He set out to inform Irish America of how much they have achieved in all aspects of American life. What he changed was that people who historically focused on their assimilation, not on their Irishness, now aspire to be recognized for their Irish connection in addition to their achievements at high levels of American society. So now people want to be on his "Irish 100" lists; they want to be in the Irish America Hall of Fame. That's a total change: people treated their Irishness as a footnote and emphasized their achievement as an American—such as, "I'm a CEO"—but now the CEO says, "One of the reasons I've done so well is my Irish heritage and my Irish upbringing." Niall did this.

Morrison and O'Dowd both recognized the challenges and payoffs of getting America involved in a new way. The biggest challenge was that for nearly 200 years, it had been the policy of the United States to regard the ongoing conflict in Ireland as an internal British matter, not an appropriate subject for an independent American policy. That deference was solidly entrenched in the State Department, and getting it changed would be enormously difficult, particularly since the British insisted that any armed activity by the Irish Republican Army was terrorism, pure and simple. That meant that anyone advocating a wholesale change in American policy could be accused of being soft on terrorism by the State Department and the FBI.

But if American policy *could* be changed, the potential that it could help bring about peace was enormous. The United States was ideally positioned to support and encourage positive developments in Northern Ireland. More and more American voices against the warfare were making themselves heard, both publicly and behind the scenes. Furthermore, given Britain's positive regard for America, if there was any nation that could influence its policies, it was the United States.

There was also a substantial domestic political dimension: Although America's pro-British policy had solid support through-out the institutions of American government, it had no significant constituency in the body politic. Simply stated, nobody much in late-twentieth-century America voted British, but there were some 40 million Americans who identified as Irish American and who could be open to voting Irish.

Both Morrison and O'Dowd understood the degree to which any peace process would have to be fundamentally a political one. It would be politicians—not academics, diplomats, or policy professionals, and not even all-knowing pundits—who would be the key to success. So it was in many respects a natural progression of the discussion when O'Dowd asked Morrison the question that would change everything: "What about your classmate Bill Clinton?"

Neither man could know it at the time, but with that ques-tion, the prospects for peace in Northern Ireland took a giant step forward.

————

What about Bill Clinton? He, Morrison, and Hillary Rodham had all been in the Yale Law School class of 1973. Clinton's reputation had preceded him there: He was a Rhodes Scholar from Arkansas, very bright and politically savvy, who pretty clearly had already set his sights on becoming president. Even as a law student in his twenties, he made a powerful first impression: Morrison said that when he met Clinton, "I knew I had met somebody."

Morrison hadn't seen a great deal of Clinton since they left Yale, but he'd followed his career with interest. In addition to becoming governor of Arkansas, Clinton was a leader in the effort to move the Democratic party closer to the center, where he believed presidential elections were won. Clinton passed on the 1988 presidential cam-paign despite the encouragement of some party leaders who liked his chances; at that year's Democratic convention, he was seen as a future star and was chosen to give the nominating speech for Michael Dukakis. But precisely what his future prospects were by the end of the convention was, to put it mildly, uncertain: His speech went on for so long that delegates started shouting at him, live on national television, to stop.

When Morrison and O'Dowd had their meeting, Clinton hadn't yet announced his candidacy for president, but it was clear he was running. Morrison already knew that he would almost certainly support Clinton, but Northern Ireland had nothing to do with it until his visit to the *Irish Voice* office. O'Dowd already knew Clinton was his man: He wanted a candidate who would make a complete break with the American policy, and to some extent, he'd settled on Clinton by process of elimination. The candidate had to be a Democrat, because George H. W. Bush and Secretary of State James Baker were in accord with the traditional policy: British all the way. Clinton was associated with the kind of bold but politically astute policy initiatives reminiscent of John F. Kennedy. Neither of the other leading candidates were seen that way: Former Massachusetts senator Paul Tsongas was a sober-sided technocratic centrist, and former California governor Jerry Brown was still saddled with his long-standing image as the far-out Governor Moonbeam. So although in early 1991 Clinton still seemed like a longshot, for O'Dowd and other Irish American activists, he was the horse to bet on. O'Dowd and Morrison both knew how seriously Clinton took politics and campaigning, and they knew that a centrist Southerner probably stood the best chance of getting elected.

Morrison liked O'Dowd's conviction that Clinton could win, but his experience and realism told him it was probably pie in the sky. The odds of Clinton defeating a sitting president were very long indeed: After driving Saddam Hussein's army out of Kuwait, Bush would enter the election year with approval ratings of 90 percent or more. But despite the odds, Morrison agreed that Clinton was the most promising candidate for a new Northern Ireland policy.

So Morrison and O'Dowd combined their strengths—O'Dowd's vision, pulpit, and contacts, along with Morrison's access to Clinton, his own newfound stature in Ireland, and his deep political insight—and made a plan. They would back Clinton and work to get him to commit to a new American approach that would help end the centuries of violent strife in Ireland. They would make sure Clinton was clued in to the political benefits of a policy that millions of Irish Americans would enthusiastically support, and they would marshal strong political and financial support for his campaign among the Irish American community.

There was good reason to believe Clinton would be receptive to all of this: A major goal of his campaign would be to reclaim the so-called Reagan Democrats—and a great many of them were Irish Americans.

When Morrison left O'Dowd's office on that winter's day, he was in a very different place than when he went in:

> I wanted to relate my newfound fame in the Irish American community to something constructive about what was starting to happen in Northern Ireland. I was thinking in terms of some kind of niche project for myself, not, "Let's go find ourselves a presidential candidate." It was Niall who tied the two of them together, making an obvious connection that I had not made. It was Niall thinking very big thoughts about what we could do.

In the ensuing months, as Morrison worked to develop his new legal practice and regain his economic footing, he and O'Dowd began to talk up and gauge support for Clinton as the most promising candidate for Irish Americans who wanted America's policy toward Northern Ireland changed. Then it would be Morrison's job to reconnect with his old classmate and learn something about what, if anything, the Arkansas governor knew or thought about the centuries of Irish warfare and the present-day Troubles.

CHAPTER FOUR

The Troubles: 800
Years in the Making

Northern Ireland became a distinct entity when Ireland was partitioned by the British parliament in 1920. At the time it had a roughly two-thirds Protestant majority and a one-third Catholic minority. In 1991, as Bruce Morrison was planning his approach to Bill Clinton, the Protestant majority was politically divided into unionists, who largely asserted their power through politics and control of civil institutions, and loyalists, who were more willing to take to the streets. The Catholics were for the most part divided into nationalists, who wanted a nonviolent unification of Ireland, and republicans, who were generally more willing to support the armed struggle being waged by the IRA.

The three decades of armed conflict that came to be known as the Troubles began in 1968. It didn't start with violence. In the midsixties, Catholics, inspired in large part by the civil rights movement in the United States, began protesting the pervasive discrimination being perpetrated against them by the unionist state in virtually all aspects of life—from voting rights to employment to housing to policing—with marches and other nonviolent demonstrations. Their efforts intensified with the formation of the Northern Ireland Civil Rights Association in 1967.

The British government and the ruling unionists in Northern Ireland were unwilling to seriously address the Catholics' grievances.

Northern Ireland Premier Terence O'Neill attempted some conciliatory gestures, but those provoked a backlash from his unionist critics. Brutal police suppression of demonstrations followed. Soon enough, a new version of the Irish Republican Army materialized and in short order it took on a fighting role, which was met by a revival of several loyalist paramilitaries. The awful violence of the Troubles was under way. In 1969, London sent in the British army to try to gain control of the situation, but the violence and killing escalated alarmingly.

The ongoing bloody conflict between the IRA, loyalist paramilitary forces, the RUC—the only armed police force in the UK or Ireland—and the British army made Northern Ireland a place of death and destruction on a scale almost unimaginable to Americans. Sniper fire, calculated assassinations, and bombings could come any place at any time. Over the thirty years of the Troubles, 3,200 people were killed in Northern Ireland—a small place with a population of a little over 1,600,000. An equivalent death toll in the United States would be around 500,000, an unimaginable rate even after 9/11.

The Troubles were the latest iteration of a course of warfare between the Irish and the British that began back in 1169, when the Anglo-Normans—Englishmen since 1066—invaded Ireland. The English king, Henry II, soon worried that his occupying knights might seek their own independence from him by making alliances with local chieftains. Henry went to Ireland in 1172 to reassert his own authority, and the Irish, despite their own frequent internal divisions, fought back. The cycle of English colonization, with its demeaning and dehumanizing treatment of the Irish, and Irish uprising and retaliation, would continue for the next three centuries.

It didn't begin as a religious conflict. In the twelfth century the English and the Irish were Catholic, although some English relished portraying Irish Catholicism as degenerate. It would be another 350 years of on-and-off fighting before Martin Luther nailed his 95 theses to the cathedral door and Protestantism came into being. The idea of a church that wasn't under the control of the Pope appealed greatly to Henry VIII, that king of many marriages, and he established the

Church of England with himself in charge. At last this Henry would be able to get a divorce when he needed one.

The fighting took on the religious dimension by which it is so often described from 1536 when Henry, in an effort to extend English control and to replace the Catholic Church with a Protestant Church of Ireland headed by himself, invaded Ireland. Over the next 300 years, it suited most British leaders to cast the conflict in religious terms, which made it easier to dismiss the Irish as irrational, impossible, and inferior and to justify the persecution and rank discrimination that far in the future would trigger the Troubles.

In 1603, King James VI of Scotland was also crowned James I of England. As King of England, he also became King of Ireland, and his strategy for gaining greater control over that difficult land was to launch the Plantation of Ulster, with Scottish and English settlers brought in to displace the Irish. James's grand plan was under way by 1610, and it greatly increased the Protestant population in the north of Ireland. The privileged position granted to the newly arrived Scots and English fueled Irish anger and resentment that has lasted for centuries. In its time it contributed mightily to the northern Catholic rebellion of 1641. That rebellion, accompanied by suitably exaggerated tales of Catholic atrocities against colonists that were already terrible enough, set off the conflict that ultimately brought Oliver Cromwell to Ireland in 1649. His arrival would bring the worst oppression of the Irish by the English yet.

Cromwell had taken power in England in the wake of his battlefield victories in the first English Civil War. After the execution of King Charles I early in 1649, Cromwell turned his attention to Ireland, leading an overwhelming invasion force of 20,000 that left a trail of slaughter and blood that seared itself onto the Irish Catholic mind. By the time Cromwell was done, enormous numbers of Catholics had been killed and some had been transported to the West Indies as slaves. Many who managed to survive faced confiscation of their lands and banishment to the barren lands of western Ireland. To this day, Cromwell represents the epitome of British oppression and brutality to the Irish.

In 1690, nearly 300 years before the Troubles, the armies of William III, Dutch husband of the Protestant Queen Mary, and the forces of the ousted James II, the last Catholic king of Great Britain, faced each other across the River Boyne, north of Dublin. James was attempting to retake the throne with the support of French and Irish allies but was soundly defeated. William's victory ensured that Great Britain would never again have a Catholic sovereign. Every July 12, members of the Orange Order, formed in 1795 and named after William's roots in the Dutch House of Orange, along with many others in the unionist and loyalist communities, celebrate his victory in the Battle of the Boyne. Parades through Catholic neighborhoods by members of the order, frequently wearing bowler hats, dark suits, and orange sashes, accompanied by fife and drum bands and attracting many other supporters, have been a source of friction and worse between the province's two populations.

In the years following James's defeat, British authorities intensified their hold on Ireland, which increasingly left the Irish as no more than tenants or landless laborers in their own land, subjected to ever greater state-imposed or -sanctioned discrimination. But a century later, the winds of change upending Europe and fueling the American Revolution blew into Ireland, principally through United Irishmen led by Theobald Wolfe Tone, a Protestant lawyer who sought to lead a united Irish force—Catholics and Protestants together—to fight for independence from Britain. The uprising claimed tens of thousands of lives and ended in catastrophic failure. Civilian fighters with little or no training, armed with pikes and far too few guns—and those guns were primitive—were no match for seasoned British troops with plenty of the best guns and artillery. Wolfe Tone was sentenced to be hanged, but he cut his own throat and died before the hangman could get to him. His vision and daring would long inspire those willing to fight for an independent Ireland.

The British further solidified their control over Ireland in 1801 with the Act of Union, which created the United Kingdom by joining

Ireland to Great Britain, the island nation made up of England, Scotland, and Wales. Episodes of futile Irish rebellion followed in the early part of the century. In the 1820s, Daniel O'Connell emerged as an effective leader of the Irish Catholics, who soon became an organized political force of great size. They made themselves felt through massive marches and demonstrations. While O'Connell himself denounced violence, the huge numbers and sheer physical presence of his supporters sent a powerful and worrisome message to the British.

In the middle of the nineteenth century, the destruction of the potato crop—the great staple of the Irish diet—by a fungus led to years of starvation from 1845 to 1852 that utterly transformed Ireland. While there was other food grown in Ireland during the Potato Famine, much of it for export, it wasn't available to the poor. The short-term result was a million deaths from starvation and disease. Although noteworthy private charity did come from Britain and the United States, the official British response to the catastrophe was largely governed by the principles of "political economy," which asserted that providing food for the starving would promote dependency, worsen their character, and destabilize society. Although arguments still persist about the complexities of food supply issues, the spectacle of such widespread starvation in the face of extensive food exports fueled an intense anti-British bitterness that can still be felt in Ireland to this day.

The catastrophe has been called the Great Famine or the Great Hunger, but the transfer of so much food to Britain in a time of such widespread starvation in Ireland leads many to believe that calling it the Great Starvation would be more accurate. Irish playwright George Bernard Shaw said as much in *Man and Superman* with this exchange:

> *Malone*: Me father died of starvation in Ireland in the black '47. Maybe you've heard of it.
> *Violet*: The Famine?
> *Malone*: No, the Starvation. When a country is full o' food, and exporting it, there can be no famine.

When the disaster was done, Ireland was a profoundly changed land. The million deaths and the emigration of some 2 million more by 1860 constituted overwhelming losses from a population of only 8 million.

In the United States, Catholic Irish America was becoming a powerful political force, as well as a bedrock of support for Irish independence, principally through the militant Fenian Brotherhood, which in 1866 invaded Canada—at that time, still a British colony—to challenge British control of Ireland. An attempted uprising in Ireland in the following year failed, but the die was cast: Ireland would continue fighting to be free of British control, and Catholic Irish American money would help.

In the fifty years before the violent uprisings that would lead to a partitioned Ireland, the Irish nationalists focused on two issues, with the great Irish leader Charles Stewart Parnell at the center of both. The first issue was land reform—fairer treatment and a stake in the land for Irish tenants. The second was Home Rule. The goal of Home Rule was to create greater political autonomy for the Irish, which could lead to substantial independence over time. Home Rule provoked strong resistance from the majority of Protestants in the north who wanted to remain an integral part of the United Kingdom, and they consistently opposed the various acts proposed. When the British did pass the third Home Rule Bill in 1912, Protestant leader Edward Carson declared that Ulster—or at least the six counties that were to become Northern Ireland—would remain part of the United Kingdom. By the time the act was to take effect in 1914, battle lines had been drawn between the unionist Ulster Volunteer Force and the republican Irish Volunteers.

The start of World War I in August 1914 caused the British to suspend the Home Rule Act until the end of the war, or for one year, whichever would be longer. But the war didn't end quickly, as the British had expected, and in 1916 armed Irish uprisings seized center stage.

The battle for Irish independence began with the Easter Rising. A small group of Irish republican radicals, supported by the Irish Citizen Army, a working-class force of meager proportions, planned an action in Dublin during Eastertime. They hoped to surprise the British, who were focused on the war with Germany. Many of the rebels realized that their insurrection was almost certainly doomed to failure, but Padraig Pearse, one of the main leaders, argued that it would be an inspirational "blood cleansing." The selection of Easter as the time for the rising was no coincidence; Pearse believed that their sacrifice would gain the sympathy of the wider world and inspire a new generation in Ireland.

British interception off the Irish coast of a German arms shipment bound for the rebels dealt a serious blow to their plans. But the rising's leaders decided to proceed anyway, and they did indeed catch the British by surprise. They seized and held the General Post Office and several other public buildings in Dublin and proclaimed the Irish Republic. Despite having no chance of prevailing, they held out for nearly a week before being overwhelmed by British reinforcements. Their leaders, Pearse and James Connolly, a longtime labor leader who had worked for years in the United States, were captured and executed along with fourteen other rebels. The execution of Connolly, who had been shot in the fighting and had to be brought out on a stretcher and tied to a chair to face the firing squad, has resonated through republican generations.

The rebels were routed, but they won the propaganda battle. Their signature document, the Proclamation of the Irish Republic, remains, despite breaches in the observance, an iconic assertion of the fundamental principles of an Irish right to independence and of the right of the Irish people to social justice.

The bold and doomed Irish action in 1916—their blood sacrifice—and the extraordinarily harsh and inept British response to it led the Sinn Féin party under the leadership of Éamon de Valera, the senior surviving leader of 1916, to a resounding victory in the 1918 general election. When the British refused to recognize the electoral verdict, the Irish Republican Army, inspired above all by Michael Collins and relying heavily on Irish American support, fought the Irish War of Independence, a devastatingly effective guerrilla campaign against the mighty British, from 1919 until 1921. The war ended with the Anglo-Irish Treaty of 1921, a compromise that established the Irish Free State, subject to the right of six northern counties to remain part of the UK.

Collins favored the treaty compromise with reluctance, but de Valera was vehemently opposed to it. He wanted a completely independent Republic with no partition of the island, although he was prepared to consider special provisions for the six counties. The split led in 1922 to the Irish Civil War. Although Collins, now head of the Provisional Government and Commander-in-Chief of the National Army, soon lost his life in an ambush, pro-treaty forces prevailed and Ireland was partitioned into a twenty-six-county Free State and a six-county Northern Ireland. The partition, followed by nearly fifty years of unrelenting discrimination against the Catholic minority in Northern Ireland, set the course to the Troubles.

De Valera, the last of the legendary Irish republican leaders standing after Collins's death and the Easter Rising executions, ultimately held high office in the twenty-six-county Ireland in all of its iterations. In 1932 he became president of the Executive Council of the Irish Free State, and in 1937 he became Taoiseach (the Irish word for chieftain, the title given to the prime minister) of Eire, a republic in all but name. The fully independent Republic of Ireland was inaugurated in 1949 and de Valera served as its president from 1959 until 1973.

In the 1940s and 1950s, Northern Ireland saw occasional violent flare-ups, but for the most part its Catholic population suffered the discrimination to which it was subjected quietly, until the civil rights demonstrations of the 1960s began, followed all too soon by the Troubles.

Bruce Morrison would later lament the inevitability of it all, which he felt was deeply rooted in British colonial history: "The British found a way to turn the opportunity for peaceful change offered by the civil rights movement into an armed struggle. They stamped out conflict in the form of marches and ultimately got themselves conflict in the form of bombs and bullets."

The violence of the Troubles began in earnest in 1969 and led, in 1972, to the British imposition of direct rule from London over the entire province, shortly after the Bloody Sunday killings by British paratroopers in Derry/Londonderry.

The warfare proceeded with unrelenting brutality and high-visibility attacks by the IRA, including the 1979 killing of Lord Mountbatten, Queen Elizabeth's beloved cousin Dickie, by blowing up his boat off Sligo in northwest Ireland. His grandson Nicholas, Baroness Brabourne, and Paul Maxwell, a local boy working on the boat, also died.

Things took a dramatic turn as the 1980s began. The British had previously ruled that captured IRA fighters would be given Special Category Status in prison, allowing them rights similar to POWs, such as being able to associate freely with other prisoners and not having to do prison work. But in 1976 a new secretary of state for Northern Ireland rescinded that status. When Margaret Thatcher became prime minister in 1979, she maintained the rescission, declaring, "Crime is crime is crime." In 1980, prisoners began a series of hunger strikes to demand the restoration of Special Category Status. The strikes would leave ten people dead and engage the attention, and often sympathy, of Irish America and much of the world.

The first hunger striker to die was Bobby Sands, who had been elected to the British Parliament at Westminster while in prison. Niall O'Dowd has written that this was his personal watershed with respect to the conflict. Bruce Morrison later said, "Maggie Thatcher had a particularly nasty and negative approach. She was the person who reneged on the deal to save the hunger strikers, so she is looked upon as right up there with Cromwell in Irish history." In 1984 the IRA came very close to assassinating Thatcher by bombing her hotel in Brighton during a Conservative Party conference.

As the fighting in Northern Ireland raged on, it was vicious and often careless. Innocent civilians were regularly killed because of mistaken identity, bungled intelligence, badly timed bombs, or simply the terrible luck of being in the wrong place at the wrong time. The ongoing violence created a pervasive atmosphere of fear and deep discouragement, which drained entire populations of hope. For thirty years, people had to wonder when and where the next explosion, ambush, or revenge killing would come. They knew it seldom mattered if the victims were actually involved in the fighting. It was a terrible atmosphere in which to try to make a life and raise children. It wasn't surprising that many in Ireland, including prominent academics, were certain the conflict would grind on indefinitely and suggested that acceptance might be the most realistic course—provided that the death toll wasn't too awful.

It was in the midst of all of this misery that the idea of resolving the conflict peacefully—however implausible that seemed—began to take hold. In 1976 two women from Northern Ireland, Mairéad Corrigan and Betty Williams, won the Nobel Peace Prize for their attempts to start a grassroots peace movement. In 1985, the Anglo-Irish Agreement established a role for the Republic in the affairs of the north, while also affirming the principle of consent under which Northern Ireland would leave the UK and join the Republic only upon the approval of the majority of its people. That agreement led to a firestorm of unionist criticism of Margaret Thatcher, who overcompensated with an even harsher anti-republican stance.

In 1986, Sinn Féin leader Gerry Adams, who was determined to persuade the IRA to pursue its goals through politics instead of military action, led his party to develop an effective political alternative to stand alongside its longtime support for the armed struggle. The strategy became known as "the Armalite [a rifle emblematic of IRA weaponry] in one hand and the ballot box in the other." While many were suspicious that it was all a ploy to put the unionists and the British off their guard, moderate nationalist leader John Hume took the initiative seriously and in 1988 opened a secret dialogue with Adams, in which the two leaders of the Catholic minority explored ways of moving ahead peacefully.

In early 1992 Albert Reynolds became Taoiseach of Ireland. Before entering politics he had a colorful and successful career as a dance hall impresario and pet food magnate. Although no one expected it, the businessman-turned-politician quickly made it clear that he intended to do everything he could to help resolve the conflict in the north. He immediately sought to establish a positive relationship with British prime minister John Major, who had replaced Margaret Thatcher two years earlier, and enlist him in the search for a resolution. Each man's overlapping service as his country's finance minister gave the pair a head start that the canny Reynolds intended exploit to the hilt. With the two prime ministers' relationship coalescing around a shared willingness to find a solution to the strife, the building blocks for what came to be known as the Irish Peace Process were in place.

Bruce Morrison's message to candidate Bill Clinton, starting in late 1991, was that there would be a great place for the United States in these promising developments in Northern Ireland if the new president radically changed America's long-standing policy of regarding the Troubles as an internal British matter, with no place for an independent American role. Morrison also spelled out for his old friend the valuable benefits that could come his way—as a politician chasing votes, as a statesman, and as an idealist trying to do some good in the world—if he took that leap.

CHAPTER FIVE

Getting the Candidate
On Board

B ruce Morrison didn't initiate direct contact with Bill Clinton
until they met at a fund-raiser in Westport, Connecticut, in the
fall of 1991. They reconnected warmly and, during their conversation,
Morrison brought up the issue of Northern Ireland. He also caught
a glimpse of the crazy chase Clinton was on: From Westport he'd go
straight to the airport and fly to Southern California and the next fund-
raiser. The competition for his attention was already intense, and Morrison knew that his follow-up would have to be catch-as-catch-can.

In January of 1992, as the primary season was getting under way,
Morrison was off on another journey to Northern Ireland as part of
a delegation sent by Mercy College, which was working to establish
a management training program there. College officials invited Morrison in hopes that his involvement would help secure grants for the
project. The trip would bring him into close contact with the Protestant community, something he welcomed. Typically, American politicians traveling to Northern Ireland were playing to the Catholic voters
back home and had no reason to spend time with Protestants, but
Morrison felt it was important to get to know unionists and loyalists as
well, in order to understand who they were and how they saw things.
It was clear to him that for the fighting to end, both populations of
Northern Ireland would need to reach agreement, and that Americans
trying to help would have to know how to connect with everyone.

A unionist politician with whom Morrison connected on that trip was Belfast councilor Chris McGimpsey, whose cousin in the United States had organized the trip. McGimpsey, a member of the Ulster Unionist Party (UUP), the major Protestant party, found Morrison to be surprisingly capable and open-minded:

> Bruce Morrison was sharp intellectually. He had a pretty good grasp of the Irish situation even then. I had met a number of Americans in those days, and often they already had their minds made up. He didn't fall under that category at all. He was fact-finding, and he was good at it. He Hoovered up the facts and he asked sharp questions. You could see that he was keen to understand both sides.

For his part, Morrison appreciated McGimpsey's own open-mindedness and his willingness to be seen with an American known to be on good terms with Sinn Féin leader Gerry Adams, something "not standard fare," as Morrison says.

Although Morrison's encounter with McGimpsey would later prove to be the most important one of the trip, there was another that imprinted itself indelibly on his memory. That happened at a loyalist housing estate called Glencairn—"your typical housing project kind of environment, pretty desolate," as Morrison describes it—with a leader "whose role was never fully described. He probably wasn't that old, but he was quite grizzled and had few teeth. He was smoking a cigarette, sitting there talking to us mostly about grievances they had with the British and how the British were catering to the Catholics. But my strongest image is the way the ash on his cigarette kept getting longer and longer . . . and longer. I don't remember ever seeing it fall." It would be years before he saw the man again.

Morrison's contact with both populations in Northern Ireland on that visit gave him a fundamentally new understanding of the conflict: Everyone was awash in grievances, especially against the British, and each group thought Britain was siding with the other. Morrison had already known how the nationalists and the republicans felt about the British, but he was surprised to learn that unionists and loyalists were convinced the British were actually favoring the Catholics. As far as many of them were concerned, the last time the British had really been on their side was in 1690, at the Battle of the Boyne.

———

When his visit to the north was done, Morrison spent some time in Dublin, where Irish president Mary Robinson invited him to lunch. In Ireland, the president is like the Queen: the head of state, staying above politics and keeping her opinions to herself. Robinson told Morrison that she had not scheduled a formal lunch because, "I thought an informal conversation would be more interesting." She spoke with a slight tone of apology for the absence of the pomp that many dignitaries expected of her, but she had correctly judged that Morrison couldn't have cared less about all of that. During the small gathering—Morrison and his wife met with Robinson, her husband, and a staff member—she spoke candidly not as president of Ireland but as the human rights lawyer she was, foreshadowing her willingness and ability, through skillful communication in the language of political symbolism rather than explicit words, to get involved in the Northern Ireland peace effort in a way unprecedented for an Irish president.

The American ambassador to Ireland, Richard A. Moore, also invited Morrison to lunch, but that one didn't go so well. During the visit, something inspired Morrison to make a snide comment about then vice president Dan Quayle, already the butt of countless jokes. The ambassador's wife recoiled and the atmosphere chilled dramatically. As Morrison learned later, the ambassador was a close personal friend and former neighbor of George H. W. Bush, the president who had chosen Quayle as his running mate. Morrison was unhappy with himself for having been an ungracious guest. It was a thoughtless faux pas that evoked for him his mother's constant reminders to watch his tongue. But it was a useful lesson for someone about to become more deeply involved in Ireland, a land where a careless word could lead to mortal danger.

An embassy event that went far better involved the new Morrison Visas. Issuance had started in October of 1991, and the embassy staff arranged for Morrison to personally hand out a number of them to recipients who had made their way through the months-long process that involved an application, a lottery, more paperwork, a personal interview, and finally an appearance to collect the visa. The gratitude of those receiving their visas from him moved Morrison deeply.

———

Shortly after Morrison returned home, Clinton's campaign, which had been heavily buffeted by the Gennifer Flowers scandal, scored a crucial success: He finished second in the New Hampshire primary. This was widely regarded as a major victory, an indication that Clinton had weathered the scandal. He started calling himself the Comeback Kid.

Soon after Clinton's encouraging finish in New Hampshire, Niall O'Dowd got a phone call he'd been waiting for, although he hadn't known when or from whom it would come. The caller was Christopher Hyland, a classmate of Clinton's at Georgetown, who said he was in charge of organizing ethnic groups in support of Clinton. It was within such groups, particularly those that were predominately Catholic, that many of the Reagan Democrats Clinton needed to win were to be found. Hyland wanted to know how to get Irish Americans fired up to support Clinton, and O'Dowd told him that activists were hungry for a candidate who would change the long-standing American policy on Northern Ireland. Hyland asked who should chair the Irish Americans for Clinton committee, and O'Dowd suggested former Boston mayor Ray Flynn and Bruce Morrison.

O'Dowd said he would announce a New York meeting in the *Irish Voice* to bring together Irish Americans interested in supporting Clinton. Hyland then called Morrison, who immediately agreed to co-chair the committee.

For the most part, the policy change that Morrison, O'Dowd, and other Irish American activists wanted Clinton to promise didn't seem to have a major political downside. Pretty much everyone who wanted American policy to remain pro-British was already firmly behind Bush. There was, of course, the danger of Clinton being called soft on terrorism, since the British considered the IRA and its allies to be terrorists. But in a pre-9/11 world, that vulnerability didn't come close to offsetting the positive gains of a new Irish policy for the campaign. That didn't mean, however, that opponents of the new policy on both sides of the Atlantic wouldn't do everything they could to tar Clinton with the soft-on-terrorism brush.

———

An important plus in the effort to help Clinton understand both the importance and opportunity involved in changing American policy on Northern Ireland was that Clinton already had some familiarity with the Troubles. So he was all ears when Morrison gave him his analysis of how an American president could help in the peace effort. The key elements involved offering the United States as an honest broker available to both sides, supporting Sinn Féin's efforts to move the IRA to a political path and helping to get all parties, especially those supporting the fighting, to the negotiating table. Recalls Clinton:

> I remember thinking that I had been interested in this since the Troubles began because I was in Oxford when they started. I'd been thinking all this time that this is something where we can really maybe make a difference, but then there was a lot of grumbling and I thought, well, what the hell, this is something I'd really like to get involved in. Bruce had really made a case.
>
> I was profoundly impressed by how much Bruce knew, how much he thought about it, and it's clear he knew what ought to be done, and he knew at that time, before the Downing Street Declaration, that it was somewhat of a long shot, but it was the only card we had to play that had any reasonable chance of defanging

the IRA violence and in the process opening up the British to a change—and that was all the strategy I needed to know.

For his part, Morrison found Clinton splendidly responsive:

> He related to Northern Ireland because of his own civil rights background in Arkansas, so there was a natural affinity for the issue. But Arkansas politics are racial, not ethnic. So it was new, but "quick study" and "Bill Clinton" are synonymous. All these pieces immediately came together in his head, so it did not take much for him to take all this stuff on board.

Clinton's former press secretary Mike McCurry saw Morrison's analysis as having been tailor-made for Clinton: "The argument that would resonate with Clinton would be the one that worked at all of those levels: You can do the right thing, you can do the historic thing, and it's good politics."

As the race for the nomination unfolded, Morrison focused his efforts on the New York primary in April. That contest wasn't typically crucial because it came relatively late in the season, when the nomination was largely settled. But 1992 was different: The whole campaign had been a wild roller-coaster ride, and not just among Democrats battling one another. Texas computer tycoon Ross Perot had mounted a third-party campaign that constantly stirred everything up, and more than a few pundits thought he might actually win a three-way race. Clinton's Gennifer Flowers scandal had threatened to destroy his campaign, but by April he was getting traction for his economic policies. It was becoming increasingly clear that the voters wanted the economy to get better, and if they thought Clinton could do that, they didn't care about the personal stuff.

It was essential for Clinton to win New York because his strongest rival, former California governor Jerry Brown, had beaten him in Connecticut just the week before and also looked strong for the Wisconsin primary, scheduled on the same day as New York's. Although Clinton was already well ahead in delegates, many observers knew there could still be a point at which his personal issues and controversies took hold and derailed his candidacy. Victories by Brown in both New York and Wisconsin could trigger that fatal spiral. Clinton was well aware that he was at a perilous moment:

> It made everybody think, that "We have a chance to derail him in New York." I think after we won on St. Patrick's Day in Michigan and Illinois it would have been difficult for them to stop us. But the outcome in New York was by no means assured. If they had a play, New York was it.
>
> I knew perfectly well that all the people in the Democratic party who didn't want me to be the nominee thought New York was their last chance to stop me, because it's big and complicated and they could portray me as some hayseed from Arkansas.

A Clinton win in New York would put him solidly in the lead for the nomination, and the state's large Irish American vote could well be the key to that victory. Morrison understood this well:

> The Clinton campaign was already focused on Reagan Democrats, of which the Irish are the largest ethnic group. But the campaign's emphasis was on social and economic policy positions that applied to all of the ethnic groups making up the Reagan Democrats. The extra thing that we added during this time was the substantive one that mattered to the Irish: Northern Ireland. And in the end, that made all the difference in the way the campaign developed, and even more so in the way the presidency developed afterward.

Morrison knew exactly what pledges on Northern Ireland would help Clinton get the Irish vote, and he knew that Clinton had to make them at the candidate's forum sponsored by New York's leading Irish American politicians and activists at the Sheraton Hotel in Manhattan on the Sunday night before the primary. This was the perfect opportunity for Clinton to show that Irish Americans should support him as the best hope for a new American policy.

Morrison was developing a comprehensive political strategy to make the most of Clinton's receptivity on Northern Ireland, a strategy that, if things went well, would play out over a span of years. It was a plan he would have to keep to himself, revealing it piecemeal as circumstances required, since the main vehicle for its execution would be none other than the president of the United States. But the Irish American Forum was a key occasion for him to get going with a critical phase of his strategy. Making sure that he crossed paths with Clinton at a Connecticut fund-raiser a week before the forum was a key tactic.

Presidential campaigns—and, for that matter, presidencies—invariably involve elaborate choreography. Morrison knew how that worked, and he was able to engineer one last connection with Clinton before the Irish forum:

> I figured out where he would go when he left the stage and just positioned myself there to say hello to him, to give him a letter that would explain what I could do to help him in Irish America. The letter was about how his friendship with me would be very valuable to him in the New York forum because of the respect I had, having done the Morrison Visas. I wrote that it would help him to say that we were friends and that he should stress his commitment to Irish immigration. I told him that the issues important to Irish America very much included Northern Ireland and that it was very important for him, substantively and politically, to focus on that.

After that encounter, Morrison was confident that Clinton understood what mattered most to those attending the forum. High on the list of changes the Irish Americans wanted was for the United States to get directly involved in helping to resolve the conflict by sending an American peace envoy to Northern Ireland. They also wanted the United States to give Sinn Féin president Gerry Adams an American

visa, despite his reputed terrorist involvement, so that he could appear
in person in front of Irish Americans to make his case for moving the
IRA to a political path, as well as acquiring increased credibility on
the international stage. In addition, nearly all wanted more immigration opportunities for the Irish and for the United States to support
economic development in Northern Ireland. Many supported the
McBride Principles, which tied American investment in Northern
Ireland to progress on human rights, just as the Sullivan Principles
had done with respect to investment in South Africa. These issues
weren't new to Democratic presidential politics: The idea of a peace
envoy had been promised as far back as Jimmy Carter and support
for the Adams visa followed in the '80s. Since neither had yet been
delivered, the expectations moved to the 1992 candidates.

Morrison knew how important it would be for Clinton to make
himself heard on this entire group of issues, since each of them was
important to a strong constituency within Irish America. As he thought
it through, it struck him that this was a lot like putting together the
coalition for his 1990 immigration bill: Everybody in Irish America
would hear hopeful words about something important to them personally when Clinton spoke about Northern Ireland. Making this happen was a central pillar of Morrison's overall strategy for moving the
United States, through Clinton, into playing a key role in ending the
warfare in Northern Ireland.

Mike McCurry, who became White House press secretary in 1995,
stresses how unusual it was for a candidate like Clinton to dive so
wholeheartedly into an issue like Northern Ireland:

> If you're the governor of a small state like Arkansas and you're
> running for president, the number one criticism that usually
> comes at you when it comes to foreign policy is that you have
> no experience in dealing in global matters. So the tendency is
> to not say anything that's going to sound naïve or like you're not
> up to speed and not to take risks when it comes to making pro-
> nouncements. You pretty much stick to whatever the orthodoxy

that reflects, in most cases, the current positions of the US government. You don't try to rock the boat at all. But that isn't the story here. I think Morrison was the one who guided Clinton to an understanding that there was a political opportunity there, as well as a substantive one.

By the Sunday of the forum, with the crucial primary just two days away, Morrison felt confident that Clinton was where he needed to be on Northern Ireland. In addition to Morrison's input, New York City finance commissioner Carol O'Cleireacain had been dispatched by Clinton's New York campaign manager Harold Ickes to give him a last-minute briefing for the forum. She and her Irish husband, Seamus, assured Clinton that positive changes really were happening in Northern Ireland and encouraged him to commit to an independent American policy there. Clinton himself felt ready for the forum:

> When they set the meeting up, I thought it was a must-do, and Bruce convinced me it was a must-do. The Irish vote was a factor: New York had notoriously low turnout, so a hardcore group of committed Irish voters could make a difference. So I was interested in the forum—I thought politically it was important, and Morrison had set it up so it looked like it was. He at least convinced me that if those people in that room were for me that I would get a hell of a vote in the Democratic primary.

Clinton triumphed at the forum. When longtime Noraid stalwart Martin Galvin asked the hottest question—would he give Gerry Adams a visa to come to the United States to make his case?—Clinton without hesitation said he would. He added that he thought it would be "totally harmless to our national security interests" and that "it might be enlightening to the political debate in this country about the issues in Ireland." In response to other questions, he said he would send an American peace envoy to Northern Ireland and made it clear that he was on board with Irish America's support of the McBride Principles and economic initiatives in the north. He wasn't asked about immigration, but because Morrison had primed him so well, he brought it up himself at the end and got warm applause when he said he was a friend of Bruce Morrison's. When Jerry Brown arrived after midnight and said many of the same things—but didn't mention immigration or Bruce Morrison—it was too late: Bill Clinton had already won the hearts of New York's Irish Americans.

In the aftermath of that long night, Clinton recognized that not everyone in his campaign was going to be happy with the pledges he'd made. "I'm sure there were people who didn't want me to go [to the forum] because they were afraid I'd do what I did." Clinton has no doubts about doing exactly what he did: "I just know that when I look back on the '92 campaign, I think one of the most consequential things that happened was that Irish meeting." He has never forgotten Morrison's role: "I depended on him to basically prep me for the meeting."

For his part, Morrison didn't feel the need to go into New York on Sunday night for the forum itself, which he knew was likely to run very late. He felt confident that Clinton was prepared and would handle it well, and, besides, his wife was eight and a half months pregnant with their son. Very soon Morrison, adopted at birth, was going to meet a blood relative for the first time. He wanted to do all he could for Clinton, but this was the time to be at home.

———

Clinton won New York by huge margin and Wisconsin by a narrow one. He was well on his way to the nomination. So far, so good for Morison and O'Dowd's plan.

Morrison and Clinton next met in June at a major Manhattan fund-raiser for ethnic constituencies. Morrison had been heavily involved in the creation and promotion of the event, and Clinton greeted him warmly. As they spoke, Morrison was startled to notice that the candidate was wearing a bulletproof vest under his shirt.

Things were really changing—Morrison remembers that that was probably the last time he called him Bill.

There was every reason to feel hopeful that a major shift in American policy toward Northern Ireland was coming—provided, of course, that Clinton could get past one remaining hurdle: He had to beat a sitting president, something that had been done only three times in the twentieth century. That was the rub, and many influential and wealthy Irish Americans were holding back their financial support because, as much as they appreciated Clinton's promises, they didn't see any way he could beat Bush.

So the challenges Morrison and O'Dowd faced in getting Irish American support for Clinton continued. There was a real danger that if Clinton did win but the Irish vote came in short, he would feel less bound by his promises. Morrison was determined to do everything he could to build the kind of support that would make it undeniably clear to Clinton that his promises on Northern Ireland had paid off at the polls.

As the summer progressed, the Clinton campaign got itself a top foreign-policy advisor: Nancy Soderberg, a member of Ted Kennedy's Senate staff and his chief advisor on Northern Ireland. Soderberg had heard about the pledges Clinton made just before the New York primary, and they didn't make her happy. She, like Kennedy, was highly skeptical of Gerry Adams and his party's links to the IRA. She hated IRA violence and was convinced that the best path to peace was the one espoused by John Hume, with his abhorrence of violence and emphasis on economic opportunity. For years, Hume had had a lock on influencing the Irish American political establishment on Northern Ireland policy. Although, to his great credit, Hume had pursued his dialogue with Adams, his Irish American followers tended to steer clear, many doubting that the Sinn Féin leader's purported efforts to get the IRA on a political path were genuine.

Despite their differences on the best approach in Northern Ireland, Soderberg and Morrison trusted and respected each other enough to speak bluntly, like two old pols. Soderberg ruefully told Morrison that if she had been on board earlier, Clinton never would have made those promises, but it was clear to Morrison that she accepted what her new boss had done and that she was willing to consider what Morrison had to say with an open mind. Her consistent availability to him, and her increasing willingness to consider that Adams might be the key to a breakthrough, made her an extraordinarily valuable ally in the efforts to get to a new American policy.

———

Clinton won the Democratic nomination in mid-July. His prospects for beating Bush got a huge boost on the very day he was to give his acceptance speech, when Ross Perot, who had promised to look under the hood and fix what ails America, dropped out of the race. By the time the convention was over, Clinton, who had often been running third in the polls, now had a strong lead over Bush. "It's the economy, stupid!" had really taken hold, and more and more voters were deciding they would be better off with Bush out and Clinton in.

As the fall campaign flashed by in a mere two months—just a fraction of the nearly two years since Clinton's fight for the Democratic nomination had begun—Morrison and O'Dowd redoubled their efforts to get Irish America politically and financially behind the best hope ever for a radical new American approach to Northern Ireland.

Bush continued to enjoy the support of people who wanted the United States to keep to the British line on Northern Ireland, but those were votes he already had. The government and the party of conservative British prime minister John Major were ready and willing to do everything possible to make sure Clinton's Northern Ireland promises never became official American policy. The Tories sent two operatives to the Bush campaign bearing absurd dirty trick ideas, including a proposal to distribute fake photographs of Bill Clinton with hippie hair waving a Vietcong flag, which the Bush campaign wisely rejected. One thing the British did do for Bush was to rummage through their passport records in hopes of confirming a rumor that

Clinton had traveled to the Soviet Union while at Oxford. They came up empty on that one, and the British paid a price when Clinton got elected and made it clear, sometimes through razor-edged humor, that he was not happy about the Tory meddling. The rift complicated the early stages of developing a working relationship between the two heads of government, though years later, Clinton would take a more benign view and even find a silver lining:

> There was this rumor that when I was involved in the antiwar movement I tried to give up my American citizenship to become British or Russian or something or other. So there was all this out-rage, including in my own camp at the end of the campaign, but it just didn't bother me: I was delighted to have them barking up that tree instead of figuring out how to position President Bush in a more positive way, which was what they should have done.

Toward the end of October, with Clinton's prospects looking increasingly positive, Morrison wanted his promises on Northern Ireland reaffirmed in writing so he could reassure Irish American activists that it was more than just campaign chatter. Clinton agreed and had Nancy Soderberg, who was still not entirely sure it was the right way to go, draft the letter. She made one last appeal to Morrison, arguing that the election was virtually won and there was no need to put it in writing—that both of them wanted Clinton to win and neither of them wanted him to stumble. From a professional point of view, Morrison understood her concern that it was important not to risk anything by courting controversy or picking a fight with America's best friend, but he held his ground. He knew that Clinton had directed her to prepare the letter, and he wanted it in his hands. In the end, Soderberg did what her boss told her to do, in spirit and with full force.

The letter reiterated most of Clinton's controversial pledges, including the appointment of a peace envoy. The visa for Gerry Adams was not mentioned: Morrison asked that it be included, and Soderberg asked Clinton, but Clinton said no. But the letter's blunt criticism of the British on controversial points—including collusion between British-backed security forces and Ulster paramilitaries and inadequate British opposition to job discrimination in Northern Ireland—tempered any disappointment Morrison and the Irish American activists might have felt over that omission. The greatest testament to the power of the letter came in the form of the intense British denunciation of it. "That letter made London crazy," Morrison told Irish journalist Conor O'Clery. And certainly anything so upsetting to the British was more than good enough for the Irish Americans backing Clinton.

For Morrison, the letter was a carefully considered building block of his overall strategy. Because it came at a time when Clinton was solidly in the lead and widely expected to win, it reassured Irish Americans that his pledges were more than the campaign promises of a candidate struggling—desperate, even—to get every vote he could. By insisting on the letter when he did, Morrison got Clinton to persuasively show Irish American activists that he was standing his ground on Northern Ireland even when there was no immediate political gain to be had, since his promises about changing American policy weren't at that point going to have much bearing on the outcome of the election.

In addition to showing Irish Americans that Clinton's commitment was genuine, Morrison also intended the letter to serve notice to the British that Clinton's concern was real and that he was willing to take risks to make peace happen. Morrison knew Clinton well enough to know that British pushback would make it all the more likely that he would keep his promises. "Resistance made the letter all the more important," Morrison said later. "In effect, the letter said, 'And I mean it!'"

Morrison's third strategic target of the letter was Clinton himself. "Politicians always say, 'Now is not the time.' But our message was, 'The time *is* now—and next week, and next month, until we get it done.'" The soon-to-be-president was on notice that his old classmate and his cohort weren't going away.

For Soderberg herself, soon to be appointed deputy national security advisor in the Clinton White House, Morrison saw the letter as representing nothing less than the commencement of planning the administration's policy on Northern Ireland.

————

On Election Day, Clinton won an impressive victory. Although he didn't win a plurality of the vote—in a bizarre twist, Perot had jumped back in—he decisively routed Bush, carrying thirty-two states plus the District of Columbia and winning the popular vote by 6 million.

Morrison and the Irish Americans who had bet on Clinton were ecstatic. But Morrison's delight was tempered by his awareness that just because a presidential candidate promises something, wins, and sincerely wants to keep his promise, that doesn't guarantee that the issue will get to the top of the agenda or that unforeseen events won't relegate it to the back burner. In other words, after the long haul that began when Niall O'Dowd asked Morrison, "What about your classmate Bill Clinton?" the job of turning Clinton's promises into American foreign policy was now just beginning. This was no surprise to Morrison: A core element of his overall strategy from the outset was the recognition that the real work would begin after Election Day.

Those who thought that throwing out long-established American policy was a terrible idea were already sharpening their knives. The British and their American allies in the State Department and the FBI had the terrorist brush ready to go. Opposition to the new policy would be intense and relentless. In marshaling supporters, Morrison knew that the road wouldn't rise to meet them and the wind wouldn't be at their backs.

CHAPTER SIX

When Clinton Wins, the Real Work Begins

I n most circumstances, getting stuck in Nashville would have its advantages. It's Music City USA, with the Grand Ole Opry and countless honky-tonks like Tootsie's Orchid Lounge. It's also the Athens of the South, with its very own full-scale Parthenon. But this was January 13, 1993, and Bill Clinton would be inaugurated in a week. Almost 350 miles away in Little Rock, Clinton and his team were in the thick of final preparations for the move to Washington. So there was nothing good about Bruce Morrison, chairman of Americans for a New Irish Agenda (ANIA), freshly rebranded from Irish Americans for Clinton-Gore, being stuck in the Nashville airport.

He was supposed to be leading a delegation of Irish Americans to Clinton's headquarters in Little Rock to collect on the president-elect's promises on Ireland. But instead of being in the midst of the post-election, pre-inauguration turmoil, here he was in an American Airlines lounge he'd managed to talk himself into, trying his best to participate in meetings via speakerphone. The visit to Little Rock could be crucial in determining how high on the new president's agenda his pledges on Ireland would get, and making the case over the speaker-phone just wasn't anything like being there.

It had been snowing in Hartford when he got to the airport that morning, but he'd gambled that the plane would take off in time for him to catch his connecting flight to Little Rock. He lost that bet: The plane sat on the tarmac for two hours. When they were finally cleared for takeoff, Morrison knew he had no hope of getting to Little Rock in time. The events yet to come in the remains of the day—a frustrating conference call followed by a long interval of airport nothingness, followed by another long flight right back to where he'd started, without ever having set foot in Arkansas—beckoned grimly. He didn't feel like much of a chairman.

Morrison was sure that there was plenty of action happening in Little Rock, and he was right. The energy and chaos that greeted Niall O'Dowd and other members of the Irish American delegation was a sight to behold. Boxes and file cabinets were everywhere. In the turmoil of aides darting this way and that, staffers trying to pack for Washington, and many interest groups jockeying to get their voices heard, little meetings were carved out among the chaos. Big shots and savvy operators were desperate to find that crucial ear or key exchange that could make all the difference in something important, and the Irish Americans were having their audience with whoever was available. They had been scheduled to meet with Nancy Soderberg, soon to be deputy national security advisor, but she got called away to meet with the president-elect about a sudden crisis in Libya.

The one real meeting the Irish Americans did get was with Christopher Hyland, who headed up ethnic outreach for Clinton and had been in touch with O'Dowd since early in the campaign. Hyland had been an unrelenting inside-the-campaign voice on Northern Ireland, doing everything he could to get Clinton's staff to understand the importance of getting Clinton involved and enduring unending eye-rolling and worse in the process. (Nancy Soderberg would later praise his ethnic outreach efforts as, "tireless and incredibly effective in a thankless job.") Undaunted, he carefully planned his meeting with the Irish Americans—he called it the Irish American Round Table—and did everything necessary to have Morrison participate by phone. Morrison did his best over the speakerphone, and when it was over, those who'd made it to Little Rock flew back to Nashville to connect for their flights home. They found Morrison still there, waiting to leave for Hartford, the second leg of his wintertime journey to nowhere. Morrison remembers their return: "They arrived from Little Rock on their way back to New York with big smiles on their faces. The good news was that they were very upbeat about their meeting with Chris Hyland. The bad news was that I'd spent the day at the Nashville airport."

Smiles notwithstanding, the Americans for a New Irish Agenda couldn't point to much in the way of concrete payoff from their visit to Little Rock. The president was never in reach, and Soderberg got called away. In truth, this was a perfect preview of the difficulties involved in turning Clinton's promises into real change. The competition for his attention was unimaginably intense. There was every reason to fear that the new Irish policy might get lost in the welter of equally worthy issues. There was also the possibility that Clinton would begin to think that his promises had been a mistake to begin with and that the risks—potential harm to the relationship between the United States and Britain and too much chance of failure—were simply too high. Certainly Soderberg might still welcome the chance to walk her boss's promises back. And there was always the possibility that Northern Ireland would get swamped by one or another—or maybe several—acute crises threatening national security or some other vital national interests.

The Irish Americans, however, did accomplish something important at their pre-inaugural visit: They showed up and they made it clear that they would keep showing up. They also knew that they had to attend to their base: Although their formidable Irish American constituency put real muscle behind their efforts, it was a constituency that would require ongoing attention and would always demand evidence that their leaders were on the right track. The key promises everyone was waiting to see fulfilled were the appointment of a peace envoy to Northern Ireland and an American visa for Gerry Adams. If those things never happened, the prospects for a real break with past American policy were bleak. And even if they just took too long, there was a danger that Irish activists, thoroughly accustomed to being let down or forgotten about by politicians, would start fighting amongst themselves and turn on their leaders.

So Morrison had plenty to worry about. But his overall strategy contained a plan to deal with that:

> Many groups like this go out of existence soon after Election Day, but our organization was about some very specific policy positions and some very specific commitments that Clinton had made. To me it was critically important not to fall back on existing Irish American organizations to carry forward that agenda, but to try to hold those groups together in some kind of alliance that would, in a coordinated, consistent way, follow up on the good work that was done during the campaign. So I suggested that we move forward with an advocacy organization, not a campaign organization. We christened it Americans for a New Irish Agenda, very consciously saying that it was a *new* agenda and was being pushed by Americans, not Irish. It would be an organization for all the various groups in Irish America to come together and support each other in focusing on Clinton's five promises from the forum in April.
>
> We were able to be a focused and effective presence on behalf of the things we'd gained during the campaign. One of the mistakes groups make in elections is that they extract commitments from candidates, but lack the follow-through after the person is in office, not just to advocate for what they want and what was promised, but also to facilitate the political situation that makes it easier rather than harder for their candidate to deliver. And that's what ANIA was. It wasn't a large organization, but it brought together a large number of organizations and people committed to the same goals.

Shortly before his would-be Little Rock sojourn, Morrison decided he had to do something that pretty much everybody working with him on Northern Ireland hated. He believed strongly that the British should be told what ANIA was planning to do. For him, this was fundamental: "Northern Ireland is British territory, even if some people don't like to acknowledge it, so we should pay them the respect of going and saying, 'Here is what we're doing and here's why and here's what you might think about it.'"

He got himself an appointment at the British embassy, not so hard for a former congressman with considerable standing in Ireland. Whether he would receive more than a polite hearing with no meaningful engagement was the real question. The embassy gave the job to two young diplomats, one of whom was Jonathan Powell, who a few years later would become deeply involved in Northern Ireland as Tony Blair's chief of staff. Powell and the other diplomat listened politely as Morrison told them that he knew Clinton personally and that the new president was serious about his commitment to make America part of the peace process in Northern Ireland. He did his best to persuade them that it was in Britain's interests to consider that the new American approach might hold real value for them. His message was that ANIA was going to Little Rock to claim what the president had promised—that Clinton meant what he said and that ANIA existed to make sure it happened. The essence of his message was, "The new president of the United States, your best friend in the world, has substantive and political reasons to want to play a role. Instead of getting upset and asking him not to meddle, you might welcome his involvement. Tell him, 'Anything you can do to help sort out this historic problem we have in our midst would be appreciated.'"

Morrison emphasized that if the British made it a matter of pride and principle—essentially, "How dare you meddle in the affairs of the United Kingdom?"—that would only make it more likely that Clinton would push to get himself involved. Morrison wanted to see them "co-opt his interest rather than reject it."

The conversation was one-sided. Politeness reigned. Morrison's hope that the British would see Clinton's promises as an opportunity instead of an intrusion seemed to get no traction at all. There was no way these young men were going to tell their superiors that a fresh

look at Clinton's plans might make sense. Morrison later summed
the meeting up as "message delivered, message received," and nothing more. But as the years passed, he became enormously proud that
he had insisted on it. It demonstrated that as the Americans injected
themselves into the peace process, they would deal straight up with all
sides, and they wouldn't go behind Britain's back. That principle would
prove invaluable in establishing the Americans as honest brokers who
would be open-minded and available to everyone. And that reputation, established so powerfully by Morrison and carried forward by
Bill Clinton and George Mitchell, was the cornerstone of the American
role that would turn out to be so crucial to the ultimate success of the
peace process.

_____

A few months after Clinton took office, it was still an open question
whether he would keep his promises—and things weren't looking
good. His pledge to appoint a peace envoy was opposed by Irish prime
minister Albert Reynolds. Morrison got a sense of Reynolds's position
early in 1993 when the Taoiseach was in Washington for St. Patrick's
Day. Reynolds invited Morrison to ride with him in his limousine
from the Irish embassy to the Ireland Fund dinner, and during the ride
Reynolds took the opportunity to tell Morrison about what types of
American involvement he thought would—and would not—be helpful. His determination not to lose control of peacemaking efforts to the
Americans was clear, and he was worried that a Clinton peace envoy
might jeopardize his own relationship with British prime minister
John Major. Reynolds knew how badly his British counterpart had
started out with Clinton, and he seized the opportunity to do Major
a favor by urging Clinton to shelve the peace envoy plan. Reynolds the
businessman was always on the lookout for the chance to do Major a
favor that might pay rich dividends in the future.

It was also evident that Reynolds had doubts about Clinton himself, as Morrison recalls: "He was probably not at all sure what Clinton was like. He had already watched him make a hash of gays in the

military, so whether he had the subtleties down sufficiently to be a player in Ireland or whether he would put a big foot in it and make a mess was probably an open question in Albert's mind."

Reynolds's comments gave Morrison a good sense of what was troubling him. He'd had reason to believe that Reynolds would welcome a strong American presence in the peace process, but now it was clear that he had real concerns about whether or not Clinton was up to it. Could the young president carry a new policy forward effectively? Would he stick with it? Would the involvement contemplated by his lavish promises do more harm than good? Obviously there was a lot more to Reynolds's urging of Clinton to shelve the peace envoy than just doing a favor for John Major.

Reynolds would go on to become one of the most important and courageous players in the search for peace. Morrison greatly valued his early contact with him:

> I came to know in retrospect how different he was from the average Irish politician: He was blunt, he really spoke his mind, and he said things that you don't expect to hear from the prime minister. He was not a typical politician; his self-image was not as a politician. He thought of himself as a successful businessman, knowledgeable about budgets; as somebody who'd been a finance minister, he thought that he was good at it. He had the sort of hard-nosed business leader view of jobs to be done. It served him wonderfully well with respect to the peace process, because there had been so much BS out of the Irish government over the years about Northern Ireland and so little constructive action. He was having none of that and was cutting to the chase at every turn.
>
> At every occasion when there was something to be done and we were trying to work constructively with the Irish government, he would meet privately with us, and he said what was on his mind—there wasn't a lot of equivocation, there wasn't a lot of papering over with fancy phrases. It was, "This is where I am, this is what I want, this is what I say." Obviously you could push

back if you thought something different, and he would listen, but he was direct and blunt and constructive. Although that got him in a lot of trouble over other things that ended his political career, it sure was what was needed at the moment.

Ultimately, Clinton followed Reynolds's advice and held off on the peace envoy. Like Reynolds, Clinton was an astute politician; he certainly understood that agreeing to Reynolds's request could help him get his own relationship with Major on a better footing.

Clinton's other key promise to the Irish Americans—a US visa for Gerry Adams—was also not looking good. Early in 1993, Adams's book publisher had applied for a visa for him to do an American tour. Morrison was unhappy that the request had been made at all—it was ill-coordinated, ill-prepared, ill-considered, and ill-timed—and he wasn't the slightest bit surprised when Clinton turned it down cold. Morrison knew there were three crucial elements that a focused effort to redeem the Adams visa promise required: The proper groundwork had to be laid, the timing had to be right, and the purpose of Adams's visit had to be lofty and broad, not self-serving or confrontational. Morrison understood that a history of visa turndowns could establish a precedent that would make it very difficult for Clinton to change course. Would he really be willing to reverse himself and take on the unrelenting opposition of the British government and his own State Department, Justice Department, and FBI?

The other serious problem was that Clinton's Irish American supporters were beginning to get skeptical and restive—the pessimistic activists were sure they were headed down the same old road of broken promises—and it took all of Morrison's powers of persuasion to get them to be patient enough to let the right visa request be presented in the right way at the right time. This was a tough job; the various Irish American groups were constantly splitting up, regrouping, forming other groups, and fighting with one another. (There's an old joke that if you get twelve Irish activists together to do something, you wind up with thirteen separate organizations.) Morrison knew that if the Irish Americans couldn't keep their own groups on track, their case wouldn't be persuasive with the new administration. And any sense that the Irish Americans who had been so excited about Clinton were starting to jump ship could seriously dampen the new president's enthusiasm for radically changing the old policy that suited the British and their American supporters so well.

These setbacks gave plenty of reason for discouragement, but Morrison never lost sight of the urgency of continuing to press the case with the White House and of giving credit when credit was due. He understood this dance exceptionally well:

> We had to play carrot and stick in the public arena. Nobody in the government wanted Clinton to do any of this stuff, so we set up an accountability structure, a mechanism by which we intended to criticize and praise in proportion to what did and didn't get done. The president would see both the political upside and the political necessity of getting engaged.
>
> The praise, what I call reinforcement, is often overlooked. A lot of people in politics only whine about what they don't get and what doesn't happen and are very spare in acknowledging accomplishment unless utopia arrives. People like to be appreciated, to have their progress noted. That was a big part of what we tried to remember, because "What have you done for me lately?" constituencies can really frustrate you when you beat your brains out to get something done and it never seems to be enough. I think Bill Clinton and his team did feel like their efforts were appreciated, and I think that was very helpful.

As disheartening as the beginning months of the Clinton administration were to the Irish Americans, the signals from the republicans in Northern Ireland were encouraging. Most communication came through Niall O'Dowd from his network of contacts in Sinn Féin and the IRA. Things might be stalled in the United States, but Sinn Féin was pressing O'Dowd to get an American delegation to Northern Ireland in the spring in order for the IRA to see that there was reason to hope American policy would change profoundly. The message to America was clear: It's time for you to come over here and show us something new.

Morrison was unavailable to go to Northern Ireland at that time, so O'Dowd asked former Boston mayor Ray Flynn to be the group's political leader. When Flynn agreed to go—and to keep the plan confidential, as Sinn Féin had requested—the trip was set. O'Dowd sent a message back to Sinn Féin that an IRA ceasefire for the duration of their visit would be a big help to the Americans in pressing their case with the White House when they returned. This was an audacious request: apart from occasional brief holiday ceasefires, this was not something the IRA did. There had been a short ceasefire years earlier that the IRA regarded as a disaster never to be repeated. It took everything Gerry Adams and Sinn Féin had, but they were able to persuade the IRA of the immense value of showing the White House that real progress toward peace could be made if Clinton carried through on his promises.

At last there was reason to be hopeful. The Americans knew how extraordinary the ceasefire promise was, and they were confident that it would make a strong impression on the White House. But as the time to leave for Ireland drew closer, O'Dowd found that Ray Flynn had suddenly become very hard to reach. O'Dowd suspected that he had broken his promise to keep the trip secret, and he was right. After Flynn finally begged off altogether (through a spokesman), O'Dowd learned that he had widely shopped the question of whether leading the trip would help or hinder his prospects for a high-level job in the Clinton administration, ultimately deciding it was too risky to go.

This was a disaster. Political leadership was essential for the success of the mission, because the key players in the peace process were politicians, and the process itself was fundamentally political: It was essentially an effort to negotiate a deal that would replace war with politics. With no experienced and skillful politician at the helm, O'Dowd had no choice but to scrap the spring trip altogether.

The credibility of the Irish American peace process venture was now severely, perhaps fatally, damaged. O'Dowd's plans were up in smoke, with major collateral damage—not to mention huge embarrassment—on both sides of the Atlantic.

The sowing of doubts among those in the administration who knew about trip was troubling enough, but the problems in Belfast were far more serious. Sinn Féin had gone far out on a limb by pushing the IRA to declare a ceasefire for the American visit. In the eyes of the IRA, the ceasefire had accomplished nothing and had placed them at a military disadvantage. Their only question was whether the Americans were playing them for fools or were just incompetent. O'Dowd's Sinn Féin contacts soon told him to get over to Belfast right away and explain the mess.

O'Dowd's journey involved the usual intrigue of getting to a secret location for a secret meeting. The driver from Sinn Féin—or perhaps the IRA itself—was constantly watching the mirror, doubling back, changing direction, and crisscrossing through the dark streets of West Belfast. As they zeroed in on the destination that would put O'Dowd in a room with men who had killed for the cause and would not like being played, the would-be peace impresario struggled to fend off worries about his personal safety.

The meeting went as well as such a thing could. Adams presided, calm but relentless. The hard men in the group were unsettlingly quiet. O'Dowd told the whole embarrassing story with complete candor. To his immense relief, his account was accepted, and Adams asked if a new trip could be organized. O'Dowd said he thought he could get one together for late summer. This time he knew that Bruce Morrison had to be the political leader.

Morrison agreed, and plans were quickly under way for a delegation of four Americans with no official government status to go to Belfast in early September. They would carry a message of Clinton's interest in helping resolve the bloody conflict, and they hoped to return with encouraging news of what the United States could do.

CHAPTER SEVEN

The Unofficial Peacemakers in Northern Ireland

In the late summer of 1993, the British border control station where Ireland's N-1 highway meets Northern Ireland's A-1 on the way to Belfast was an unmistakable reminder that to enter the north was to enter a land at war.

After passing through the main gate, all travelers were subject to being stopped for interrogation and search by the British soldiers and the RUC. Behind those who decided who got stopped were more soldiers in full combat gear, some of whom watched from observation towers equipped with "general purpose" machine guns.

If reinforcements were needed, soldiers at a British army encampment housed in an old linen mill a short way up the road in the village of Bessbrook were at the ready, along with pilots at the improvised heliport outside the village that had become the busiest in all of Europe, with its constant bellowing and batting of engines and rotors. The military helicopters blanketed the border area, patrolling for terrorists and smugglers, who ducked border control by taking narrow back roads. The British regularly blasted holes in those roads in an effort to force everyone—travelers, smugglers, and paramilitaries alike—to keep to the main route.

Plenty of cars were stopped for questioning and maybe a search, but the car carrying a small party of unofficial American peacemakers was allowed to continue on to Belfast, now less than forty miles ahead, without incident. Riding with Bruce Morrison and Niall O'Dowd, impresario of this audacious journey, were Chuck Feeney and William J. Flynn, two Irish American businessmen of radically different styles.

Feeney was a brilliant, hard-nosed entrepreneur who cofounded a chain of duty-free shops in 1960 that became a multibillion-dollar venture. He became one of the richest men in the world, but he was no stereotypical big-time billionaire. His personal style was one of complete self-effacement—he had a plan to give away nearly all of his fortune, including hundreds of millions to his alma mater Cornell, though he never wanted anything named after him. He was obsessively private and hated being photographed. Feeney dressed modestly— there was even a story that he was once spotted with his pants held up by a safety pin. As Morrison describes him, "Chuck is very low-key, respectful, and inquisitive, the opposite of the table-pounding and demanding Donald Trump type. He's always human scale, as opposed to grand and pontificating."

By the time the Americans met up in Dublin, Feeney was no longer the multibillionaire that *Forbes* had reported him to be; he had already given almost all of his assets to Atlantic Philanthropies, a mysterious foundation that made grants anonymously to people and organizations that hadn't asked for them. Feeney was now in the business of charity, driven to use his resources to make a difference in the world, undeterred by what others might think.

Feeney's commitment to peace in Northern Ireland reached its peak when he saw the horrific images of the 1987 IRA bombing in Enniskillen, home to some of his forbearers, on television. He was moved to tears as he listened to the transcendent response of a father who held the hand of his grown daughter, a nurse, as she died in the rubble: "I bear no grudge. Dirty sort of talk is not going to bring her back to life. She was a great wee lassie. She loved her profession. She was a pet. She's dead. She's in heaven and we shall meet again. I will pray for these men tonight and every night." Feeney was determined to do anything he could to help end the violence.

The other businessman in the delegation, William J. Flynn, was entirely the corporate man. Chief executive officer of the insurance giant Mutual of America, he was tall and elegant, with beautifully tailored clothes. An ex-marine and a very devout Roman Catholic, he was the very model of the fully arrived, establishment-certified Irish American business success and was entirely at home at the University Club on Fifth Avenue near St. Patrick's Cathedral in New York. As a prominent CEO, Flynn was always willing to call upon his contacts—moneyed, social, corporate, political, and academic—to support and advance the struggle for peace in Northern Ireland. He was also a serious student of foreign policy, and his involvement in that arena would prove invaluable as the process moved forward. He did business and made connections in a direct and personal way, belonging not only to the high ranks of corporate America, but also to Ireland, where his parents had been born and raised and where he visited frequently. Flynn was eager to get other CEOs behind the developing peace process, but he never hesitated to tell the Irish republicans that the violence had to stop or they'd lose corporate America.

————

The members of the little American team landed in Dublin in the early morning hours of Monday, September 6, 1993. They met in the Westbury Hotel coffee shop off Grafton Street. Niall O'Dowd pulled out the letter from Sinn Féin that had been delivered to him by courier in New York, confirming that there'd be an IRA ceasefire for the duration of their visit. Sinn Féin demanded that it be kept secret; if word of the ceasefire got out, the IRA would cancel it and get right back to the bombs and guns. Because one of the goals of the trip was to show that Sinn Féin had the ability to deliver a ceasefire in response to American involvement—what Morrison called a "demonstration ceasefire"—its cancellation would deal a serious blow to their prospects for success before they even got out of the Republic.

One by one, Morrison, Feeney, and Flynn read the letter. It drove home, in a way nothing else had, that their journey was about war and peace, life and death. When everyone had finished reading it, O'Dowd, as he'd been instructed, destroyed it right there at the table, tearing it into the tiniest of bits.

The Americans spent the rest of their day in Dublin meeting with top officials. Although Morrison was fond of describing the American group as "nobodies," he was well aware that they were nobodies who could get meetings at the highest levels. "I remember being impressed that we got such good access," he said later, recalling the day in Dublin when they met with a prime minister, a president, and an ambassador. Money may be the mother's milk of politics, but access to the powerful is the coin of the realm.

Taoiseach Albert Reynolds had held the office for a little more than a year, and he was already deeply involved in the situation in Northern Ireland. Reynolds, who saw himself as more of a businessman than a politician, was certain there was a way to negotiate a resolution to pretty much any problem.

When the Americans arrived, Reynolds cleared everyone else out of his office for a full two hours. He brought his guests up to date on his secret exchanges with British prime minister John Major and laid out his vision for getting to peace. It was a productive meeting, and the Americans found Reynolds open to new approaches. He treated them as teammates, but it was clear to Morrison that this wily character's mind was whirring fast with thoughts of how he could make them the instruments of his strategic vision. For their part, the Americans remained true to their promise to Sinn Féin and didn't tell the Taoiseach about the ceasefire.

Irish president Mary Robinson received the Americans at her official residence, *Áras an Uachtaráin*, as warmly and as sympathetically as the constraints of her post allowed. She was the head of state but had no substantive governmental role, and the meeting was largely ceremonial. But because Morrison had met with her the year before and they'd had a long off-the-record discussion about human rights issues, he was confident that peace in Northern Ireland was profoundly important to her and that she would do whatever she could on the issue.

The last stop on that long Monday was a visit to the American embassy at Ballsbridge. When the Clinton administration had started the search for a new American ambassador to Ireland, Jean Kennedy Smith decided that she wanted the job. Her brother was Ted Kennedy, chieftain of everything Irish in the US Senate, so when a simple message—"Jean wants it"—went out, the search was basically over. When Smith was officially chosen in March, Ted Kennedy wrote that she was "returning in the spring," thereby redeeming the promise their brother President John F. Kennedy had made at the end of his last visit to Ireland but didn't live to keep.

It was immediately clear to her visitors that the ambassador was still new to the job. Because her brother Ted was so influenced by moderate nationalist leader John Hume, Smith seemed to have zero enthusiasm for her visitors' plan to engage with Sinn Féin and support a visa for Gerry Adams. In fairness to Smith and Ted Kennedy, the terrible legacy of the assassinations of their brothers John and Robert made the prospect of seeking a way to peace through contact with those close to the IRA deeply unappealing.

"She was clearly uneasy with being drawn into a conversation on this," Morrison recalled. "She was guarded and holding back, unsure of her role and unsure of her facts because she hadn't spent a lot of time on this issue. She'd only been there a few months, and here we were with a grandiose plan—we were going to meet with everybody and talk about the peace envoy. On some level it was, 'What are you doing here in Dublin? You should be in London talking to that ambassador.'"

The Americans left the meeting with Smith with a shared sense of disappointment. "We expected more engagement," Morrison says. "She was a bit detached. I would say that at that moment, she was more than anything Ted Kennedy's sister. She was in the position because Teddy wanted her to be, and Teddy's view of Northern Ireland was whatever John Hume said, so it was unclear where we sat in the picture." But it wouldn't be long before this Kennedy sister became entirely her own person and a major player in the peace process— "jumping in," as Morrison said later, "with both feet."

————

By the time the Americans were preparing to head north to Belfast the next morning, two important decisions about how they'd operate in the north had been settled: The first was who would do the talking; the second was what they would talk about. Although it was clear that each member of the American group—not a shrinking violet among them—would speak his mind without hesitation throughout the visit, the group needed a spokesman. Because O'Dowd had organized the trip, it was his call who that person would be. Without hesitation, he chose Morrison.

O'Dowd had previously determined two crucial attributes the American spokesman would need to have: He should speak with an American accent and he shouldn't be a Catholic. Morrison, a Lutheran who grew up on Long Island, fit the bill. His adoptive father had some Irish blood and reportedly his biological father did as well, but Morrison had once been described as resembling—of all things—a benevolent British army colonel. It had to be the pale skin, sandy hair, thick mustache, and merry laugh.

O'Dowd also knew how important it was that the spokesman be skilled and knowledgeable in the art of politics, and having worked closely with Morrison on the passage of the 1990 Immigration Act, he had the highest opinion of Morrison's political understanding and skill. He also knew that Morrison had a masterly command of the complex and subtle issues involved in Ireland, both historically and in modern times. Lastly, O'Dowd knew that Morrison was so revered throughout Ireland that he was literally a household name. And, of course, his friendship with Bill Clinton couldn't hurt.

When O'Dowd told Morrison that he wanted him to be the spokesman, Morrison's immediate thought was the age-old response of someone eager to get into the thick of the action: "Put me in, coach!" Worries and concerns wouldn't creep in until later.

The other important decision—later described by Morrison as, "What are we gonna say about why we're here?" —had been resolved before they left the United States. Morrison had convincingly argued that they needed a substantive focus—and, to a considerable extent, a cover story. They all agreed that the story should be that they came to Northern Ireland to discuss and gauge support for the appointment of an American peace envoy to Northern Ireland.

Although enthusiasm for the peace envoy plan ranged from muted to nonexistent in Dublin, in London, and—with the exception of Sinn Féin—in Belfast, it was the kind of idea that could win wider support if efforts to get all-party peace talks under way remained stalled. As a basis for conversations that were aimed at exploring common ground, the topic of an American peace envoy was a reasonable focus. The other major Clinton promise—a US visa for Gerry Adams—would be a polarizing nonstarter; bringing it up would guarantee that their discussions in Northern Ireland would go nowhere good.

At the heart of the group's planned approach in the north was the shared understanding that any solution to the conflict would have to accommodate Catholics and Protestants alike. The Americans didn't know what that solution would look like, but they knew that it would have to come from the people on the ground in Northern Ireland. All of that meant they would be meeting with the widest possible range of political and activist groups, listening with respect to all viewpoints, making it clear that the Americans were there with open minds, not favoring any one side over the other and not holding a predetermined agenda. Their success depended on their being seen as honest brokers, not shills for Sinn Féin.

Morrison describes their approach this way:

> We would make talking to everyone a defining characteristic of the visit. Our talking to everybody would not connote agreement or disagreement with who they were or what they were doing or

what they might have done in the past. We would pay respect
to everybody's point of view. We had no agenda for settlement.
We would make the point that Northern Ireland could not move
forward economically if it didn't resolve the political conflict and
that it couldn't move forward politically if people weren't talking
about economic opportunity for everyone. There should be a
shared vision of the future.

Because Irish America was traditionally aligned with the republican cause of unifying the six northern counties with the rest of
the Irish Republic, it was particularly important that the Americans
meet with people representing the unionist political parties. Both the
establishment Ulster Unionist Party (UUP) and the radical breakaway
Democratic Unionist Party (DUP) had tentatively agreed to meet
with them. But when the newspapers reported shortly before their
arrival in Dublin that they would also be meeting with Sinn Féin
and its president, Gerry Adams, the firebrand cleric Ian Paisley, who
headed the DUP, immediately denounced Morrison as a trouble-
maker (this was actually mild language for Paisley, who had once
been removed from the European Parliament for loudly interrupt-
ing Pope John Paul II and calling him the antichrist; he would later
refer to his unionist rival David Trimble as a "loathsome reptile"). He
declared that his party would never meet with anyone who would
meet with Sinn Féin. A party spokesman said sarcastically, "If you
want to exclude yourself from a real say in Northern Ireland politics,
meet with Sinn Féin."

The response from the UUP also made it clear that their willingness to meet with the Americans was now in question. Party secretary
Jim Wilson said, "the meeting with Sinn Féin throws a whole new light
on the matter. It's something I will have to address first thing tomorrow morning." Tomorrow morning—Tuesday—was right when the
Americans would leave for Belfast. The comments of John Taylor, a
UUP member of the British Parliament, made it clear that it might
be a rough morning for the Americans: he called them anti-Ulster

meddlers and said they were "at the forefront of the campaign to get Northern Ireland out of the United Kingdom."

This wasn't a good start. Morrison asked the American consulate in Belfast to do everything possible to persuade the UUP to meet with them. If the situation couldn't be turned around, the American initiative would basically be dead in the water. Irish Americans coming to the North to meet with Irish Catholics would be the same old story: all green. It wouldn't be news, it wouldn't break new ground, and it wouldn't advance the new American approach. Although the mission could survive the DUP refusal—these were angry extremists for whom rejection and refusal were their stock-in-trade—a refusal by the mainstream UUP would be fatal. Suddenly the success of the mission was hanging by a thread. But unbeknownst to the Americans, they had a rescuer, and he was hard at work turning things around.

Chris McGimpsey was a UUP councilor from Belfast, a big man, hearty and bold, more left-leaning than the typical UUP politician, and never afraid to put himself out there against the odds. A few years earlier, in defiance of IRA attacks on trains running between Belfast and Dublin, he had organized what became known as the Peace Train: a broad coalition that made highly publicized train runs, saving the crucial link between the two cities.

When he heard about the UUP's reluctance, McGimpsey took it upon himself to change their mind, since he felt that Morrison, whom he had been so impressed by during the 1992 Mercy College trip, was exactly the sort of American the UUP needed to connect with. He hadn't spoken with Morrison since 1992 and never expected to see him again, but now that he was on his way to Belfast, McGimpsey went right to UUP headquarters, ultimately taking his case directly to party leader Jim Molyneaux. As he recalls:

> I thought to myself, "a significant opinion-former on Ireland, both now and potentially even greater in the future, is coming over here, and we're saying we don't want to talk to him?" I

wasn't worried about whether it would reduce their credibility in America, I was worried about the credibility of the unionist case.

I was still an officer of the party. Although I had no input into that decision, I advocated hard that we should meet with these guys. Not meeting with them because they were meeting with Sinn Féin was just so ridiculous. My counterargument was, "Sure, they're meeting with Sinn Féin, but they're meeting with lots of people. Why shouldn't they hear our position—unless you want Sinn Féin to explain our position, which is exactly what they'll do."

I told them, "I've met this guy, he's not a new Teddy Kennedy, he's not part of the John Hume Appreciation Society. He's an independent and he's keen to learn. He is influential and he will continue to be influential." To be fair, I wasn't 100 percent convinced that he didn't lean towards the other side. I felt he had over-listened to the republican-nationalists, but I wouldn't have faulted anybody for that because of Unionism's inability to sell its case.

So I told Molyneaux directly: "This guy is worth seeing," and the agreement was made to meet them. It was the right decision. I think the fear was that there would be a major fallout within the party with the extreme right wing and also with the DUP. Unionists felt that God was on their side so they didn't need the Yanks. So maybe a factor in our final decision was that people thought it was time for us to say we're a different party, to stand up to the DUP.

En route to Belfast on Tuesday morning, the Americans learned to their great relief that McGimpsey had prevailed. UUP leader Jim Wilson, drawing heavily on McGimpsey's arguments, deftly spun the meeting as an opportunity they shouldn't pass up: "We certainly would not meet Sinn Féin, but I don't think I have ever asked any visitor to unionist headquarters which office they have just been to or where they were going next. It would cost a fortune to send an Ulster unionist delegation to the States, so it would be downright stupid for us not to take this opportunity to put forward the unionist case and tell them eyeball to eyeball exactly what we think about the peace envoy plan."

Morrison cites the McGimpsey story as evidence that life is "cumulative," meaning that doing a good thing might pay off later in some completely unanticipated way. As they drove toward Belfast, the unofficial peacemakers had reason to hope that their mission would accomplish something.

But another foreshadowing of the difficulties and complexities in Northern Ireland occurred during the car ride itself. Niall O'Dowd noticed that their driver was paying unusually close attention to their conversation, which led him to believe that the car wasn't a safe place to talk. So discussion about what they planned to do in the north and how they thought events might unfold stopped. Anything important was communicated by passing a note.

As the car sped north in relative silence, Morrison had plenty to think about. Exactly what might he and his companions face in Northern Ireland? In truth, he had no expectations of what lay ahead, and this uncertainty wasn't comfortable for him. He was seriously concerned that beyond the very basic elements of their approach, the American team had embarked on an unscripted venture with a totally unknown outcome. It felt to Morrison, with his master's degree in chemistry, like an off-the-cuff science experiment in which almost nothing is known but a hypothesis.

Although he knew that he was pretty fast on his feet and could react effectively to the unexpected, his strong preference was to have a strategy and a well-developed message before undertaking an important mission. He was capable of winging it, but it wasn't the way he preferred to operate, especially when the stakes were so high. The unavoidable truth, however, was that they'd be making it up as they went along, with important meetings arranged or rearranged on the fly.

One area where Morrison did feel confident was that he knew what happened when he got "in the room" where powerful people were deciding important things. In his early days as a politician, he was no stranger to anxiety about how well he'd measure up and how well he could perform. Soon enough, though, he'd learned that the rooms weren't filled with geniuses and that there was no reason to be shy or trim his sails.

But to an extent that he couldn't yet know, Morrison's ability to be comfortable and assertive in Northern Ireland would be affected by what he refers to as the "adopted child syndrome:" an ongoing uncertainty about where you belong, if anywhere at all. Morrison found himself genuinely distressed when an Irish journalist he liked and respected exclaimed in an *Irish Times* article about his activities that he wasn't even Irish. The observation left him feeling like a man without a place in a land where identity is literally a matter of life and death. But however much the lack of clear identity made him feel diminished, it also had its advantages as he moved between groups and communities in Northern Ireland. He was never "one of us," but at the same time he was never "one of them."

––––––

It was already clear to Morrison that the purpose of the trip was evolving. The original idea had been to respond to the request from Sinn Féin that the Americans meet with them in Belfast and then return home with a message to the new administration that Sinn Féin was ready to do serious business—and that it was capable of getting an IRA ceasefire as evidence of its intent and effectiveness.

For their part, the Americans had a message they wanted to deliver: Bill Clinton is personally involved and cares deeply about Northern Ireland, and if events move ahead on the right path, the president himself will come. They wanted to show that Clinton got it, that the issue resonated with him because, as a son of the American South, he knew firsthand about discrimination and what happened when groups were stuck in protracted conflict with each other. The core message was that Clinton had a new approach, recounted years later by Morrison: "The defining element was that the British and the Irish spent thirty years of the Troubles trying to make a deal in the middle that excluded the extremes. The Clinton analysis, which we pushed hard, was that you needed the big tent. You had to bring the political extremes into the political process because the war was caused by extreme feelings. The moderates were not the ones making war, so having them talk to each other wasn't going to make peace."

Morrison had plenty to work on as he thought through how he'd deal with all of the variables. He had to present the case for American involvement in a way that would fully realize the opportunities that might present themselves in Northern Ireland, while avoiding the pitfalls that had plagued so many American politicians before him.

It wasn't long before his analysis of the challenges gave way to thoughts of the high wire, a worrisome image familiar to politicians in situations in which they have to stand out front, very alone, and speak about important matters with all eyes on them. It's a place where stakes are high and mistakes are costly.

Morrison had been on the high wire many times in his political career, but never like this. He believed he could perform well up there, but the fact was that it had been nearly three years since he'd had microphones shoved in his face by clamoring reporters shouting questions that were often meant to do little more than reveal what a liar or jerk the politician before them was.

It was also true that the last time he'd been in the public eye, running for governor of Connecticut, it had ended in the epic defeat that made him a pariah in his own party and a political nobody in his own state.

Morrison was painfully aware of all of this, but he was sure he could do this new job well. He was excited by the challenge and grateful for the confidence and trust O'Dowd had placed in him.

———

Because the approach to Belfast from the south is fairly flat, a traveler from Dublin sees the Black Mountain and other high hills on the western edges of the city, but never a commanding vista of the city itself as it spreads out east of the motorway toward the water—only such glimpses as roadside buildings, trees, billboards, and road signs allow. The twin spires of St. Michael's Cathedral in West Belfast—Sinn Féin territory—stand out, as do the gigantic yellow cranes known as Samson and Goliath in the Harland and Wolff shipyard, the place where the *Titanic* was built and where there were almost no jobs for Catholics.

Belfast sits near the mouth of the River Lagan; as the river passes through the sandy and muddy flats that gave Belfast its name, it opens out into the Belfast Lough, which in turn opens out to the Irish Sea. From that point, Scotland, ancestral homeland to so many in Northern Ireland, is just twenty miles or so eastward across the water.

People have lived in the place that is now Belfast since the Bronze Age, but the city came fully into its own in the nineteenth century, first as a center of the linen industry and later as the biggest and busiest shipbuilding center in the world. The great buildings of Belfast are for the most part products of the imperial eras of Queen Victoria and her ne'er-do-well (for a king) son Edward.

When the Americans arrived in 1993, the city had a population of about 250,000. It was unquestionably a war zone: There were checkpoints everywhere, and British army troop carriers and RUC armored Land Rovers were constantly patrolling the streets. Neighborhoods were often separated by high walls of brick, steel, or mortar, topped by high chain-link fences and razor wire and loaded with graffiti and partisan murals. These "peace walls" were intended to separate nationalist and loyalist working-class neighborhoods that were crammed too close together. They were usually erected at the request of residents who felt safer with high barriers between the different populations. To outsiders, the walls were a profoundly depressing sight, but to those who lived there, they were a crucial part of whatever sense of security they could muster.

The heart of the militant working-class unionist and loyalist population of Belfast, including the notorious Ulster paramilitaries, was centered on Shankill Road. The heart of the militant working-class nationalist and republican population, and with it the IRA, was centered on Falls Road. There were a few places in Belfast where these roads came absurdly close to each other. Residents took to painting the curbstones to identify who lived there. If you saw green and orange, you were in a republican neighborhood; if the curbs were painted in the colors of the Union Jack, you were in a loyalist neighborhood. If you were in the wrong place, you better get out fast.

These Belfast neighborhoods were the epicenters of the violence of the Troubles. IRA fighters and Ulster paramilitaries trudged along year after year on a treadmill of provocation, shooting, bombing, and killing. From 1969 to 1998, nearly 1,500 people were killed in the fighting in Belfast, a staggering number for a city of 250,000; in New York City, a comparable death toll from political warfare would be 48,000—basically a 9/11 every other year for thirty years. In the face of such a frightening and pervasive level of death, it wasn't difficult to understand those who believed Northern Ireland would never see an end to the age-old cycle of violence. But to those who knew it had to stop—that people just couldn't continue to live this way—it was clear that if anything was going to get better in the north, Belfast would be at the heart of it.

When the Americans arrived at Dukes Hotel, a compact Edwardian pile in a handsome area near Queens University, and bade farewell to their nosy driver, their concerns about security continued. Niall O'Dowd, ever alert to the possibility of intrusion, encountered strange bits of conversation whenever he picked up a hotel phone. Morrison was more casual, even somewhat fatalistic, about security concerns, especially in light of the omnipresence of the British internal security agency MI5. "On the scale of careful to not careful, I was much closer to the not-careful end of the spectrum," he said, "I was just like I was in New Haven. I'm sure it was prudent to care about security, but there wasn't anything to do about it. MI5 knew everything we were doing. They had moles everywhere. So there were no secrets. If they wanted us killed, we would have been dead. They probably didn't want us dead."

———

Finally, after all the planning, agonizing, maneuvering, and traveling, the meetings that had brought the unofficial peacemakers to Northern Ireland were at hand. The Americans' agenda for their first day in Belfast included a visit with the moderate nationalist who had recently defeated Gerry Adams in his bid for re-election to the British Parliament, followed by a trip to the Stormont Estate in Ballymiscaw, just east of Belfast, to meet with the British secretary of state for Northern Ireland. After that, they would be off to the now-salvaged meeting with the Ulster Unionist Party leadership. The UUP meeting had to be held on the day they arrived in Belfast: As a condition of agreeing to meet, UUP insisted that the visitors meet with them before they met with Sinn Féin.

Although the Americans had no clear sense of how much media attention their visit might attract, on the day before they arrived in Belfast, the two major papers were already beginning to square off in their coverage.

The headline of the unionist-leaning *Belfast Telegraph* screamed, "Clinton Slams Britain." The paper's political correspondent wrote that the *Telegraph* had "today" gotten hold of a copy of a letter Bill Clinton wrote to Bruce Morrison about Northern Ireland, in which he criticized the British for not doing enough to oppose job discrimination against Catholics. The letter also discussed his idea of sending a US peace envoy to Northern Ireland. The article noted that Morrison "is a keen supporter of the envoy option." Anyone reading the article would have thought Clinton had sent the letter to Morrison on the eve of his departure for Ireland and would assume that despite their claim to be arriving with open minds, the American team—or at least Morrison—were coming with a firm anti-British and anti-unionist bias.

The *Telegraph* article reflected the considerable unionist opposition to the American visit. It was also seriously misleading. The letter in question had actually been written and widely publicized nearly a year earlier: It was the letter Clinton wrote at Morrison's insistence just before the presidential election. So it was definitely old news, but the *Telegraph* obviously felt it could get a maximum jolt from the inflammatory headline by withholding basic facts. The paper saw nothing good for the unionist community in the American visit. The next day, an account of the team's plan to meet with Sinn Féin breathlessly claimed that the party's deputy leader Martin McGuinness had recently been labeled as "Britain's No. 1 Terrorist."

The story in the nationalist-leaning *Irish News* had a quieter headline: "Fact-finders Strengthen Case for US Peace Drive." Obviously the *News* had a much warmer feeling about the American visit than its unionist rival. It did, however, predict accurately that "the decision to meet with Sinn Féin and support for the envoy proposal is likely to irritate the unionist parties."

Combat via newspaper headline was obviously preferable to the more violent alternatives so familiar in Belfast, but it still didn't bode well for the ability of the American team to engage constructively with all sides of the conflict. It further revealed the challenges Morrison would face as American spokesman as he tried to communicate openly and honestly across the partisan chasm.

When the American team set out from Dukes Hotel for the first day's meetings, they found themselves leaving the starting gate not with a confidence-inducing, powerful stride forward but with an embarrassing stumble. They were supposed to meet Joe Herndon, the MP who had defeated Gerry Adams, at his office in a complex known as Twin Spires, but they were taken to the wrong Twin Spires. They hustled to the right one, arriving late, appearing not a bit like a well-connected American political/corporate/media powerhouse. Morrison feared they "looked like rubes" and that Herndon might feel disrespected. But he was gracious, and the brief event went well, although Morrison did have some jitters about facing the Northern Ireland media for the first time. Even though it was a low-key event, he remembers it as his "baptism under fire" and recalls "the body tension of being thrust to the fore." He would soon discover just how gentle a baptism it had been.

The Americans managed to leave for Stormont more or less on schedule.

———

Stormont Estate, purchased in 1921 to be the seat of the Northern Ireland government, is dominated by the gargantuan white parliament building that was opened in 1932 for what unionist leader James Craig called "a Protestant Parliament." When the Americans arrived it was a parliament building without a parliament, since the British had imposed direct rule from London years earlier. The building's design mission, not uncommon in Europe between the World Wars, was to convey in no uncertain terms who's who and what's what. No one approaching the parliament building by way of the enormously long and wide rising mall that leads up to it could fail to be impressed by how powerful the state can be and how small and insignificant an individual human being can be made to feel.

The Americans' meeting with the British secretary of state for Northern Ireland, Sir Patrick Mayhew, was to be held at Stormont Castle, also unique but more benign. Since Mayhew was Britain's top official in the province, Morrison expected increased media coverage at Stormont. He was picturing the kind of stodgy press events so common in Washington when a member of Congress—at least one not embroiled in a scandal—faces the media. How wrong he was.

As the Americans approached the castle, they found themselves in the midst of what ex-Gaelic footballer O'Dowd called "a media scrum:" a tumultuous crowd of reporters, broadcasters, and camera crews covering their arrival like sensational breaking news. About two dozen microphones were thrust toward Morrison. Television cameramen were jockeying for position. Niall O'Dowd might have been the prince of Irish American journalism, but this frenzied coverage took him completely by surprise.

For Morrison, "Put me in, coach!" immediately gave way to "Oh shit, I'd better do a good job." Suddenly the high wire was far higher than he'd imagined, and all of Northern Ireland (not to mention London, Dublin, and Washington) was watching. There was no longer time for him to worry about how rusty he might be or how badly things had gone just three years earlier. He took in the great weight of his responsibility, with stakes far beyond those involved when he ran for governor. Back then it had merely been about an election he would either win or lose. This time it was about war—a war that so many were sure would grind on for many more generations—and peace. If he did well, new opportunities for peace could materialize. But if he slipped, even a little, the chance for a constructive American role in the process might not be fully realized, or, worse still, it might be lost altogether. And even worse than that, the future prospects for peace in Northern Ireland might be set back terribly. This time his success or failure would be measured not in votes but in human lives.

Morrison faced the media's questions, delivered in tones from skeptical to aggressive, with aplomb. It was obvious to O'Dowd that the journalists were trying hard to trip the American spokesman up, but they weren't succeeding. Morrison was pressed hard about the group's intention to meet with Sinn Féin and was grilled on the controversy over the willingness of the unionist parties to meet with them. This was yet another vivid reminder of how potent the idea of Americans meeting with Sinn Féin was. The unionists and the British couldn't understand why any group claiming to be, as Morrison had said earlier, "coming with no preconditions or preconceptions but with open minds," would want to meet with them at all.

Morrison robustly defended the plan. "I believe there isn't anyone here that I would not meet with if they were willing to meet with me. I do not think that one adopts the views or sanctions the particular actions of one or another group by talking to them. I think that one of the barriers to progress in this community is too many preconditions rather than more communication."

In the closed-door meeting that followed, Morrison found Mayhew to be "an aristocrat through and through" and "the epitome of the British diplomat." Mayhew was a large, full-faced, somewhat overbearing man with wild and impressive eyebrows. He had been attorney general of the United Kingdom from 1987 to 1992, when he'd been appointed to his current post. He was confident in his abilities and sure of the correctness of his nation's cause.

Mayhew was cordial but thoroughly dismissive of the notion of the United States sending a peace envoy to Northern Ireland. He told the Americans that while he received the idea as "an act of friendship," he regarded it as irrelevant in the face of his conviction that the stalled peace talks would go forward "in one form or another." Morrison had already gone on the record with his view of how likely it was that there would be talks anytime soon: "A combination of circumstances makes it clear that the prospects for the talks going forward are zero." Still, they'd heard each other out, and that was why the Americans had come.

On the way out, Morrison faced the same media throng. He candidly told them that Mayhew had "expressed skepticism about the usefulness of techniques like the envoy." He also previewed the defense of the envoy plan that the UUP would doubtless hear: "The most important thing is that no one should use it as an excuse to not do something they otherwise would do to promote peace and reconciliation. Everyone should see it for what it is: an attempt to be helpful and not an attempt at meddling or to interfere or deprive people of their legitimate point of view."

Then the unofficial peacemakers headed to the on-again meeting with the UUP. The obvious damage from the recent bombing of the party's headquarters on Glengall Street in the center of Belfast set just the right tone. The press was still covering the American visit like breaking news.

The UUP leaders meeting with the Americans included party general secretary Jim Wilson—who the day before had told the *Belfast Telegraph* that the visitors "would be left 'in absolutely no doubt' about unionist opposition to 'outside interference'"—as well as Chris McGimpsey, who had played the crucial role in keeping the UUP meeting on track, and two UUP members of Parliament at Westminster. One of the MPs was David Trimble, who would later become the party's leader and win a Nobel Prize for his role in the peace process—though at that point there was no hint of his future. "David was pretty awkward and out there," Morrison recalls. "No one would've predicted that he was going to play such a central role." Morrison also found Trimble to be somewhat dandified in his dress and downright bizarre in his manner of greeting the Americans: Upon being introduced, he clicked his heels like a proper German officer. Morrison couldn't fathom why a member of the British Parliament would do such a thing, apparently oblivious to its Nazi associations. For his part, O'Dowd had no idea how to interpret the gesture; he wondered if it had been meant as a sign of disrespect.

The UUP leaders and their American visitors wasted little time in getting down to the matters at hand. Morrison described the business part of the encounter as "a real meeting, not scripted, not like a stiff bureaucratic or diplomatic meeting." As the UUP members spoke, Morrison became aware that yet another dimension of the journey was starting to reveal itself: The people living through these harsh times desperately needed to be heard. That need, pervasive throughout the Protestant community, would become more powerfully evident in the days to follow.

The discussion between the UUP and the Americans was reported by the *Irish News* as covering such contentious issues as "political talks, the lack of democratic structures, British-Irish relations, paramilitary activity, and American financial support for the IRA." For their part, the UUP leaders fully delivered on their promise to tell the Americans "exactly what we think about the peace envoy plan," insisting that the majority in Northern Ireland opposed it. They added that because Clinton had, as they saw it, backed the peace envoy plan during the election campaign as a result of Irish American pressure, the sincerity of anyone he would subsequently appoint "would always be suspect."

In Morrison's equally direct response, he stressed that his team had come to Northern Ireland not as official representatives of the president, but as his friends who were supporting his program, especially the appointment of the peace envoy. He recognized that with this group, the peace envoy was a hard sell, but despite that challenge, he made considerable headway presenting the United States as "an honest broker: ready, willing, and able to listen to all the sides," and sincerely interested in doing whatever it could to advance the prospects for peace. This really was the man McGimpsey had told his party about, and Morrison clearly did well: After the meeting the UUP issued a statement that described the discussions as "harmonious and constructive."

———

The main event of the team's second day was a trip to Derry, seventy-five miles away, to visit moderate nationalist leader John Hume at his summer home outside the city. He was cordial and generous with his time, but, as expected, he countered their call for a peace envoy, who would have a broad mandate from the president, with his preference for an economic envoy, whose focus would be much narrower. His stance was that the Americans could best contribute in the economic sphere while leaving the politics to the political leaders in Northern Ireland. Morrison felt that Hume's confidence in the ability of economic change to drive political change gave short shrift to the necessity for a fundamentally new approach in the political sphere: "I was consciously pushing against the Hume analysis because you won't get investment and economic change in a war zone. These things have to go hand in hand; the idea of the peace envoy is to work on changing the political environment to make this a place where people would want to invest." In Morrison's view, this involved getting a clearer picture than Hume had about where the republicans fit into the political landscape, as well as greater emphasis on the development of grassroots political participation throughout the nationalist community.

Morrison recognized that for him John Hume was a complicated proposition, just as Morrison and his ideas surely were for Hume. In an Irish American political world long divided between IRA supporters and those who condemned the violence, Hume's moderate nationalist stance gave him an absolute lock on the opinions of the mainstream Irish American political establishment, which included Edward Kennedy, House Speaker Thomas "Tip" O'Neill, and New York senator Daniel Patrick Moynihan. (Along with New York governor Hugh Carey, they came to be called "The Four Horsemen.") Indeed, Hume had set Kennedy straight years earlier by rebuking him for a brief flirtation with hard-line republicanism. But as Morrison saw it, the Hume approach was, in terms of American policy, leading nowhere new.

It was Hume's confidence that the Catholic community could not be held down if you gave them economic opportunity, which is an important thing—it's not to be dismissed, but it just doesn't ever turn the corner. It doesn't require people to create common cause in any particular way. If you are asking people to share the community, you cannot ask them to give up what they have. Asking unionists to give up their jobs or houses so the Catholics can be equal is a fool's errand. You have to grow more jobs and houses, if you want that to happen. But there's more to it than economics. There had been a lot of change in the economic circumstances of Catholics in recent decades, but that didn't root out the IRA, because the problem wasn't just things, wasn't just material problems. It went to the heart of identity: recognition of identity, proper respect for identity, and all of that. So you couldn't just do economics.

It's fair to say that it was easier for Morrison to think beyond Hume's influence because he was not himself part of the Irish American establishment—not a Kennedy, not a Catholic, and without much Irish blood—and therefore regarded by Hume as an outsider, not someone of great importance on matters of war and peace in

Northern Ireland. But then along came Bill Clinton, another out-sider, and he was listening to Morrison and others like him instead of the establishment over which Hume held such sway. This other flank of political Irish America was a new world for Hume, and by the time of his meeting with the Americans, he had not entirely adjusted to it.

In the meeting, the Americans, as Morrison put it, "went to the mountain" to pay their respects to an important leader he considered "a great man, with all the limitations and attributes of a great man." Morrison summarized the visit with a bit of an edge: "The gospel according to John had been preached over and over, so there was no new news there." The Belfast newspapers saw it the same way: The fact that the Americans went to Derry to meet with Hume was reported as news; what they talked about wasn't mentioned.

Although Hume wouldn't be an important part of the story of the groundbreaking 1993 visit, a day would soon come when he, like so many other leaders involved in the peace process, would be sum-moned by history, and he would answer courageously and unselfishly. As Morrison later said, "At every critical stage, John did what was right about inclusion, not what was in his personal interest. But sometimes he had to be roughed up a little bit to get him to see."

———

Throughout the week-long Americans' visit, the great news story, as far as the media was concerned, was that the Americans would be meeting with Sinn Féin and its president, Gerry Adams. These were the politicians closest to the IRA. It was widely believed (often accu-rately) that many of those who were in leadership positions in Sinn Féin had been or still were active in the IRA. Some, like Sinn Féin vice president Martin McGuinness, have since acknowledged that they were IRA fighters. Others, like Gerry Adams, have said they weren't, despite the belief of many that he was commander of an IRA brigade in Belfast; whether he was active IRA remains unproven.

Because Adams was on terrorist watch lists in Great Britain, Ireland, and the United States, and because his image and voice had been banned from British and Irish broadcasting, any sign of respect toward him from conventionally respectable quarters had enormous impact. When Irish president Mary Robinson shook his hand before the cameras in June of 1993, the effect was seismic and a huge step forward on his path to political acceptance. When an influential group of Americans close to the new American president, among them a former member of the United States House of Representatives, announced that they would be meeting with Sinn Féin and Gerry Adams in Belfast, the earth shook again.

Precisely how newsworthy these meetings really were depends on what the big story of the American journey was. If the story was that a group of private citizens friendly with Bill Clinton had come to Northern Ireland to meet with a wide range of political parties and leaders, then, of course, the meeting with Sinn Féin—especially since they had mastered arts of public relations in ways that their rivals had not—was the biggest part of the story. But if the story was that the Americans' visit was making historic connections in the process of helping bring peace to Northern Ireland and that it was cementing the American role as honest brokers without an agenda other than peace and a better future for all who lived in Northern Ireland, then the most important story was completely missed by the media. In fairness, they missed it because everyone involved kept it secret—some because they feared it could be dangerous for them if the wrong people learned about it.

Each member of the American group understood the importance of meeting with leaders in the unionist community, which is why they were so concerned with getting the UUP meeting back on track. But they wanted to do more than meet with establishment politicians. They wanted to hear the voices from the Shankill, the loyalist heart of Belfast.

They first met with Jackie Redpath, a longtime unionist community organizer, born and bred in the Shankill, who agreed to see them at Dukes Hotel. He later recalled that of the nearly twenty Irish American delegations that had come to Belfast two years earlier, only one sought out the perspective of the Shankill. Redpath recalls describing a community "under siege and in retreat":

> Belfast was becoming basically a nationalist/republican-dominated city, which it was in the early stages of then. The retreat was not only territorial but also political, because unionism had lost its political control of Northern Ireland under direct rule. It was economic, because of the decline of traditional industries like shipbuilding and engineering and linen. So much of the cultural and intellectual arena was dominated by people from a nationalist/republican background.
>
> I tried to explain to the delegation that unionism felt itself in retreat and that wasn't healthy. No community should find itself with their back against the wall, because then you tend to respond in an extreme sort of way and violently.

The Americans were deeply impressed with Redpath's presentation, and he was impressed with them. As Redpath recalls, "That was my first serious interaction with political Irish America. Because the meeting was organized that morning, I'm not sure who they thought I was, and I'm not sure who I thought they were. But it was a good discussion. The fact that this delegation reached out to unionism and loyalism was very, very significant." In time, of course, Redpath would learn a great deal more about the American visitors:

> My job in meeting Bruce and his colleagues was to try and explain to them that there's another community here that has a case, and this isn't an issue of right or wrong—this is an issue of how you bring conflict to an end. All sides need to be taken account of in an equal and embracing fashion. Bruce did do that, even though he was perceived as leaning towards nationalism and republicanism. He had an ability to transcend that. I saw him as the pathfinder—in many ways he was able to open stuff up that Clinton and George Mitchell were able to follow into.

> I can see that at key times he had a crucial role to play. Obviously that first visit and the seven-day ceasefire was of critical importance in a whole range of things. He was also persistent in coming back again and again and again, so there were other occasions that I met him, but that now gets wrapped up in a whole race of events that gathered pace. But this was the first—like somebody said, "the whole banquet is in the first mouthful . . ."

After the meeting, Redpath was asked to arrange another meeting, one far more audacious and potentially dangerous than any meeting with Sinn Féin: The Americans wanted to meet with loyalist paramilitaries. This would be like meeting directly with the IRA. Redpath reached out to Gerry Vinton, a member of the Ulster Volunteer Force, one of the largest and most violent Ulster paramilitary organizations. Word came back that Vinton and three other UVF men would be willing to meet with the Americans the next morning, but only on the condition that the meeting was kept secret. The UVF men—two of them convicted killers—would slip into Dukes Hotel, go to a pre-arranged private room, and await the Americans.

By any measure, the idea of representatives of Irish America meeting with an Ulster paramilitary group was extraordinary. By 1993, Sinn Féin was making headway as a political party, so it wasn't completely unheard of for Americans visiting Northern Ireland to meet with them. Nor was it unheard of for American supporters of Noraid to meet with IRA men. But *nobody* met with the loyalist paramilitaries. These were groups of varying degrees of organization with names like Ulster Defence Association (UDA) and Red Hand Commando. (The story behind the red hand, a central element of the Ulster flag, captures how far paramilitaries on both sides were willing to go: In the legend, a long-ago chieftain, racing another to be the first to touch the shore and claim Ireland for himself, sees that his rival is likely to beat him, so he cuts off his own hand and throws it ashore to win the race.) The loyalist paramilitaries were widely seen as being even lower than terrorists, because of the involvement of so many of them in criminal activities like robbery and drug trafficking. Terrorists claimed their violence was in service of high objectives; robbers and pushers had no such cover.

Although criminal activity wasn't unknown among its members, the IRA was widely seen as an organized army, not just a ragtag bunch of killers. It had a command structure, it was disciplined, and it was capable of delivering orders and ensuring they were carried out, top to bottom. For all of the viciousness behind so many of their actions, the soldiers of the IRA enjoyed respect in many quarters. Their bravery and sacrifice, as well as their bold exploits and harsh circumstances and choices, were recounted in songs and ballads, and reflected, not always flatteringly, in the poems of Yeats, the plays of O'Casey and Behan, and in great movies like *The Informant*. The IRA was a political and cultural institution with an impressive pedigree: Its predecessor from the earlier part of the century had defeated the mighty British and won the independence of Ireland after centuries of domination. That tradition lent the IRA of the Troubles more of a glow than was deserved, perhaps, but when Sinn Féin spoke of them as "the Army," it never sounded absurd.

Because the IRA had succeeded in being seen by many as an actual army, with the attendant trappings of authority and the nobility of their bravery and sacrifice, they stood, despite their terrible acts, on a different plane from the Ulster paramilitaries. Members of the republican and nationalist communities might have deplored their tactics, but the IRA was an abiding symbol of the struggle. To be sure, the Ulster paramilitaries saw themselves as having gone to war to protect their community from attacks by the IRA and from the unreliability of the British, but even in the eyes of much of their own community, they weren't seen as a noble, disciplined fighting force.

For Morrison, the difference between the various paramilitary forces fighting in Northern Ireland boiled down to politics:

The IRA had a clearer political orientation and was far more effective in presenting its cause and its political justification. The loyalist paramilitaries were a more splintered band, and there was probably more overt lawlessness unrelated to political objectives. Most importantly, the loyalists failed to establish an effective working-class political base of their own.

After breakfast the next morning, Morrison and his companions approached the hotel meeting room where the UVF men waited. They were confident that the loyalist paramilitary men wouldn't kill them when they entered the room, but beyond that, they had no idea what to expect. Morrison acknowledged years later that the prospect of meeting with such men was strange and a little frightening.

As the door opened, the first sight—"emblazoned in my memory," Morrison says—was of an older gentlemen in a tweed jacket smoking a large, curved-stem pipe of the sort favored by Sherlock Holmes and Santa Claus. He looked more like a kindly professor emeritus than a murderous paramilitary soldier. This was Gusty Spence, a UVF leader who had been convicted of murder years earlier. During the time he'd spent imprisoned for a crime he denied committing, Spence started to think that a political path might be preferable to the violent one the paramilitaries had so far taken.

Two other loyalists in the room had also served long sentences: Billy Hutchinson, who had been convicted of murder, and David Ervine, who had been caught in a car loaded with explosives, likely on its way to its intended target. Hutchinson and Ervine got to know Spence in prison and had been strongly influenced by his evolving views, which, ironically, had been influenced by those of an IRA member serving his own sentence for murder. The fourth member of the group, Gerry Vinton, had never gone to prison. He later pointed out, in a tone of quiet pride, that he "was never convicted." His ability to blend into the background, unnoticed in a group, was one of his strengths as a paramilitary man.

Despite Spence's warm and welcoming demeanor, it was possible to see the hard man underneath. Ervine and Hutchinson—the first stocky with thinning dark hair and a bushy mustache, the other balding and lean as a greyhound, and both with piercing eyes—had the look of hard men right then as well. It wasn't difficult to imagine them as younger men with guns they had used before and were willing to use again.

But then the men from Ulster began speaking, and with that, an entirely new chapter in the quest for peace in Northern Ireland—and a new role for the United States—began.

They spoke in a straightforward way, with deep feeling and candor, of their fears: fear of falling behind, fear of being abandoned by the British and the unionist political establishment, fear of what would happen to them as the Catholics continued to ascend, and fear of how bad it would be for them if word got out that they were meeting with the Americans.

They spoke of what they didn't have: There was no urban working-class political party that offered a path other than the give-and-take of violence and death that had consumed the paramilitaries on both sides for so long. Unlike the IRA and Sinn Féin, the loyalists had no community in the United States bolstering them with money and political support. They didn't even have the respect of the predominantly middle-class and rural unionist parties. On the contrary, they were denied and disdained by both the British and the established Northern Ireland party leadership as thugs and criminals. But when the respectable men of London and Ulster needed dirty work done, they would turn again and again to the paramilitaries, all while publically deploring the awful things these violent men had done. Even the radical Ian Paisley, who, in Morrison's words, "engaged in fiery rhetoric that seemed to justify violence, but denounced the violence when it occurred," left them feeling that they were merely being "used as cannon fodder."

What struck Morrison as he listened to the UVF men was how their grievances sounded just like those of the republicans. He was reminded of the way it had been in the Jim Crow days of the American South, when the white establishment looked down on the poor whites—except when they needed dirty work done—but kept them stoked up with such a sense of superiority over the blacks that it was unlikely that the common economic interests between the two groups would threaten the established order. He lays it out this way:

> Close your eyes and listen to the words, and the working-class people of each community have a grievance with the ruling class, which has essentially been playing divide-and-rule and causing the struggling people at the bottom to hate and kill each other as a way to manage control from the top.
>
> Nothing was done in a way that would cause shared opportunity or shared progress. Nobody was told that new housing will be built when it's shared—"You guys will have to agree on the allocations or it won't happen at all." There should be a benefit in cooperation and conciliation, instead of, "See those pricks over there? You ought to kill them because they're getting what you aren't getting." I'm sure that they weren't sitting at Whitehall planning this. But to the people in MI5, and Army and RUC types, this was their idea of how you control this uncontrollable heathen population.

More than anything, Morrison and his companions heard the pain and uncertainty of human beings faced with massive changes that were completely beyond their control. Yet they also heard, astonishingly, voices of once-violent men who were hopeful about the possibilities for peace. All of this profoundly changed the sense the Americans had of who they were dealing with. Recalls Morrison:

> The upshot of that meeting was a clear realization that the situation of the working-class Protestant community was much more complicated than people liked to talk about, and that if we cared about a resolution, we needed to pay attention to their grievances and feelings. They had to be brought along. They didn't

have a natural constituency in the United States, the way the Catholics had the Irish American community—even though half the people in the United States who trace their heritage to Ireland are Protestant.

On the unionist side, the two major parties took all the political oxygen and the grassroots loyalists didn't have a Sinn Féin–like political organization, which they still do not. It is really a tragedy for working-class loyalist people in Northern Ireland that their political analysis has always been done by rural, middle-, and upper-class leadership that actually disdains these people. They have taught these people that they had a birthright entitlement to an economic place, when, of course, in a modern competitive economy, there is no such thing left. So these people are unemployed and they don't blame the right people.

The very thing they told us—"the Catholic communities are ascendant and we are being left behind"—is absolutely true, because the leadership of the unionist community left those people behind and blamed the republicans.

The meeting was revelatory not just for the Americans, but for the loyalists as well. For the first time, they experienced a group of Irish Americans as warm, sincere, and open-minded. Morrison seemed to understand the situation in all of its complexity and subtlety. They became open to receiving the Americans as trustworthy facilitators who'd come to Northern Ireland not to impose their predetermined solutions on the people who lived there, but to listen with engagement and respect. And they began to imagine that one day they could receive a warm welcome in the United States. According to Hutchinson, "The Americans gave us a fair hearing. They seemed to be on board for all the right reasons. Bruce gave assurances with his words and body language that he was serious and fair."

That's not to say that they weren't apprehensive: Vinton, in particular, couldn't disregard the possibility that the working-class men of the paramilitaries were being conned by these educated and accomplished Americans. But he and his companions responded to that fear in the way men of action do: They pressed ahead full force, making their case without holding back.

Hutchinson remembers the meeting as a chance to be heard and to see a new side of Irish America:

> From my point of view, it was important to actually talk to those people at that time, because one of the things we were trying to find out from Irish Americans was in terms of the amount of money they were giving to the IRA to fund the war against British citizens. We wanted to make sure that in any future process, all that would be stopped.
>
> I think overall, what they were saying made sense from my point of view. I suppose in many ways it changed my opinion, particularly of Irish America in terms of having a stereotype, being sort of cheerleaders for the IRA.
>
> Morrison was the one who stood out in the whole meeting. It seemed to me that he was a strategist and had things well thought out. I warmed to some of the stuff he was saying—some I probably wasn't comfortable with, but I could also see that if we were working on that basis, I could get more comfortable, I could put my feet up. He was an intelligent man—I think the things that stood out from him was, he was a negotiator, he was a strategist, and you could do a deal with somebody like him.

Hutchinson says the meeting led to "a totally new dynamic" between the loyalist paramilitaries and the United States:

> Whenever we accepted all the things that came after—the American role itself and also George Mitchell as chair of talks and so forth—I think we wouldn't have got there if we hadn't have had that meeting. That was the meeting that cracked it for us.

Although the gathering was secret and the talk concerned conflict and fear, it felt to Morrison like a thoroughly engrossing session in the dark-paneled office of a distinguished professor at an ancient

university. Years later, he'd look back on it as one of the most compelling and rewarding meetings he ever participated in at any time
in his career.

———

The meeting with Sinn Féin, so highly anticipated by the media, was
held in two parts. The first was the public part: a skillfully orchestrated
and impressively media-savvy event at which the American visitors
and the very excited media could hear directly from the people of
Sinn Féin's community. It was held in a large hall on the fifth floor
of Conway Mill, a converted linen mill off Falls Road that was partly
surrounded by British army barracks. High windows on the side, iron
pillars, and long diagonal bracing secured by huge bolts evoked the
place's linen-making days and provided an open space for the throng
packing the room, 200 or more. There was barely enough space for
each community group's table and for the journalists covering the
event. The thick walls of the mill kept it cool, even in the late summer.

Sinn Féin offered the Americans the chance to meet with a wide
range of ordinary members of the republican community who had
terrible but sometimes uplifting personal stories to tell. Each member
of the American team could move from group to group and hear the
stories. Traditional Irish music lifted spirits and boosted the energy
in the room. The *Irish News* reported that it was "a lively reception."

Although Morrison makes the point that, in light of the tragic
stories being told, the event certainly wasn't a party, still there was an
aspect of celebration in the proceedings. This was a moment at which
Sinn Féin and the republican community had plenty to celebrate:
American friends of the new president had come, the ceasefire was
holding, and Sinn Féin was getting unparalleled access to the world
stage. Morrison was tremendously impressed with the skill and verve
with which they seized the opportunity:

> We'd had all these meetings with all these officials that were
> very somber, the usual office meeting. Then we go to Sinn Féin
> and the meeting is like a performance—all these groups, all

kinds of Irish music and dancing, plenty of Irish speaking. There was a whole different approach, which made sense because our visit let them get this kind of coverage. Everybody else was just reacting to our presence, but they had a plan. Somebody might say we were being used by them, but it wasn't really like that, because the fact that they had a plan sort of fits with my general take about them. Whatever else is wrong with them, whatever bad things they did, they had a vision, which at the end of the day was central to how it all came out. These guys were thinking about making history.

Beyond the politics of it, the people of the republican community were telling their stories and being listened to with warmth and respect. Niall O'Dowd remembers an older woman with a heartbreaking account of her son's death. After finishing her tale, she held his hand firmly, looked straight at him with tear-filled eyes, and said with heartfelt gratitude, "Thank you for not treating us like animals." It was all O'Dowd could do to maintain his composure, and he didn't fully succeed.

In political and diplomatic terms, Gerry Adams and the leadership of Sinn Féin were being treated like legitimate leaders, not terrorists who should be isolated and silenced. This was something far beyond Adams shaking hands with Irish president Mary Robinson earlier in the summer. It was the arrival of a Sinn Féin and its leaders at an entirely new level—a long way from the days the British home secretary mocked Adams as "Mr. Ten Percent" after his party had turned in a dismal showing at the polls. Although Great Britain would continue to fend off Sinn Féin's efforts to be included in peace talks for years—often at ruinous human cost—the gathering at Conway Mill marked the beginning of the end of the marginalization of the party.

When the enormously successful and deeply moving presentation was done, it was time for the second stage, in which the Americans would meet privately with the top Sinn Féin leadership. That part was held in a harsh, plain space utterly devoid of creature comforts; there weren't even any of the minimally comfortable chairs one would expect to find in the waiting room of a public agency, just backless stools.

Despite the hard seats in the hard room and the tense feeling the discomfort engendered, the glow of the public event could still be felt. It was an easy transition to the initial business of the private meeting, in which the Americans laid out what the republicans could expect from the United States in response to movement away from violence. Morrison and the others stressed that the involvement of the new Clinton administration offered an unprecedented opportunity for peace and the establishment of an effective political process that Sinn Féin and the IRA should seize quickly and without hesitation. They made it clear that they themselves—friends of the president, influential people in the worlds of politics, journalism, and business— were willing and able to ensure that any moves toward peace would be met with corresponding political and economic benefits from the United States. These benefits ranged from getting Clinton to authorize a visa for Adams, to aggressively encouraging the American business community to invest in a Northern Ireland that was making its way toward peace.

As the discussion progressed in this positive vein, Morrison saw how easy it would be to let everyone continue to bask in the afterglow of the public event. But a powerful realization overtook him, brought on in part by the hard atmosphere of the room itself: He knew that keeping things comfortable was not his duty. Though it brought him little pleasure, he knew that the moment demanded he take a serious risk and tell the Sinn Féin leadership the truth about the need for the violence to stop.

This wasn't the first time Morrison had been in the presence of people who'd been involved with violence and killing in support of causes they believed were so compelling that terrible acts were justified. As a member of Congress committed to advancing human rights, he had gone to Nicaragua to meet with the Sandinistas and to Cuba to meet with Fidel Castro. On each occasion, the welcome was warm and the people charismatic. How bluntly to speak was a matter of judgment: Would directness be constructive, or would it create greater problems? Should the focus be on making a connection, with the tougher words left for another occasion? Apart from knowing that nobody likes to be the skunk at the garden party, Morrison was aware that keeping things pleasant is often the smartest way to behave: "In many circumstances, it's called diplomacy."

But in that hard, spare room in Belfast, it was inescapably clear that the moment demanded straight talk of the sort Irish republicans almost never heard from visiting American politicians. He also knew that Sinn Féin and the IRA never responded to such words and entreaties directed at them; they just took them in and discussed amongst themselves later. But he knew that "we weren't there to get Sinn Féin on British television; we were there to make peace." And he believed that the integrity of the American mission was on the line. So he did his duty and laid it out.

Morrison told them that while he and the others understood why the IRA violence seemed necessary to so many in the republican cause, it was time for it to stop. He explained that the violence gave the British their most effective weapon: the ability to label the IRA and Sinn Féin as terrorists. It was that word that enabled the British to marginalize Sinn Féin and keep its members out of the peace talks that were necessary to end the conflict. The IRA had it within its power to take that word away from the British and force them to find a new way of dealing with the republicans. If they stopped the violence, the peace process could move forward and Clinton would feel free to engage Sinn Féin as a valued and essential partner in ending the war. But if the IRA wasn't willing to meet these demands and stop the violence—if they lacked the understanding or perhaps even the courage—then this extraordinary moment of opportunity could be lost and the conflict could grind on indefinitely.

As he spoke, Morrison felt the discomfort that comes when the hard message clashes with the warm tone of the moment: "The whole atmosphere was that they had put on this performance very successfully. But now we were not going to tell them that they're right and they should go blow up Big Ben—we were going to tell them that they're right, there is suffering and discrimination and wrongdoing here, but the way to stop it is to find a political process through which their grievances can be heard."

In that moment, Morrison was acutely aware of how much he didn't know about Gerry Adams, Sinn Féin, and the IRA. He knew the history of the 1986 split within Sinn Féin that had the Adams faction advocating the establishment of a political agenda in addition to the IRA's armed struggle. He felt confident that his assessment of Adams as primarily a politician was correct, but he couldn't be certain. The challenge Morrison and the Americans faced was to get the republicans to lay down the gun so the ballot box could be fully engaged. Recalls Morrison:

> It's not that Adams disdained the violence of the IRA—I don't know that he ever did. Like most revolutionary leaders who have been part of the struggle, he accepted that violence comes with the territory. But I knew Adams was a politician and a gifted political leader, and that a gifted political leader would gravitate to politics if it was on offer, if you could convince him that it would work. That was his strength. That doesn't mean that I knew in 1993 exactly how committed he or the IRA was to stopping. That was a question mark. It wasn't a question mark that politics was a viable way forward—but what would it take for that way forward to happen?

True to their way, the Sinn Féin leaders listened intently and betrayed no reaction. But Morrison was relieved at what their body language didn't show: Adams and the others remained completely still on the hard stools—there was no stiffening or bristling. The Americans were hopeful.

———

At a news conference following the Sinn Féin meetings, Morrison offered a comprehensive summary of both the Americans' visit and what he saw as the way forward. He said that despite the unionists' continued opposition to Clinton's appointing a US peace envoy, he remained convinced that the idea still had value. He told the press:

> We have heard a variety of viewpoints, but most of what we have heard is constructive contributions on how a US role can be helpful, and I think an envoy is part of that role. All people of goodwill should be looking to end violence. Ending violence is more than making ritualistic denunciations of violence; it is looking for ways that alternatives can grow. The best alternative I know comes from compromise and particularly negotiation, and that is what I think the envoy idea is all about.

This was a politician speaking, a politician with an abiding faith in the capacity of a democratic political process to achieve great ends. He was speaking from the absolute heart of his credo. And it was precisely this—a political process in the highest and best sense of the word— that would in time lead to the end of the war and the establishment of a society in Northern Ireland that accommodated its entire population.

Morrison also, of course, stressed the importance of ending the violence: "I want to see peace given a chance and all guns put away. I want to see the people of Northern Ireland have their disagreements through a political process that works for everyone, not through a violent process that at the end of the day works for no one."

———

After the press conference, the Americans left Northern Ireland for Dublin. O'Dowd, Feeney, and Flynn would fly home, but before Morrison left Europe, he had a date at Cambridge University in England with the elite of the British and Irish establishments, as they gathered to discuss Northern Ireland.

When the car bearing the American team crossed the border into the Republic of Ireland, the IRA ceasefire was still in effect. It would be another day or two before the world became aware of it. Irish prime minister Albert Reynolds learned about it only by reading the *Irish Times*, although the White House knew about it much earlier. Gerry Adams later revealed that the ceasefire itself had been a very close call—really it was an "informal" ceasefire (which was not the way it had been described in Sinn Féin's letter to O'Dowd) that hadn't been fully communicated throughout the IRA, and in fact allowed for the possibility, of which the Americans were blissfully unaware, that local commanders might carry out actions that had already been planned. So while the Americans believed they were under a confirmed ceasefire, there was actually the constant danger that someone who hadn't gotten the message would blow something up or shoot somebody. But luck was with them, and the White House saw that Sinn Féin could deliver a ceasefire if there were solid signs of progress toward letting the republicans into the political and diplomatic process. Of such close calls, history is made.

In reflecting on that crucial visit, Morrison recalls the extent to which the busy Americans were isolated from the world around them and not cognizant of the historical import of their achievement. "I couldn't have told you whether there was or wasn't a ceasefire. I was living in the moment. It wasn't like, 'This is the first step in how the world changes.' That's all retrospect."

Morrison did feel uncomfortable about one thing. Although the administration had been told that Americans were going to Northern Ireland, he had carefully avoided in any way seeking White House permission for the trip, because he knew it wouldn't have been given. But when the trip was over, one aspect of what he'd done didn't sit well with him: "I was trading heavily on my friendship with the president without his permission."

Apart from that concern, Morrison was happy with what the Americans had achieved and how he had played his crucial part in the mission. He attributed it to something very basic:

Nobody ever talked straight to the media in Northern Ireland before. People spun everything through their own rose-colored glasses. It was a propaganda world. It was all such a game; you know, "You can't talk about it—there are these two communities that don't talk to each other." We are the Americans dropped right in the middle of it to talk to all the people in this place where people don't talk to each other. In a democracy, that's how people solve problems: They talk to each other.

Although it would be some time before the two communities actually began talking directly to each other, in those late-summer days of 1993, nearly everybody with a stake in the future of Northern Ireland talked to the Americans. A vital new chapter in the process that would ultimately lead to the end of the centuries-old conflict had begun.

It was also clear to Morrison that the absence of expectations and a well-worked-out strategy hadn't been an impediment but a boon. The constant need to improvise had definitely contributed to the success of the journey: "Because we didn't know what to expect, we didn't know what the right way was. So we were making it up. If I went back to try and do it now, I would probably be much more circumspect—and it wouldn't be as good." But as it was, the Americans presented themselves well: "The media had come out to watch the silly Americans get it wrong, and we weren't getting it wrong. We knew exactly what we were talking about."

From a political perspective, Morrison said later, the trip was everything it needed to be: "One of the great advantages of our group was that we were nobodies. We were accountable to nobody; we were completely deniable. If things went badly, so what? But if we brought back any goodies, they belonged to the president. That is a perfect thing in politics."

Morrison's notion that any credit goes to the president reflects a fundamental—and for a politician rare and admirable—credo that Morrison adhered to throughout his involvement in Northern Ireland: "It's remarkable what you can accomplish if you don't care who gets the credit."

Morrison got high marks for his performance as the mission's public face and its explainer-in-chief. Veteran Belfast reporter David

McKittrick of the London paper *The Independent* says that Morrison presented to the unionist community an entirely new view of American involvement, adding, "This is when everything changed."

Niall O'Dowd summarized his man's performance in two words: "Just right." To Bill Flynn, Morrison's performance had been "letter perfect."

Flynn's assessment evokes memories of Yankee pitcher Don Larsen's perfect game in the 1956 World Series, an unmatched feat from which Larsen—like Morrison, no stranger to the agony of defeat—draws a modest and generous principle: "I think everybody is entitled to a good day." No one who was there denies that in Northern Ireland in September of 1993, Bruce Morrison had one good day after another.

CHAPTER EIGHT

An American Nobody Meets the Elite in Cambridge

C ambridge, embraced by the deep curve of the River Cam as it flows gently through the flat landscape of England's East Midlands, has been a university town since 1209, when a group of Oxford scholars fleeing hostile townspeople set up shop there. Across the sea to the west, the Irish had already been fighting the British for more than two generations.

In September of 1993, Cambridge University was the venue of an important conference on Northern Ireland, and Bruce Morrison was an invited guest. The occasion was the annual proceedings of an ever-so-British organization known as the British Irish Association. This rarefied gathering of elite policy and opinion makers, along with selected guests, met each year to talk off the record about what should be done in Northern Ireland. The meeting location alternated between Cambridge and Oxford Universities—never in Ireland or Northern Ireland.

In Morrison's eyes, this was basically a collection of wise men (and a few wise women) who "know all there is to know" about whatever topic they turn their attention to. Sinn Féin would be conspicuous by its absence; only representatives of those groups the organizers considered to be legitimate political parties were invited. As Morrison saw it, it was the kind of gathering that would engage in "the kind of endless conversation about structures that would somehow fix this, but without a whole lot of confronting the fundamentals. It was a proper British gathering." For him, this approach of devising the solution first, followed by an earnest effort to explain to everybody else why this was what they should do, was the antithesis of the brick-by-brick politics on the ground that he knew it would take to make real and lasting change in Northern Ireland.

> A lot of people believe that change works like this: You say the way the world should be and you wait for the world to do it. Which of course is a joke. Nothing ever happened this way. Change takes action at a granular level, really down and messy. Grunt work. Every important thing that's ever been done was done one brick at a time.

But Morrison had been invited to the conference, and he was determined to do his best to convey the reality and the promise of Clinton's new policy.

The guest list also included Inez McCormack, a labor activist from Belfast who had managed to rise to the top level of the man's world of organized labor in Ireland. McCormack radiated energy and intense commitment. Her fearlessness and relentlessness were legendary. One of the maxims she lived and worked by was, "We don't wait for the change, we make it," which, as she was well aware, was "anathema to the elites." She made no effort to conceal her frustration with the difficulty of improving the lives of those in Belfast who held no power: "This is a very small place. Change here is very doable. In a sense, you have to work very hard to keep conditions as bad as they are." McCormack was under no illusions about how she was regarded by the overwhelmingly male power structure she was constantly up against. "In the corridors of power, I was seen as an uppity woman. I didn't know my place."

Additionally, Ambassador Jean Kennedy Smith was at the conference, as was an American foreign service officer who, without a doubt, would be more in tune with the traditional State Department line on

Northern Ireland than that of his new president. John Bruton, an Irish politician who would later become Taoiseach, was also present, along with many other influential opinion makers.

The first day there was a reception, to be followed by a dinner. Toward the end of the reception, Smith approached Morrison and asked him to take a walk with her. It was a perfect late summer day in Cambridge—a brilliant blue sky, with the late summer heat cut by the crisp air of the coming fall. They walked through the university grounds and out on to the rugby fields at the brisk pace to which both were accustomed. As they began to speak, Morrison noticed right away that Smith was spontaneous, direct, and confident—all the things she hadn't been back in Dublin. This time, outdoors instead of inside her embassy office, less hemmed in by her position and its formalities, with no embassy staff watching over her, she was Jean Kennedy Smith, not Madam Ambassador.

She promptly got down to business. As Morrison described it, she "jumped right into the middle of what was on her mind," and what was on her mind was Gerry Adams. She was clearly aware that Morrison had met with Adams in Northern Ireland just days before, and this was her chance to pick the brain of someone who had been in the cage with the lion.

She really wanted to know if she could trust Adams. Could she do business with him? Would he stab her in the back if she reached out to him? These were clearly the questions of someone who wanted to get more directly involved in efforts to stop the warfare.

Morrison knew she could have a major impact on the peace process, so he told her everything he knew about the Sinn Féin leader from his personal experience. He said that Adams was an intellectual and a theoretician, a writer and speaker, striving to articulate big ideas and aspirations. He added that Adams, whatever his history may have been, now functioned as a politician, not a soldier, and that he thought and dealt only in political terms. Morrison said he was confident that Adams, like most people, gravitated to what he did well, which in his case was politics. He added that when he'd met Adams, he hadn't thought "hard man" the way one so often did with Sinn Féin members, and that in the six years they had been in communication with each other, Adams had never misled him.

As Smith listened to Morrison's assessment, he could see that she wanted to find an opening—that she felt that this was the real reason she had been sent to Ireland. She wanted to believe that Clinton's plans offered real possibility, but she really didn't know. Morrison understood fully: "This was fact finding, but I was honored that she cared what I thought and that she wanted to take time and hear what I had to say. I was one of the few people who had actually seen the 'monster', so she was taking advantage of it."

Morrison made the point that by seeking American support in advancing his political role, Adams was submitting to certain useful constraints: He knew the United States opposed terrorism, and that by engaging the administration, he would be subjecting himself to constant pressure from Washington to do all he could to end the IRA violence.

Morrison didn't shrink from offering Smith the big picture, stressing the opportunity that Adams's initiatives presented: "This is something that has lots of potential, so it's well worth the risk. The payoff is huge and the signs are pointing in the right direction. This man is asking the United States to get involved politically. If you are willing to engage, I don't think you're going to be sorry." Smith gave no answer, but the intensity of her attentiveness was palpable.

So it was no surprise to Morrison that in the coming weeks and months, Smith charted her own bold course on Northern Ireland, which caused mighty consternation in her embassy and at the State Department, but had an immensely positive impact on the developing peace process.

Reflecting years later on the difference between Smith-in-Cambridge and Smith-in-Dublin, Morrison thought there was more to it than "official versus private or one-on-one versus part of a group." He realized that in Dublin his group had approached her as "Teddy's sister" and held her to an activist standard that she probably didn't yet possess. He understood that what had seemed in Dublin like a lack of interest in getting involved in Northern Ireland was more of an uncertainty about what should be done. He also knew that in all likelihood she had been told before his group's arrival at the embassy that they were a dangerous bunch—or at least pushing dangerous ideas.

———

During the proceedings of the British Irish Association, Inez McCormack's fierce commitment to social and economic justice was on full display. It was a bone-deep proposition with her that real and lasting peace required an equality of economic opportunity, freedom from discrimination in all realms of Northern Ireland society, and respect for basic human rights.

> I didn't like the bombs, but I understood you had to change the conditions that caused it. It was far beyond fair employment—it was the conditions that brought that about. Everybody had to accept responsibility for a role in the conflict. If you just stopped the gun, you weren't going to change the way things were done before. As I articulated this principle, I was constantly attacked for being an apologist for violence. The British even argued in the US that I was a member of the IRA Army Council, or close to it.

McCormack's pro-labor and pro–social justice orientation wasn't characteristic of the participants in the proceedings at Cambridge. With the way she saw things—"This is a world in which there were insiders and outsiders, and the insiders demonized the outsiders"—she knew her mere presence provoked a big question: "Who was I to mix in their world?"

McCormack regarded Morrison, who had attained such stature throughout Ireland with his immigration bill and his visas, as a kindred spirit. "Bruce has always shown me that when you get to the table, the question is 'Who ought to be at the table but isn't here yet?' His approach was, 'Is there a democratic approach to the problem?'"

For the skill and constancy with which Morrison supported and advanced her positions with well-crafted arguments of his own, McCormack felt a deep gratitude. With such wholehearted support from the man who had so recently and impressively made the case in Belfast for American involvement in the peace process, she didn't feel like a woman alone among uncomprehending establishment males. And she understood the significance of how the Americans had profoundly altered the terms of the debate on Northern Ireland: "The whole argument was about dominance, but Bruce and Clinton changed it to dialogue and deal."

For his part, Morrison cherished his acquaintance and working relationship with the fearless woman from Belfast. He enjoyed the irony of finding himself introducing McCormack, a Belfast resident, to the Reverend John Dunlop, who lived in a Belfast suburb and had just finished his term as moderator of the Presbyterian Church in Ireland. "She was a Northern Ireland Protestant labor leader, and he was a Northern Ireland Protestant religious leader. They were introduced by me, an American, in Cambridge. That's Northern Ireland. It's not a big place, but there's a big separation."

In a breakaway session attended by a dozen participants, Morrison said that he thought Sinn Féin would get a chance to make its case in the United States—in other words, that Clinton would make good on his promise to give Gerry Adams a US visa. The American foreign service man, confidently—smugly, really—sought to soothe those troubled by such a notion: "I can assure you that will never happen," he said. But Morrison came right back with: "There's a new president elected, and I expect him to keep his promise." He said that, based on their long personal relationship, he believed that Clinton "intended to make a different way forward on this." Morrison knew he wasn't making the diplomat happy: "He didn't like being contradicted by this smart-ass former congressman in the midst of this meeting of British and Irish elite."

The group, apart from McCormack, responded to this exchange with a bit of a gasp, a sense of disapproval at Morrison responding so firmly. This was simply not the style to which the British Irish Association was accustomed.

McCormack, of course, heartily approved: As she recalled shortly before her death in 2013, "Bruce made it clear to the State Department that it wasn't a matter of handling the Clinton pledges—the expectation was that he would carry them out. He was very cool and yet not offensive in telling the State Department official: 'You're here for the State Department. I'm describing the wishes and pleasure of the president of the United States, who is your president too.'"

Toward the end of the proceedings, it came time for Morrison to give his own speech, and he laid out Clinton's promised new policy on Northern Ireland. Coming fresh off his week in Northern Ireland and thoroughly energized by the sense of possibility he'd found there, he spoke without hesitation or trimming of sails. As in the north, he focused on the peace envoy. He told them it had the potential to be useful and argued that it would be a mistake for any party to the conflict to disdain such an initiative by the leader of the free world. He added that each side should try to co-opt the peace envoy idea for their own purposes, later calling this the essence of politics: "Take somebody else's idea and see whether you can make it work for you."

Morrison recognized that what he was advocating was not in tune with the kind of conversation generally heard at the British Irish Association. "That was very crassly political, talking to people as if they were politicians with political objectives. That's not the British conversation." But for Morrison, it was *all* politics: The underlying conflict was fundamentally a political one that had been created in large part by politicians, so the solution had to be a political one developed not by academics, diplomats, or think-tank wizards, but by politicians on the ground, listening to their constituents but unafraid to lead. "What's important," he said, "is for political leaders to create a set of circumstances in which doing a deal is the expectation of their constituents—where people want to do a deal instead of planting the flag and standing firm." Morrison concluded his talk by stressing that change would only be achieved with the big tent that Bill Clinton was committed to bringing to the peace process.

His parting sense of the British Irish Association gathering was that it was "a little tent filled with people who didn't blow people up or work openly with those who do"—representatives of what were termed "constitutional parties," along with others trying to devise what he called "magical structures" to fix the problem. Those in the little tent were talking about people who "really did blow each other up, people who felt so disenfranchised that they took up arms." But neither those people nor their political friends and associates were in the room.

One participant from Belfast who was very impressed by Morrison was distinguished journalist David McKittrick.

I had heard and read various things about Bruce Morrison, but I didn't know what to make of him and his campaign because he didn't fit into any of the usual categories. He wasn't a deep green republican, he wasn't US administration.

We had seen coming from Irish America series of congressmen and lobbyists and so on, who may or may not have been politically motivated and careerist in their interventions. They would present their way of thinking, but then when you started to question them in detail, they had no detail; it was kind of a couple of paragraphs off a campaign platform. That gave the sense that they were saying things for political effect rather than out of any deep political or personal commitment. Morrison had detail, he had it thought through; he was clearly a very intelligent person. He basically knew what he was talking about, which was not always the way with Irish America.

Bruce was a different kind of animal. We wanted to know, "What's his angle?" It didn't seem to be for self-benefit—he was just doing something he figured was right. That was a completely new experience for us. After all the years of guys in pubs in America collecting for the IRA, everything softened—even Paisley accepted White House involvement. That wouldn't have happened if Morrison's altruism hadn't appeared on scene. It made people more

open to seeing Clinton that way—a president who was taking big
risks on something of no strategic value. It was a new era.

Once Morrison's Cambridge sojourn had drawn to a close, John
Bruton, the Irish politician and future Taoiseach, offered him a ride
to the airport. There was no hefty exchange of ideas; Bruton's objective was not to pick Morrison's brain but to have his company as he
shopped for a present for his wife. Connecting in that simple human
way, completely outside the formalities that can so easily restrict a
leader's freedom of movement, helped give Morrison valuable access
to Bruton when he became Taoiseach (although, as things developed,
Bruton would prove to be no match in the peace effort for either
his predecessor Albert Reynolds or his successor Bertie Ahern.) The
informality perfectly suited what Morrison was striving to create in
all of his interactions throughout the peace process: "The real contribution of this project was getting beyond all the formalities and urging people to step out of their role and take a risk and do something
because it's the right thing to do."

After Bruton found the right gift for his wife, there was still a
little time left before they had to get to the airport. So he and Morrison did what tourists do and went to Great St. Mary's, the university
church in the center of Cambridge, to take in the view from the top
of its centuries-old tower. The tower was dark and the climb was
steep—123 high stone steps, just narrow wedges, rising and twisting
tightly, around and around. It was a disorienting place, like Yeats's
tower, where "Rough men-at-arms, cross-gartered to the knees / Or
shod in iron, climbed the narrow stairs . . ."

The Irish politician and the American peacemaker climbed past
looped bell ropes that at first glimpse suggested the gallows, up past
the bells, coming at last into bright daylight high above the city streets,
and beheld the panoramic view of Cambridge—magnificent buildings
of England's great ages, with King's College Chapel, a cherished jewel
of late gothic architecture, right there, and Blake's green and pleasant
land encircling in the distance. It was well worth the climb.

Then for Morrison it was back to America, to rejoin his Northern Ireland–traveling companions and take the next steps toward peace. The long flight home gave him time to take stock of the Northern Ireland journey and to think about where it could lead. Years later he spoke of how it all looked:

> This trip, this delegation, was only one step along the long journey, but it was a very important step in changing the terms of debate. It was the introduction into Northern Ireland of the Clinton difference, the idea that there was an active American leader who could take actions that would matter on the ground. That was the idea of an envoy, of people coming and talking to everyone, and this trip embodied a demonstration of what that would mean.
>
> The temporary cessation by the IRA in its campaign of violence was another indication that there was a crack in the door, that there could be a way through. The meeting with the UUP that came so close to not happening and the secret meeting with Protestant paramilitaries demonstrated that something important was happening. That got them thinking that maybe the American role would be something different from a one-sided intervention—actually a friend to all, working on behalf of peace.
>
> Before the visit, people had a lot less hope than they had after. I think the message back to Washington was that this was the fruitful path: Something could be done, people can be talked to. It wasn't as hopeless as people had said in the past. We could take risks on the road and maybe win the prize.

CHAPTER NINE

Helping the President
Go First for Peace

By the fall of 1993, after so many failed attempts to kill the flamboyant loyalist assassin Johnny "Mad Dog" Adair, head of the West Belfast Brigade of the Ulster Defence Association (UDA), the IRA was desperate. They knew that Adair often met with other paramilitaries in a room above Frizzell's Fish Shop on Shankill Road in the heart of loyalist Belfast. They did surveillance, put together their plan, and got it approved up the line. Then they waited until word came through that Adair was there. This was their chance, and it had to be seized right away, carried out fast, no hesitation, no hand-wringing about endangering noncombatants who would be crowding the shop and the busy street early in the afternoon on a bright, crisp October Saturday.

The IRA gave the job to two younger operatives, Thomas Begley and Sean Kelly. Here was the plan: First they would steal a car and go to the fish shop disguised as delivery men bringing in fresh cod. Begley would carry the big plastic fish tray to the counter, with a layer of fish hiding a five-pound bomb underneath, while Kelly waited at the doorway to call out a warning and get everybody in the fish shop out before Mad Dog and his pals, who wouldn't have time to get down the stairs before the bomb went off, were blown to eternity.

They figured an eleven-second fuse would do it. The bomb itself was designed to drive the force of the explosion upward toward the second story where they were sure Mad Dog would be.

But as is so often the case with bombs, things just didn't work out as planned. Before Begley was able to put the fish tray down on the counter, before Kelly had any chance to call out a warning, the bomb went off, instantly killing Begley and nine other people, two of them on the sidewalk outside. The fish shop owner and two young children were among the dead, and dozens more were injured, including Kelly, who lost an eye and the use of his left arm. The deafening roar of the explosion was followed by another terrible sound: the collapse of the building's second story onto the first, burying the poor souls lying there, the living sprawled alongside the dead under heaps of debris. Then the sirens and the racket of rescuers digging through the mess, rescuing survivors, and bringing out the dead. It took hours. Jackie Redpath later called it "our 9/11."

The reporters and the cameras got there right away. There were conflicting accounts about the whereabouts of Mad Dog. All agreed that he'd left the building long before the bombing. Some had him sauntering back from a nearby pub to what was left of the building; others said he was long gone from the scene.

Then came the reprisals, which began swiftly and lasted for the rest of October. The first to die were two Catholics, a deliveryman lured to an ambush and an elderly pensioner. Then two more in a single attack. The big payback operation came just before Halloween. Three UDA/UFF gunmen, one in a mask, two in balaclavas, burst into a Halloween party at the Rising Sun bar in Greysteel, outside Derry. The lead gunman shouted "Trick or treat!" as he opened fire with an AK-47, killing everybody—Catholic, Protestant, who cared?—who happened to be in the path of a bullet. Eight people, ranging in age from twenty to eighty-one, died (six Catholics and two Protestants), and thirteen were injured, one of whom later died. The killers were said to be laughing as they made their escape.

When it was done, the body count stood roughly even: ten in the fish shop, counting Begley, and twelve by UDA/UFF guns, although two of those were Protestants.

The Shankill bombing was a tragic fiasco, unforgivably dangerous to the civilians the IRA had promised to safeguard after the Enniskillen disaster of the previous decade, but from the IRA point of view, it had been an official operation in which a volunteer was killed. There would be a funeral with full military honors. As president of Sinn Féin, Gerry Adams had to help carry the coffin. Pictures of him doing so rocketed around the world. Adams understood and accepted the responsibilities of his position, but to the rest of world, he didn't look like a man of peace.

The Shankill atrocity and its aftermath gave the unofficial peace-makers what Morrison, in a model of understatement, called "a bigger mountain to climb." In truth, it would be difficult to imagine a more devastating blow to the plan of action they had carefully devised and begun to carry out upon their return from Northern Ireland in September. The combination of such wanton disregard for the lives of innocents, the added insult of sheer incompetence, the endless possibilities of how plans for violent action can go so very bad, and the sadistic glee and cruel randomness of the reprisals added up to a deeply repellent and disturbing episode. That it threatened Gerry Adams's growing reputation in the United States as the man to move the IRA from war to politics deepened the gloom considerably. Adams was their best hope, but here he was helping to carry the coffin of a killer. It was true he had to do it to maintain his credibility with the IRA and also that he'd denounced the bombing, calling it a stupid operation. But nobody was in any mood to think about that.

What a mess, when the task at hand was to persuade an American president, over the vehement objections of his State Department, his Justice Department, the FBI, and the CIA, not to mention the British, America's closest ally in the world, to give Adams a visa that would allow him to come to the United States and make his case. The only hint of a silver lining was that the bombing and its aftermath didn't become a major media event in the United States. The challenges it created for Morrison and the group were immense, but it did leave them with a little more room to maneuver than they would have had in full media glare.

It might have seemed to Morrison and the others that this was as bad as it could get, but obstacles kept coming. While the reprisals were still under way, in a thoughtless, spectacularly ill-timed move, New York mayor David Dinkins, desperate to give his flagging re-election campaign a boost with the Irish, asked Clinton in a widely publicized letter to give Adams a visa. The administration's response was swift and devastating: Giving a visa to the man so entangled with the terrorists behind the Shankill Road slaughter was beyond unthinkable. Absolutely not.

It was no surprise to Morrison and the others that the visa request was rejected and no surprise that the Shankill Road attack was cited so forcefully as the underlying reason. But still it was a huge setback—yet another occasion where Clinton had to take a stance against what he had promised during his campaign. Morrison knew that a pattern of precedents would make it more difficult for Clinton to ever start taking steps in support of the new approach he had promised. It was impossible to know where the point of no return was or when it would be reached, but once it was, it would be very difficult to get Clinton back on track. It wouldn't necessarily be a case of repudiating his promises or changing his outlook on Northern Ireland; more likely just a busy president with an abundance of worthy endeavors in front of him making a hard-nosed judgment that other issues were more likely to give him a better return on his time and effort, not to mention fewer headaches.

It was precisely because Morrison completely understood how Clinton could reasonably move his focus away from Northern Ireland that alarm bells were going off in his head. He was already worried that the earlier request for a visa for Adams's book tour had been strike one. Now Dinkins's botched request looked like strike two.

Still, it was clear that the president had to make good on the Adams visa soon in order for the new strategy to succeed. Only that fundamental breakthrough would demonstrate to the IRA and their American supporters that the United States was really going to support the shift to the political path Adams was urging and show the

British that the break with past policy on Northern Ireland was thoroughgoing and genuine. In short, it was the only way to demonstrate that Morrison and the others could actually deliver the goods.

For the visa drive to succeed, three major things had to happen: There had to be a compelling event in the United States for which Adams's presence was necessary, there had to be overwhelming political support among Irish Americans for Clinton to grant the visa that would allow Adams to attend that event, and events in Ireland and Britain had to unfold in a way that would support, not undercut, the visa push.

When Morrison met with O'Dowd, Flynn, and Feeney in New York after returning from Cambridge, they all agreed that they needed to find a worthy event in the United States that required Adams's attendance right away. Flynn and O'Dowd were charged with finding—or, perhaps, creating—such an occasion. Meanwhile Feeney would continue his essential analysis, oversight, and blunt truth-telling—what Morrison sometimes referred to as Feeney's adult supervision—along with his generous financial support for their endeavor. (Morrison was prepared to pay his own way, but it was a welcome thing when Feeney, as he often did, picked up a check.) The other great, enormously complex task, would be primarily Morrison's responsibility: Keep Irish America behind Clinton by pushing him to keep his Northern Ireland promises and creating political conditions to help him do so.

Morrison's responsibility for maintaining the support of Irish America required him to persuade the activists not to lose heart, not to see this as just another political letdown, even though Clinton hadn't yet taken a single public step to carry out his promises. Or, put differently, every public step Clinton had taken on Northern Ireland since his inauguration seemed to be moving *away* from what he had promised. It would take every shred of political acumen Morrison possessed to keep the now-restive activists behind the president. There was a real danger that Irish Americans would decide Clinton wasn't going to keep his promises and would lose faith in him entirely or, worse still, begin to actively oppose and undermine his policy. If the activists jumped ship, there was little reason to believe that Clinton would ever make good on his promises. And, as Morrison always remembered, while Clinton had promised the visa, he never said *when* he would deliver it. Morrison knew it was up to his group to determine the timetable by the impact of their own actions. A deadline was needed, and his group would have to bring it about.

Morrison would also, of course, continue to press the White House directly to take long-overdue positive steps in support of the promised new policy. That meant dealing effectively with Clinton's deputy national security advisor Nancy Soderberg, who now held the NSC portfolio on Northern Ireland. Although Morrison had managed to work well with her after she joined Clinton's campaign, she had her doubts about the plans he was pushing, so it was a challenge keeping her on his side.

> Dealing with Nancy Soderberg I always considered a challenge because she is always at the top of her game. There's an intensity to her personality—because she really does her homework and she really cares about what she works on. She's a fun person, but it's not always fun to have to negotiate with her, to have to satisfy her, to convince her. She can be quite intense and demanding. I always felt under enormous pressure to rise to her standard of what we needed to persuade her.

After the White House rejected Dinkins's request for an Adams visa, Morrison went out of his way to affirm to Soderberg that he understood why the administration had done so. That was important for his credibility, and it made a good connection between them. Beyond that, he worked hard to understand the administration's concerns in order to provide them with whatever was needed to make it easier for Clinton to grant the visa and to move forward on his other promises. He strove to give Soderberg the information and analyses she needed to advance the case.

Years later, Soderberg described the give-and-take of their working relationship and the strengths Morrison brought to it:

> I'm sure I got mad at him and I'm sure we argued. I remember arguing with him about that week-long ceasefire in 1993. He tells me what a big breakthrough it was, and I say, "Bruce, a week's nothing." He goes, "No, no—it really is something." I said, "Well, it may be something for you but not for me. I mean, it's progress, but there's no way that a week ceasefire is going to be enough to get the president of the United States to move."
>
> But he was so persistent and so responsible in how he presented issues. He would listen and he understood the politics of it for the president. He's a smart guy: he's been in government, he knows how decisions are made. He understood the need to build up a base of facts, and he also understood the role of Congress. He was masterful in laying the groundwork and not rushing it. He was a genius about orchestrating a yes out of Clinton. Bruce and Clinton were on the same page. Clinton really wanted to do it, and Bruce knew that because he'd had enough conversations with Clinton directly. I never got tired of his persistence because I respected it. That's the White House—you're there to get pushed to do things.

Without a doubt, the quality of their working relationship was a key factor in Soderberg's growing receptivity to Morrison's overall view that engaging and supporting Adams was fundamental to progress toward peace. For Morrison, this was an encouraging evolution from her long-held view that the approach of moderates like John Hume was the right way forward and that Adams and Sinn Féin were best avoided.

In pursuit of his responsibility to maintain and increase Irish American support for the new course on Northern Ireland that Clinton had pledged, Morrison worked relentlessly to convey the unprecedented opportunity presented by the developing peace process and the active role for the United States Clinton had promised. To the segment of Irish America that had largely avoided involvement in issues relating to the conflict because of the violence, he continued to stress his belief that Adams's commitment to a peaceful path was genuine and that it was in the interests of those who wanted the violence to stop to engage Adams and his supporters in their peaceful aspirations, rather than to regard them as permanently tainted by IRA actions. He consistently made the case that supporting Adams and condemning IRA violence, even when Adams himself did not do so, were not incompatible.

Morrison knew that to keep Irish American activists—a diverse array of people who were often at odds with each other—on track with the strategy, he had to show them that his group's efforts with the White House were getting somewhere. "Meetings of ANIA (Americans for a New Irish Agenda), which were held more or less weekly in New York, reverberated with complaints of betrayal and beliefs that the visa promise had already been breached," he recalls. "So what was to be done? My idea was to arrange for a meeting at the White House to achieve some communication, some expressions of concern from the outside, and to elicit words of support from people on the president's staff." To do that he would need Soderberg's help, and he would have to persuade her that the invitees needed to include the full array of activists, not just the politically safe moderates. "You don't get to the White House unless the White House says okay. To get in, even in 1993, you needed to be vetted fairly seriously." What it came down to was that Morrison would have to persuade the deputy national security advisor to the president of the United States to invite Martin Galvin to the White House.

Galvin was a longtime official of Noraid, which was widely seen as the major American base of support for the IRA, channeling extensive financial support for weapons purchases, and often weapons themselves, into Northern Ireland. The development of the peace process complicated life for Noraid. Warnings of British perfidy fell easily from Galvin's lips in the face of encouraging developments in the direction of peace. Morrison was under no illusions about the challenge he had set for himself: "Martin had been denied access to the White House by other administrations on the basis of his role as a leader in Noraid. This time it had to be different."

Morrison knew it was essential that Galvin not be excluded from direct participation in the White House meeting, because exclusion would give him and other hard-liners a powerful weapon to undercut support for Clinton's initiatives. Better to let him into the room—just another guy with a strong point of view—than to have him make a ruckus at the gate, shouting about censorship. Galvin was controversial and polarizing, but he was part of ANIA. Morrison told him, "We're going to the White House and you're going to come." Galvin, no stranger to exclusion from the White House and other bastions of polite society, scoffed, "It'll never happen." Morrison said it again: "We're going to the White House and you're going to come."

Selling it to Soderberg was another matter. When she spotted Galvin's name on the list, she was incredulous: "You want me to vet *this* guy?" So Morrison explained why it was better to include Galvin than to make him the martyr he had been in the past. Recalls Morrison, "I said to Nancy, 'You don't have to listen to what Martin has to say. But if you keep him out, you empower him. If you let him in, he's just a Joe Blow at a meeting.' Nancy got it."

Soderberg's acceptance was a harbinger of an important shift she would undergo as the new American policy gathered steam. Morrison's abiding perspective, which he was not at all shy about urging on Soderberg, was, "Do the deed, take the risk, reap the reward. What do we use power for? What's the downside? You've got a possibility of doing something important." He adds, "Nancy bought into that perspective. She evolved from 'Why?' as she came on board in the campaign to 'Why not?' as the visa was being considered."

The meeting was constructive and enjoyable for those on both sides of the table. But its overriding significance was that it happened, that the full range of Irish American activists were present, and that they all got to speak their piece and experience a White House that listened with respect and engagement. This helped reinforce to all that Clinton's promises still mattered and that he was still worth supporting.

———

Meanwhile, Niall O'Dowd and Bill Flynn were still looking for an event that would provide Clinton with a solid justification for granting Adams a US visa so he could participate. Flynn had recently become chairman of the National Committee on American Foreign Policy, a respected and well-established activist organization focused on resolution of conflicts that threatened American interests. He asked O'Dowd if he thought a peace conference in New York sponsored by his organization might be the event they were looking for. O'Dowd agreed enthusiastically and soon began to promote the conference heavily in the *Irish Voice*. Over the next several weeks, the group worked hard to build support for it among top Irish American politicians like Ted Kennedy and leaders from Northern Ireland like John Hume.

As the push for the Adams visa gained momentum, its supporters were assisted considerably by something over which they had no control: developments overseas. In November of 1993, it became known that the British government, which had steadfastly denied Adams any legitimacy—even to the point of banning his image and voice from television and radio—had in fact been conducting secret talks directly with the IRA itself. That revelation severely undercut Britain's claim to the moral high ground when it came to talking to what they themselves called terrorists and made their claim that allowing Americans to hear from Adams amounted to yielding to terrorists seem hypocritical.

Then in mid-December, another significant step forward came when British prime minister John Major and Irish prime minister Albert Reynolds announced the Downing Street Declaration. The essence of the agreement was that the people of Northern Ireland would determine its future status, whether it would remain a part of the UK or rejoin Ireland. This signaled a willingness on the part of both governments to hear and honor the wishes of the people who actually lived there.

The declaration also addressed the question of participation in peace negotiations by political parties like Sinn Féin that were linked to paramilitary organizations, demanding a renunciation of paramilitary violence as a condition of participation. Morrison saw the declaration as a definite step forward:

> The Downing Street Declaration had many faults and many limitations, but it was an important step in the right direction. In many ways it was the formal start of the peace process as far as the Irish and British governments were concerned. Its very existence was promising and more helpful than anything that had happened between the two governments up to that point.
>
> For the British government to say quite explicitly in an international communiqué that the people of Northern Ireland could leave the United Kingdom on a majority vote was remarkable. It would have surprised most prime ministers of the United Kingdom going back hundreds of years.
>
> The agreement communicated to the republicans that the outline of a final agreement would require taking on board not a formula for a United Ireland but a formula for self-determination of the people of Northern Ireland. This would be a concession for them, and it was ultimately at the heart of the Good Friday Agreement.

One aspect of the agreement that Morrison saw as singularly *un*helpful was its lecturing tone: "Downing Street was the 'good guys' lecturing the 'bad guys' on how to do the right thing. It's words versus deeds. Lecturing versus doing." It was a valid critique. But soon enough, Bill Clinton would offer a compelling and historic example of doing versus lecturing.

———

The New York peace conference was scheduled for February 1, 1994. Flynn's organization took out a full-page ad in the *New York Times* in early January to promote it and to put pressure on political leaders like Kennedy and Hume to support it—and, by implication, to support the Adams visa, since his presence would be necessary for the conference to be seen as meaningful. Flynn also delighted Morrison with his willingness to augment more genteel methods of advocacy with old-fashioned political pressure: he reminded Hume that he had generously supported an earlier conference that Hume wanted in Northern Ireland and let him know clearly and firmly that now he needed Hume to back the Adams visa. This "I did this for you, now I need you to do this for me" is essential to the effective political give and take by which agreements are forged, and Morrison enjoyed the spectacle of the distinguished executive getting down with it.

By late December, the visa proponents had gained support from important political corners. Irish prime minister Albert Reynolds had felt for some time that granting the visa was the right thing to do and that it would give the peace process a boost; the Downing Street Declaration only strengthened his conviction. US ambassador Jean Kennedy Smith became convinced as well, despite her belief that the men of the IRA—and perhaps Sinn Féin—were, as she told journalist Conor O'Clery, just like the men who had murdered her brothers. But Smith had well-developed political instincts, and it was clear to her that the support of both her brother Ted and John Hume were essential to getting Clinton to issue the visa. Smith had already clashed with members of her own staff at the Dublin embassy over her support for a strong new American policy, and she brought that same zeal to bear in her relentless effort to persuade Hume and her brother that the visa would help bring about peace and that they should join her in urging Clinton to issue it.

For Ted Kennedy, backing the visa would bring him politically closer to the IRA, something that had gotten him into trouble years earlier, when his strong pro-republican and anti-British stance had brought him a torrent of criticism. At that time Hume counseled him that the solution to peace in the region needed to come via economic progress and politics, not violence. Kennedy gratefully accepted

Hume's advice and followed it for twenty years, often uncritically. But now Hume came to Kennedy encouraging him to support the visa for Adams. Kennedy worried that he could be seen as reverting to his 1972 stance, but Hume presented it as a matter of supporting a peace process, not rewarding the IRA. In 1972 the focus had been on injustice and human rights violations. Now the focus had shifted to advancing the peace process by helping Adams establish a political path. The exchange squared the circle between the two men, redeeming Kennedy and exalting Hume.

Hume's own political situation around the visa was more complicated and perilous than Kennedy's. For years he had been the preeminent nationalist leader, both in Northern Ireland and in Washington. His SDLP was by far the strongest among Catholics, and his grip on the opinions of figures like Kennedy, New York senator Daniel Patrick Moynihan, and House Speaker Thomas Foley was nearly absolute. As a nationalist leader untainted by violence, he also had wide support from Irish Americans upset by the violence. But the charismatic Adams was now a real threat to his political position, both at home and among the Americans. There was no doubt that any political rising of Adams and Sinn Féin would diminish the power and influence of Hume and his party. Hume knew that giving Adams a visa was the right thing to do, but in raising his rival's stock and conferring legitimacy on a man both the Irish and the British had banned from the airwaves, he put himself in real political peril. Ultimately, his support for the visa would be tremendously influential, but in the years to come, he would pay a big political price as Sinn Féin eclipsed his SDLP as the majority nationalist party.

Hume's great moment, as recounted by Irish journalist Conor O'Clery, came in early January as he spoke with Ted Kennedy at the funeral for former House Speaker and Irish American icon Tip O'Neill. Kennedy asked Hume point blank whether or not he would support the visa for Adams. Hume had everything to lose, but his answer was unequivocal: yes. Kennedy immediately said he would do the same. In one brief exchange, these two heavyweights were onboard, and the push for the Adams visa now had major momentum.

For Morrison, the man from Derry had truly answered the call of history:

> John Hume owned America, but once Gerry Adams came, Hume's role was different. It was not marginalized, but Gerry is a much more charismatic human being than John is. Gerry's a little professorial, but John is very cerebral. He is not charismatic, in an American political sense, so it was never going to be the same again. For John to be a sponsor of Gerry's role was huge. John is a real patriot, and he wanted the right outcome. He never let the cost to him get in the way of the goal. So I think he is pretty special.

Morrison himself worked hard to get the support of another heavyweight: the editorial board of the *New York Times*. He had extensive conversations with board member Susannah Rodell, who wrote their editorials on Northern Ireland. Her strong support for the visa helped turn the tide of the public debate.

The gathering momentum did not go unnoticed by the British and their American supporters, among them House Speaker Thomas Foley, Irish by blood but Anglophile by heart, as well as the State Department and the Department of Justice, especially the FBI, which had all long opposed anyone having anything to do with the IRA. The British, however, were surprisingly slow to grasp the serious possibility that Clinton would actually give Adams the visa. When they finally realized that it really could happen, they were all over Washington, grabbing whatever ear they could to fend off the dreaded possibility.

State Department spokesman and future Bill Clinton press secretary Mike McCurry remembers the British onslaught vividly:

> I was getting creamed by all of my friends over in the British embassy. I remember Jonathan Powell, who, as young, very talented foreign services officer in the British embassy, had traveled

with me in 1992 when I was with the Bob Kerry campaign, calling and just howling and screaming about what a disastrous idea the whole visa was and how this was going to besmirch the special relationship between the United States and the UK. They were just frosted about this, and particularly upset that they had been outflanked by what they then later came to understand was a pretty determined behind the scenes effort that was certainly guided by Morrison but I think had a lot of very deft and capable help from Nancy Soderberg.

It wasn't just diplomats who were getting upset. The actor Hugh Grant went to a reception at the British embassy and then to a dinner at which Clinton official George Stephanopoulos was giving a talk unrelated to Ireland. Grant loudly interrupted him to denounce White House encouragement of terrorists.

As the conference drew closer, efforts to influence Clinton's decision intensified. The big labor unions, many with Irish Americans in top leadership posts, strongly favored the visa. The British and the State Department argued that the visa would imperil US/UK relations. The FBI was certain it would send the wrong message to terrorists.

Clinton felt the full weight of the moment and the opposition to an Adams visa:

> First Bruce's trip happened and then the Downing Street Declaration and then we got word that he wanted to come to America and speak and wouldn't fund-raise. And that if he got a visa, we might be able to get a ceasefire. So by then, the major players who had been talking to Bruce and to Nancy Soderberg and Tony Lake had come around to the prospect that it was better for me to give him a visa than to appoint an envoy, because then the play would still be between Ireland and Britain but we would have injected ourselves into it.
>
> The State Department was, to a person, crazy against it. Warren Christopher thought I had lost my mind. Admiral Crowe, our ambassador to England, who had been a chairman of the

Joint Chiefs of Staff under Reagan and who had endorsed me for president, which was hugely important to me at the time—it made a major contribution to my credibility as a candidate—was wildly against it. Of course he would be; I mean, he was there in the UK, he was hearing one side of the deal. And Foley, who was Speaker, whom I needed desperately to pass my program, thought it was crazy. Dodd thought I should do it, and Kennedy also wound up thinking I should do it.

Clinton's decision-making process went as far down to the wire as it could. On Saturday afternoon, January 29—a mere three days before the conference—he met with top White House advisors George Stephanopoulos, Tony Lake, and Nancy Soderberg to talk it through. All three favored giving Adams the visa, but Clinton was still concerned about the likely impact it would have on America's relationship with the British. His advisors told him that they were sure the relationship was strong enough to withstand this disagreement. Clinton finally told them he saw it the same way, even though he was eager to get British support for his plans in a different region of the world:

Keep in mind, the world was focused on Bosnia and I had tried to get the allies early in '93 to agree to have NATO take action there. Warren Christopher got stiffed everywhere, including in the UK, but we still knew that the UK was the most likely country to come on quickly along with the Dutch. I'd wanted to go into Bosnia earlier, but I knew I couldn't do it without the Europeans because of just the geography—they had to live with the aftermath, not me. So I was in no great hurry to destroy our relationship with Britain, but I just thought, *if this works . . .*

Nancy said they'll get used to it, and even though they'll never admit it, they'll think it was the right thing to do—and if it doesn't work, then we'll be back with them.

Soderberg confirms her analysis: "I never bought the argument the State Department made that they wouldn't continue to cooperate with us on Bosnia. They weren't doing it as a favor—it was in their interest to do it."

At that moment things couldn't have looked better for the Adams visa. But the drama never seemed to let up. At the last minute, a potentially fatal obstacle emerged: a strange and highly suspect story from San Diego. The report was that fake bombs had been placed in British businesses, and that the real thing would be next if Adams didn't get the visa. The "South California IRA," which no one had ever heard of, took credit. Investigators later found blue training grenades at a pub, a British curio shop, and the federal courthouse, but the name, the place, and the exquisite timing of the threat gave plenty of reason to be skeptical about it. Many suspected that the whole thing was a trick—by the British?—to block the Adams visa. But there was no time to get to the bottom of it. If Clinton was going to grant the visa, he would have to authorize it on Sunday morning in order for Adams to have time to collect it at the embassy in Dublin on Monday and get to the United States in time to attend the conference Tuesday morning.

All of this meant that the fake California bombs had to be treated like a real threat. The White House needed Gerry Adams to denounce the whole thing, publicly and in writing. The task of getting that statement, *still* with no guarantee that the visa would be granted, fell to Soderberg, who decided it was time to talk to Niall O'Dowd directly. Before this, all of their contact had been through intermediaries, principally Kennedy staffers, in order to keep the man who seemed to have so many friends close to the IRA at a safe remove from the White House. But now Soderberg needed to reach Adams immediately, and O'Dowd was the one who could get her to him.

O'Dowd's heart sank when he learned of this new obstacle and what he had to do. He called Adams right away, fully prepared for the Sinn Féin man to take out his frustration on the messenger. But Adams surprised O'Dowd by taking it in stride: He was ready to oblige with whatever would help Clinton feel comfortable granting the visa. His only expression of annoyance was ruefully asking whether he'd have to prepare a statement every time an Irishman and an Englishman got into a fight in a bar.

Adams's statement on San Diego was faxed to the White House and then hand-delivered to Clinton at a dinner at Washington's Alfalfa Club. The dinner had nothing to do with Ireland, but the seating arrangements gave those who favored the visa a last-minute fright: Clinton had been placed between Secretary of State Warren Christopher, the most vehement visa opponent in the administration, and House Speaker Thomas Foley, the most vehement visa opponent in Congress. (Foley later told Conor O'Clery that he briefly raised the issue with Clinton but concluded that the president had already made his decision.)

On Sunday morning, Clinton told his staff that he would give Adams a forty-eight-hour visa with numerous restrictions to keep him on a short leash. He called his unhappy secretary of state, who tried hard for half an hour to talk him out of it. Then he called Janet Reno, his unhappy attorney general, who didn't mount a major argument but was thought by some to have been the source of a leak that made it impossible for staffers to tell the British about it before they heard it on the news, a breach of protocol that made the British feel all the more wounded and outraged.

But the overriding reality was that despite terrorist watch lists, Gerry Adams was coming to America.

Years later, Clinton described his analysis:

I just decided to do it. I figured it was our best chance ever to try to settle this thing, and I did not personally believe that the politics in the UK would permit it to happen unless we could trigger some sort of jolting event. They couldn't do that—there was nothing they could do for Gerry Adams that would change the internal calculus of his politics. But I could. It was very simple to me. In the end we did it and NSC [National Security Council] was for it, and everybody else was against it. Thank God it worked.

For Morrison, the magnitude of what Clinton had done cannot be overstated:

> This was the history-changing moment: the powerful one, the president, goes first and takes the risk for peace. Now there's a huge moral claim that the less powerful one should take the same risk. It's easy to *tell* someone to do the right thing, but with the president going first. . . . He doesn't lecture, he takes action, and now the ball's in Adams's court—there's a clear expectation of a ceasefire.

Nancy Soderberg was a bit rueful, as she had been during the campaign when she learned Morrison had already gotten to her candidate before she could put the brakes on. But she offered a gracious tip of the hat to her worthy opponents:

> None of us were happy about the peace conference. I was very annoyed by it. But it was brilliant. I was like, "Why are you jamming this down our throat? We're not ready!" But they just forced the decision on us, which was great. It was really brilliant the way they did it. How do you oppose a peace conference? But I hated it at the time.

The British, of course, were unhappy in the extreme. As Soderberg recalls, "I don't think they thought we would do it, and when we did they were just dumbfounded. Major didn't take Clinton's calls for a week."

———

It was well past midnight in Ireland by the time everything was in place for Adams to pick up his visa at the American embassy in Dublin the next morning, and he barely managed to catch the last flight out that could get him to New York in time for the conference. For Morrison, the last-minute hurry-up was all too typical of how things had worked throughout the peace process:

> It so often came down to the last minute, being held in doubt as to whether things would move forward or they wouldn't—the visa, the ceasefire, the Good Friday Agreement. It really does test one's faith and energy, waiting for the shoe to fall and hoping it falls on the right side.

It was 4:30 in the afternoon on January 31, already getting dark in New York, when Aer Lingus flight EI 105 landed at Kennedy airport and the clock started running on Adams's forty-eight-hour visa. Inside the terminal he was welcomed in true rock-star style, with a media mob, old friends, fans and nonfans, and curious people of all stripes. Morrison and Republican Congressman Peter King, a longtime supporter, greeted the Sinn Féin leader at customs. Adams gave a brief press conference, and then he was off to Manhattan. Morrison recalls the momentous culmination of so much of his work:

> Gerry's arrival was very exciting. There was the media, but most of all the reality of meeting Gerry on his first time coming to the States. It was another huge leap forward in the project that started years before. It was rewarding and overwhelming—feeling like you had a very big role in why it happened.

Bill Flynn's security man Bill Barry rode in the front seat of the limousine carrying Adams to Manhattan, but it was the man riding in the back with Adams who was interesting in a wonderfully ironic way. He was George Schwab, a CUNY history professor and president of the National Committee on American Foreign Policy. Decades earlier Schwab had been a member of the Stern Gang, Jewish guerillas fighting the British in Palestine. He had helped with the running of guns and ammunition from New York to Jerusalem and had been trained at an estate in New Jersey for surveillance and assassinations of British officials in the United States. Everything the British said about Adams had also been said about former Stern Gang members, including future Israeli prime minister Menachem Begin. So Adams and his host had plenty to talk about on the way to the hotel.

Adams was familiar with the Stern Gang and the controversy surrounding its members who later became politicians. As the two conversed, Schwab says, "We became, so to speak, friends." As the magnificent sight of Manhattan, sparkling brilliantly on that winter's night, came into view, Bill Barry spoke up from the front seat. "We were in deep conversation," Schwab says, "so he interrupted, saying, 'George, maybe we should let Mr. Adams look at the skyline of New York.'" Schwab remembers taking the Queensboro Bridge into Manhattan—Jay Gatsby's route to the "city rising up across the river."

"Anything can happen now that we've slid over this bridge . . . Anything at all . . ." Nick Carraway had mused in *The Great Gatsby*, and in every sense, this crossing too was filled with possibility for Adams, for Clinton, for all who had worked so hard to make it happen, and for all who longed for an end to the warfare. The miraculous possibility was that America could help Northern Ireland break free of the current that had for so long borne it ceaselessly into the violent past.

In time the possibility of that moment would be realized, but at this point, it stood only as a beginning—a fine beginning, but soon to give way to the very down-to-earth demands of fitting everything Adams wanted to do into the allotted forty-eight hours.

———

It was early evening when they arrived at the Waldorf Astoria and Adams registered under the assumed name Schwab had given him: Shlomo Breznitz, a prominent Israeli psychologist. As Schwab and Adams parted company, the Irishman solemnly told his host: "George, I promise we won't go back to the old ways." It was clear to Schwab that for Adams, "coming to New York was an eye-opener. He had always looked through the lens of Northern Ireland, and now he was amazed at the wider view from New York City, where you could speak to anybody about anything."

Adams was exhausted after the long day of travel, but his visa clock was running fast and his schedule was packed. Before the evening was out, he would go to a small reception at the Waldorf, a secret meeting with a senior member of Ted Kennedy's staff, and over to the CNN studios to do the *Larry King Live* show, live for the entire hour. This would be America's first opportunity to see and hear Adams on live television.

During the show, King labored mightily to get Adams to give a blanket renunciation of IRA violence, but the Belfast man, who came across as thoughtful, charming, and more than a bit funny, would go no further than saying he "wanted to get the gun out of Irish politics." King continued to prod him, but Adams knew he'd reached the limit of what he could say and still retain his credibility with the IRA fighters.

The hour concluded pleasantly with a discussion of the feasibility and safety of King doing the show from Belfast. When it was over Adams had charmed King—and America. It made the British furious, but it was obvious that their policy of banning him from television and radio had only increased the impact of his appearance. Nevertheless, policy was policy: When the show aired in Europe, an actor read Adams's words. (Not long after, the British rescinded the policy that made them look so foolish.)

Although it had been Bill Flynn's conviction that the peace conference would be much more than merely a vehicle to get Adams his US visa—that its proceedings would make a substantive contribution to the peace process—the facts suggested otherwise. The hoped-for broad cross-section of speakers from the Northern Ireland political parties never materialized, because, of course, leaders of the unionist and loyalist parties refused to participate if Adams would be there.

So when the conference opened the following morning, the audience got to hear only from Adams, Hume, and John Alderdice of the Alliance Party, which tried to appeal to both populations of Northern Ireland. By then, Adams was tired and off his game, and it is generally agreed that the best speech came from Hume. Morrison, who knew the goal had been achieved the moment Adams walked into the terminal at JFK, was sure that nothing new would be said or done at the conference, so he went back to work in New Haven.

With only three speakers covering familiar ground, the conference itself was over quickly. For Adams, the rest of the day was a blur of sightseeing, as many TV appearances as he could squeeze into the time remaining on his visa, and a huge gathering with supporters at the same Sheraton Hotel where, nearly two years earlier at the Irish American forum on the eve of the New York presidential primary, Clinton had promised that he would give Adams a US visa.

The Sheraton blowout was the event Morrison wanted to go to:

This was the fulfillment of one of the promises made to these activists, many of whom had been in the room in April of 1992. It was a demonstration that politics had its place and could work. They had stood up and asked Clinton to give them an answer before he was president, and now they were there to see he'd kept his promise, that he'd done this deed and could be counted on to do more to advance the prospects for peace in Northern Ireland. It was an affirmation of what these folks had set out to be part of. It was also a demonstration to them that there was a reason to have supported Clinton and a reason to stay the course and continue to support the process.

In virtually no time after Adams's arrival, the visa clock had run out, and then it was back to Ireland. But everything had changed. Today Adams speaks of the drama of it all with understatement that can only be called . . . British: "I was a bit surprised by the whole furore," he allows mildly.

It was clear that the visa plan had succeeded. Adams got heard and seen in the United States, he abided by the restrictions, and he would be allowed to return and continue to make his case. The door was also now open for leaders of the unionist and newly developing loyalist parties to come and make their case as well. Adams was now in the mainstream, and the United States was a full partner in the peace process.

Years later, Morrison took stock of how the long-view political strategy he and the others had done so much to develop, implement, and support had played out:

> Clinton did not know the plan. He did not sign up to be leveraged. He played his role, as some of us believed he would, given the chance. It's not like we, marionette style, moved Clinton around. But we did create a political environment in which somebody with Clinton's skills and political inclinations was more likely than not to do what we hoped would get done. Our goal was to create a political environment where the right things would happen. He had to choose, but we had to make the choices attractive, and I think we did that. We were overjoyed at the level of success. No one would have predicted the enormous amount of energy he poured into the process or the enormous satisfaction he felt at being involved in it. So it was much better than anyone could have bet on.

––––––

Now the question was: What next and when? Although it hadn't been an articulated quid pro quo, it was now clearly up to Adams to deliver an IRA ceasefire. If he did so, the peace process would continue full force. If he failed, his influence would wane, and many who had welcomed him would wonder if they had been tricked. Nancy Soderberg, at once pragmatic and philosophical, figured it was win-win regardless, since Adams would either deliver a ceasefire or he would be seen as ineffectual, which would leave him without influence in the United States.

Adams knew full well what he had to do, but neither he nor Morrison nor Clinton knew how much time he had to deliver it before the president, whether from discouragement, frustration, or second thoughts—or because a new crisis grabbed center stage—turned his attention to different matters and the precious moment was lost.

CHAPTER TEN

The Road to Ceasefire:
It Took Forever and
Happened in a Flash

The mood at the 1994 White House St. Patrick's Day party was celebratory. Adams had come and gone, the world had survived, and the United States had carved out a major independent role in the peace process. Movie and television stars like Paul Newman, Michael Keaton, Conan O'Brien, and Roma Downey were there, as was the renowned classical flautist James Galway, a Belfast native. There was plenty of Washington star power too, including Senate majority leader George Mitchell, House Speaker Thomas Foley, and Ted Kennedy. The great chieftain of Irish American activists, Paul O'Dwyer, now eighty-seven and in a wheelchair, was thoroughly enjoying his first visit to the White House. He'd been invited back in 1933 but couldn't come; he was invited again during the Carter administration but, in vintage Paul O'Dwyer style, refused to enter when some members of his group were turned away at the door because of their Noraid ties. But now he, like everyone else, was filled with hope about Clinton's new policy.

Morrison, O'Dowd, Flynn, and Feeney mingled with the stars and top administration officials like Tony Lake and Nancy Soderberg, looking terrific in a long, emerald green dress. Irish prime minister Albert Reynolds was a happy partier, and SDLP leader John Hume probably was, too, though his characteristic dour mien made it difficult to be sure until he joined Clinton and Reynolds in singing "When Irish Eyes are Smiling" at the end of the evening.

For Morrison and his wife, it was a wonderful occasion. "I'd been at parties at the White House when I was in Congress," he recalls, "but I had never had a friend like Bill Clinton to go visit there." There was also a moment of comedy when a flustered military officer in formal dress shooed them out of chairs on which they had briefly perched, exclaiming, "Sir, sir, you're in the Newman seats!" When Paul Newman and Joanne Woodward arrived just as the Morrisons stood up quickly, they greeted each other warmly as longtime Connecticut political activists.

But there was also a dark undercurrent to the occasion. There had been a series of IRA mortar attacks—all with dud shells—on London's Heathrow airport earlier that month: three of them, at two-day intervals, each targeting a different part of the airport. The message was clear: Even as the peace process seemed to be advancing, the IRA hadn't gone away. It was ready, willing, and able to bring the fight—with live ammunition—to Britain's front porch at any time.

When New York senator Daniel Patrick Moynihan, who had been a somewhat reluctant supporter of the Adams visa, learned of the attacks, he sent a note to Ted Kennedy, who had pressed him to support the visa, saying simply: "Have we been had?" His question revealed a deep well of anxiety and dread to which many of those who had set aside their doubts about Adams were still vulnerable. Clinton was plainly angry and perplexed about the IRA action as well. When he said in his formal remarks that it was "difficult to know what to make of the latest attacks at Heathrow," Niall O'Dowd was convinced that Clinton was glaring straight at him.

But despite the reminders that there was still a war on, this St. Patrick's Day was a cause for celebration. When Clinton began his remarks in Gaelic with the traditional Irish greeting *Céad míle fáilte*— a hundred-thousand welcomes—the crowd answered with thunderous applause and raucous cheers. These sons and daughters of Ireland felt their time had come, and they were going to enjoy every minute of it.

————

As spring made its welcome appearance, even those who understood that Adams couldn't snap his fingers and produce a ceasefire were becoming increasingly restive, needing to see something from him. The question of Sinn Féin's response to the Downing Street Declaration became an interim focal point since Adams hadn't yet embraced the accords, although he'd offered general statements that the declaration held promise for a way forward. But he wasn't prepared to commit to it, particularly the requirement that any political party that wanted to participate in the negotiations had to renounce the use of violence. The problem for Adams was fundamental: If he was going to bring the men of the IRA to politics instead of war, it was essential that he maintain his credibility with them. They had to believe that he understood and respected the reasons for the armed struggle and that he wouldn't ask them to give it up unless he was confident that the politics was a viable way to achieve their long-term goals. And they had to believe he understood that, as an army that hadn't been defeated, they could accept no resolution that looked like surrender. If Adams lost them on any of these points, he would lose them altogether, and his ability to lead them to a peaceful path would be destroyed. Although he understood the frustration many of his American friends felt, Adams held steady to the reality of the circumstances and his obligations as the leader of Sinn Féin. He also never lost sight of the human dimension involved when ordinary people find themselves in circumstances so desperate that they turn to violence. As he saw it, those deploring the violence should offer a better way:

> There was no point in condemning the IRA. It's a waste of time. Whatever you think about it, there was not in the mind of the IRA a peaceful and democratic way to go forward which has the same efficacy as what it was doing. So if we want to persuade

them to stop doing that, then let's bring forward another and better way, or at least another way which has the same potential. These weren't career soldiers—there is no Sandhurst, there's no military aristocracy. These were ordinary citizens, ordinary folks who got involved in armed actions.

Morrison was no stranger to Irish republicans' endless talking and splitting of hairs, the mysterious deliberations behind closed doors, the complex qualifications and sub-qualifications of almost anything that managed to get put in writing. For him, the way Adams held steadily to his bearings and responsibilities in the face of his newly acquired international celebrity was a true measure of his greatness. Adams never allowed himself to believe he held such power over the IRA that all he had to do was demand a ceasefire—as so many of his international supporters were urging him to do—and the IRA would declare one without hesitation, yielding to the overwhelming force of his celebrity.

Morrison holds a distinctly unsentimental view of Adams-as-celebrity:

People over here had sort of fallen in love with Gerry Adams, because he is charismatic and so much not the image of the terrorist. So there was all this stuff about how he should denounce the IRA and separate himself from them—which is ridiculous, because the only reason Gerry was important was that he could bring the IRA into the peace process, he could end the war. This is the great confusion of celebrity politics.

Despite recognizing the constraints under which Adams operated, Morrison and the unofficial peacemakers were determined to do everything they could to help get to the ceasefire. They went to Northern Ireland later in the spring as Sinn Féin prepared to gather at Letterkenny for its annual party conference. There was rampant speculation that this was the time—that the IRA would announce a ceasefire during or right after the conference. Morrison and his group shared those hopes: They met with Sinn Féin members to help formulate a list of what the United States government and Irish America could do to create conditions that would support a ceasefire.

Expectations were high, but expectations were wrong. In the spring of 1994, nothing about the IRA's ways of doing business had changed. They worked behind closed doors in their own way and in their own time; any effort to rush them only slowed things down.

For Morrison, who had an especially good grasp of how important it was to be steadfast and patient in these matters, the sliding of spring into the summer with no ceasefire—no sign of when it would come, no certainty it ever would—was a maddening time. Many in the administration and in Congress who had supported the Adams visa experienced increasing doubt and discouragement. Nancy Soderberg candidly acknowledges that her confidence in what Morrison and the others were telling her was getting shaky:

> They would always say, "It's about to happen, it's about to happen," and in retrospect I think they really were trying, but I was increasingly skeptical. I put the president's political credibility on the line, saying, "Okay, if Adams gets the ceasefire, we'll win. If he doesn't get the ceasefire, it will show that they weren't sincere and we can further isolate them." So I was on the start-further-isolating-them track and had basically given up.

But in truth, there was nothing for anyone on the outside to do but to be at the ready, help when called on, not lose hope, and wait (at least until Clinton himself lost patience and decided to walk away from the whole business).

Looking back on that time of exasperating silence, the rising and falling and rising and falling again of hope, when the fear that it might all turn to ashes was no longer manageable by distraction and denial, Morrison marveled at how, when the waiting was over, a process that felt as if it was taking forever seemed to have happened in a flash.

Sinn Féin hadn't been dragging its feet: It was clear to the Americans at Letterkenny that Sinn Féin had been working hard for a ceasefire, but the IRA just wasn't ready. Morrison described Sinn Féin as "getting to yes with a process that was respectful of their constituency," but acknowledged that "living it was excruciating. But what's seven months when you're changing the whole world?"

The first sign that the long wait might be over came in early August when a Sinn Féin contact told O'Dowd that they needed a detailed statement in writing of what support the American group felt the United States would be willing to give in response to a ceasefire. The Americans were able to provide that quickly because the document had already been largely prepared during their visit to Letterkenny. Finishing touches were quickly applied and off it went to an intermediary in Dublin for hand-delivery to Sinn Féin by whatever cloak-and-dagger method they would devise.

So when an attractive woman appeared out of the mists of a mid-August Dublin night and asked the man standing outside the offices of the *Irish Independent* whether he thought Dublin would win on Sunday, the detailed written summary of what the Americans could offer in support of the ceasefire was handed over and on its way to the IRA. The list included regular access to the United States for Adams and other Sinn Féin members, the opening of a Sinn Féin office in Washington with considerable financial support from Chuck Feeney, curbs on deportation from the United States of those with ties to the IRA, direct government support for the peace process, and promotion of American business and investment in Northern Ireland.

The message delivered, there was, once again, nothing to do but wait.

This time, blessedly, the wait was short. In a matter of days, O'Dowd was told by his contact that he should take his holiday in the last week of August. That was code for: "Get the group over here right away."

"The group" now numbered six—Morrison, O'Dowd, Flynn, Feeney, and top labor leaders Joe Jamison and Bill Lenahan—and they arrived in Dublin on August 25, 1994. Ceasefire rumors were flying all over the city: Would the IRA really do it? Would it be long-term or short?

Before heading north to Belfast, the Americans met with Albert Reynolds and Foreign Affairs Minister Dick Spring. Reynolds was unusually agitated and intense; he told the Americans, with a vehemence that took them aback, that as far as he was concerned, only a complete ceasefire would be acceptable. He said that if they came back from Belfast with a limited ceasefire, whether three months or six, he would not be with them. Morrison didn't agree:

> If we had been told by the IRA that ninety days was all that was on offer, we would not have walked away, because we were in it for the long haul. We didn't have the high standards of John Major, which were that the only ceasefire worth having was a permanent ceasefire. That, of course, is malarkey. Anything, any positive step, is better than no step, because you can build on it.

But Reynolds would have none of it; for him, it was all or nothing. So as the Americans headed to Belfast the next day, they discussed the best ways to get the IRA to agree to an unlimited ceasefire. It wasn't a good sign that the Belfast rumor mill was dominated by talk of a limited one or even no ceasefire at all but just a pullback to a "defensive posture." The Americans ultimately decided that they would simply ask straight out when there would be a ceasefire and how long it would last.

Shortly after arriving in Belfast and checking into their hotel, the Americans were taken to Sinn Féin's Connolly House headquarters above Falls Road. It was a media mob scene, with questions being shouted from every direction, and the Americans literally had to force their way into the building. After appearing briefly before the press with Adams and other top Sinn Féin leaders, they were ushered into a small room for a private meeting. They were completely geared up to make every argument they could in favor of an unlimited ceasefire.

Feeney and Flynn, the businessmen, were confident that the IRA would do exactly that, but Morrison didn't share their certainty; his world was practical, political, where you strive to get as much as possible but know that if you overreach, you may well get nothing.

During the meeting, Morrison pressed hard for as much of a cease-fire as Adams could get. He also addressed the question of how Sinn Féin and the IRA should present whatever ceasefire they ultimately declared to the world. He returned to the basic point he had made at Conway Mill the year before: It was necessary to do whatever they could to take away the terrorist label that the British used so effectively against them. The only way he saw that happening was for the IRA to just say, "We've stopped." He was sure that any attempts to embellish or explain further would result in endless semantic entanglements with the masters of the English language. In essence, his message was that less is more: "I told them that nobody has to listen to you because you're terrorists. The day you say, 'We've stopped,' you change the world, because the British have no other language with which to deal with your grievances, other than to keep calling you terrorists."

As always, Adams and the others listened carefully, making no direct response to Morrison's entreaties. When Adams did speak, he said simply, "The Army is going to call a complete cessation." He made no mention of a time limit, but he didn't say unequivocally that there wasn't one. And he quickly added that there were still problems to be resolved before the IRA would make an official announcement and asked the Americans not to tell the media what he'd told them. There was no further clarification and no time for questions or additional discussion. Then they were ushered out to face the media. "We had to say something without saying anything," Morrison recalls. "We beat around the bush as only good politicians could."

As the Americans left Connolly House, Feeney and Flynn remained confident that the only feasible decision was an unlimited ceasefire. O'Dowd concluded from Adams's confident and relaxed demeanor that the IRA's decision was a very good one. Morrison, perhaps now more lawyer than politician, knew what had been said and what hadn't been said, and he knew that the term "complete cessation" didn't answer all of his questions—it certainly seemed to imply that as long as the cessation was on, there would be no military operations. But it didn't say how long it would last or if it had any kind of conditional expiration date. He would have to wait for the official IRA announcement to learn more.

Morrison flew home where he waited . . . and waited—saying later that it was the longest weekend of his life—for the announcement. He knew it would come only when—and if—the problem Adams had only alluded to was resolved. Once he was back in the United States, Morrison learned that the issue was indeed serious, with the potential to derail the ceasefire. The IRA was offering the ceasefire only on the condition of receiving another controversial visa, this time for Joe Cahill, someone whose terrorist status was beyond any doubt. They wanted Cahill, an elderly IRA man, to go to the US to explain the ceasefire directly to the IRA's hard-line American supporters. (Some unionists later insisted that the real reason Cahill had to go was to formally stand down IRA units that were rumored to be operating in the United States.)

It's unlikely that any visa applicant ever had a more appalling record: Cahill had been sentenced to death by the British in 1942 for his part in the shooting of a Northern Ireland policeman. He escaped the noose with a reprieve from the British when one of those arrested with him took responsibility for the crime and was hanged, and he later made his way to the United States, where he helped establish Noraid. In 1973 Cahill was arrested off the coast of Ireland on a ship carrying five tons of weapons and explosives that had been donated to the IRA by Libyan dictator Colonel Muammar el-Qaddafi. The Irish sentenced him to prison, and after getting an early release because of ill health, he snuck back into the United States, where he'd been barred as a terrorist since 1971. Once there, he began raising money for the IRA. The US deported him again in 1984.

This new visa request was preposterous on its face, but both Albert Reynolds and Jean Kennedy Smith became convinced that unless it was granted, there would be no ceasefire. Nancy Soderberg vividly remembers their efforts to persuade her:

> Jean Kennedy Smith started calling me, telling me that we had to give them another visa. I was on vacation in LA, and I said, "You're crazy, go away, no way." By the time I was back in DC, Albert Reynolds was calling me. I still didn't believe him. He faxed me the text of the ceasefire agreement and then, I'm like, "Whoa, this is real!" It wasn't the usual mumbo jumbo. This was unequivocal. It was very different than normal statements that were coming from the IRA.
>
> I sent the text to Clinton and said, "I really think this is going to happen." I got on the phone with Albert Reynolds and told him Clinton agreed to give Cahill the visa, and they announced it the next day.

Cahill collected his visa at the American embassy the morning of August 30 and immediately flew to the United States to begin explaining the ceasefire decision. The way was now clear for the long-awaited IRA announcement.

———

Shortly before noon on Wednesday, August 31, 1994, a muffled cassette recording by an IRA spokeswoman interrupted a broadcast on Irish radio and announced "the complete cessation" of operations by the republican fighting force. It wasn't limited in any way whatsoever. Morrison recalls hearing the announcement at last:

> It was my wake-up call. It's five hours earlier over there, so it was on the news at seven o'clock in the morning. It was great, but as with most good news in this process, there was always, "Well, what's next?" We made these promises, some of them requiring persuasion at the highest levels of the American government, and so the first thing on my mind was, "Oh my God, our bluff has been called." We had a lot of work to do, so there wasn't a

whole lot of time for celebration, except getting invited to be on *Larry King*. I was accused by one caller of being a Catholic, although for the most part it was a very celebratory show.

Much of the world responded with unqualified jubilation. Morrison was named ABC News's Man of the Week. Political leaders who had gotten on board with the new American policy felt vindicated, and some who had opposed it so strenuously, like House Speaker Thomas Foley, graciously acknowledged the breakthrough. It was an unqualified triumph of Clinton's radical new policy on Northern Ireland.

The joy the ceasefire engendered was felt and expressed in Catholic neighborhoods throughout Northern Ireland. Morrison saw the response as confirmation of Sinn Féin's political acuity:

On the ground in Belfast it was seen as a very positive event, and it really was the first example of what I would say was the ultimate skill that Adams and others working with him, have exhibited in this process, which is knowing their own community—being in one sense ultra-cautious, but in another sense ultra-smart about preparing the ground for movement, such that whatever dissenting voices there were would be drowned out by the bang of garbage cans on the street. It really was celebratory, a sense of victory, and not at all the sense of being backed into a corner and forced to do something.

Ironically, that response would, in months to come, seriously complicate Britain's ability to respond constructively to the ceasefire. The nationalist joy aroused destructive suspicions among the unionist community that if the Catholics were happy, the Protestants must have somehow gotten screwed or that maybe there was a secret deal in which the British sold them out.

But all of that would be a problem for another time. On Day One of the ceasefire, the overriding question was whether the British would, in Morrison's succinct phrase, "take yes for an answer."

CHAPTER ELEVEN

The British Respond to
the Ceasefire:
Words, Words, Words

It was generally accepted by participants and observers alike that the peace process would never move forward to all-inclusive political negotiations and settlement without the IRA taking the crucial step of declaring an unconditional, unlimited ceasefire. When the IRA finally did take that action in late August of 1994, it was announced in four brief paragraphs. The first kept it simple:

> Recognizing the potential of the current situation and in order to enhance the democratic peace process and underline our definitive commitment to its success, the leadership of *Óglaigh na hÉirann* [Soldiers of Ireland] have decided that as of midnight Wednesday, August 31st, there will be a complete cessation of military operations. All our units have been instructed accordingly.

The next paragraph paid tribute to IRA fighters and supporters and reiterated their "commitment to our republican objectives." The third expressed their belief that a settlement of the underlying issues was within reach, and the last acknowledged the Downing Street Declaration while asserting that, as Morrison and many others had maintained, "a solution will only be found as a result of inclusive negotiations."

The statement concluded with a declaration that the purpose of the ceasefire was "the creation of a climate which will encourage" a political settlement.

Now that the IRA had taken the action so long sought by those who wanted the conflict resolved by politics and not warfare, all attention turned to London: What would the British do in response?

British prime minister John Major's first reaction came the very afternoon of the announcement. In response to questions asked during an interview, he said:

> Firstly, let me say I think the statement that has been made today is very welcome and it is a very great advance, and to have this cessation of violence is a remarkable move forward. But I think we do have to be clear that this is permanent, that it isn't a temporary ceasefire that will be turned over at some stage and the armed conflict, as the Provisionals call it, will begin again. We must be certain it has ended.
>
> [Gerry Adams] doesn't actually have to use the words I did, but I think he has to make it clear unambiguously that this is the end of the use of violence, that they aren't going to return to violence in pique if they don't get their way at some future stage . . .

Major's words left little doubt that the wait for reciprocal British action to advance the peace process would be a long one. In fact, there was reason to worry that instead of any action, the British response would amount to nothing but words, words, and more words. Major, like so many of his illustrious predecessors, had an impressive arsenal of words at his disposal—words capable of defining, deflecting, demeaning, disparaging, avoiding, and reframing anything or anyone.

While no one begrudged the British a reasonable period of time for the ceasefire to show itself to be genuine, Major's primary plan of action seemed to be the constant deployment of torrents of words, many of which systematically erected obstacles to all-party talks. This alarmed and discouraged those who had for so long called for the ceasefire, which they expected would lead quickly to real negotiations. Major's words are a more accurate indicator of the way the British responded to the ceasefire than any actions they took. By insisting that the ceasefire be "permanent," Major was demanding something much more than a ceasefire. By its very nature, a ceasefire involves a decision by a combatant to suspend fighting in order to pursue something else—anything from collecting the dead and wounded to celebrating a holiday to discussing settlement of a conflict. Major's insistence that the IRA completely renounce the use of force forever, no matter what the British, the RUC, or the Ulster paramilitaries did, was worlds away from any credible notion of what a ceasefire is, as well as a practical impossibility given the mission and history of the IRA. Even though he regularly denied it, Major was essentially demanding a surrender.

His words were also noteworthy for their belittling tone, suggesting that the IRA might return to violence "lightly" or "in pique." That was a powerful indication that it would be a far distant day before this British prime minister would be ready to deal with these old adversaries with any measure of respect and awareness of the challenging circumstances they faced, which would be essential to productive negotiations.

Less than a week after the IRA declaration, Major repeated the same demand for a "permanent" ceasefire, but this time he added that he might see things differently after the ceasefire had been in place for three months:

> We need two things, don't we? We firstly need it to be made clear that this is intended to be a permanent cessation of violence, and then of course we need to see those words carried out, we need to see the deeds, we need a period in which violence actually ceases. And as we set out in the Joint Declaration, if it is clear that it is permanent and if the violence then ceases for a period up to three months, within that three-month period we will begin to talk to Sinn Féin about how we bring them into the constitutional talks, and that is a great prize for everyone.

These words offered some hope that Major would no longer cast a cold eye on the ceasefire and that all-party negotiations could really begin at the end of three months. But then his statement on October 13—two-and-a-half months after the ceasefire began—again made it crystal clear that he was in no hurry to move things ahead:

> We still have to reach the situation where we are satisfied it's permanent. When we have reached that situation, I will make a judgment upon those matters. But I repeat the point I made a moment ago: if we snatch at these things, it is going to slip away. We need to retain the confidence and trust of all the people in Northern Ireland, and they expect us to be cautious. They have had 25 years of misery, with bombings and killings in Northern Ireland. I think it is right to take this at a measured pace, and I propose to continue doing so.

For Morrison, Major's steadfast avoidance of all-party talks, even as the ceasefire was showing itself to be the genuine article, was sad confirmation of Britain's inability to adjust to the new world created by the ceasefire:

> The cessation unsettled the expectations that the British had over the decades developed about the republicans: that they would always do the wrong thing, that they would always be on the outside, and that at the end of the day peace would be made by excluding and by marginalizing them. When the republicans stopped doing that and started a campaign to make peace rather than a campaign to make war, the British weren't ready. They hadn't thought it through; they didn't have a strategy. I think you hear Major being called upon to say things and having nothing to say. But of course politicians can never have nothing to say, so he filled the air with words he had learned before the facts changed.

By December 13, the three months were long gone. The ceasefire held, but there were still no all-party talks on the horizon.

Instead, Major moved the goalposts by introducing the precondition of decommissioning IRA weapons before beginning all-party negotiations.

> Sinn Féin and the political representatives of Loyalism have declared that they wish to enter the political arena as peaceful democratic parties. It is a declaration that people across the communities in Northern Ireland had longed for for more years than they care to remember. And so Sinn Féin and the political representatives of Loyalism are now beginning an historic dialogue with the government about how this should come about and how their weapons and explosives may be safely taken out of commission.

Although Major made it sound like something the republicans had agreed to, his new precondition was a nonstarter. There was no possibility the IRA, which saw itself as an army that hadn't been defeated, would ever agree. To them, giving up arms before talks began would be surrender, plain and simple. But Major nevertheless clung to it repeatedly, ultimately at great cost to the peace process.

Morrison found Major's unwillingness to get all-party talks under way disappointing, but he wasn't entirely surprised:

> The British view always was that there is no legitimacy to the IRA's war and therefore that there is no legitimacy to their peace terms. All there was for them to do was acquiesce to the British view of what they must do to cleanse themselves of their sins. I'm sure the British aren't the first people to think that way about an enemy, but it's not an operational thought; it's a moral thought or something for a speech. It's nothing for the negotiating table.

On May 3, 1995, nine months after the ceasefire and still with no prospect for all-party talks, Major introduced yet another reason why they couldn't start: Until Sinn Féin met the ongoing British demands of permanency and of prior decommissioning of IRA weapons, the unionist parties would never agree to negotiate with them, even if Britain itself were willing to do so.

> The decommissioning of arms is perfectly clear. If people are prepared to enter into the democratic process, then they don't need arms. If they need arms, then there must be a question about how serious they are about entering into the democratic process. Now, we need to examine this matter. It isn't a matter of semantics, it isn't a matter of detail, it is a matter of principle and it is a matter of practice. The reality is that if Sinn Féin are to move forward as I wish to see them do, and enter fully into the democratic process as I wish them to do, and to enter into the talks with the other political parties as I hope they will do, then they are going to have to put themselves in a position where the other political parties will sit down and talk to them.

Spring passed into summer and summer into fall, still with all-party talks nowhere in sight. Major's characteristically wordy statement of September 21, 1995—more than a year after the ceasefire was declared—was liberally sprinkled with protests that all he really wanted to do was get the talks under way as soon as possible, coupled with a plea for understanding that he as prime minister simply had no way to get the unionist parties to the table if they didn't want to come and that only IRA compliance with the British preconditions would get them there:

> Let me add just a couple of points about the future. Firstly, all-party roundtable talks—the sooner that I can convene all-party roundtable talks on a constitutional settlement, the happier I will be. I would be perfectly happy to do so this afternoon if that were feasible. But in the reality of politics, there is no purpose whatsoever in calling all-party talks unless there is a pretty good chance that all the parties are going to be there if we were to do so, and if parties began to absent themselves, perhaps

permanently, perhaps in large numbers, then we would have made a mistake in our move forward.

I can't force people to the conference table, I can't coerce them to the conference table. I can only encourage them to go to the conference table. The plain truth is simply this: The majority parties in Northern Ireland, representing the majority of the people in Northern Ireland, will not come to the conference table until Sinn Féin / IRA have begun the process of actual decommissioning.

Major's newest statement ignored the obvious point that he was prime minister of the United Kingdom, of which Northern Ireland was a part, and he was head of a powerful political party that was formally named the Conservative and Unionist Party. Further, because Major himself had devised the preconditions at the heart of the stalemate, he certainly had the ability to withdraw or adjust them in order to take advantage of the opportunity offered by the ceasefire.

As Morrison sees it, there was plenty for a leader to work with:

The ceasefire was a dream come true and there was real momentum. With that momentum and the upswing of hope, it would have been difficult for the unionists to reject full talks. But instead of building on that momentum, Major stonewalled and coached the unionists in resistance. It was time not for speeches but for taking action. Major had real opportunity, but instead he talked himself and others out of it, killing the momentum. The unionists were not the ones who listed the reasons not to talk. Major created the reasons not to talk, and eventually the unionists said, "Right, that's why we won't talk." But it was hardly their initiative. So whatever the problems may have been with unionist reluctance, Major never really tested it. On the contrary, he stoked and encouraged it, and prolonged by years the period that it took to get down to the hard bargaining that led to the Good Friday Agreement.

Major's defenders argue that he was handcuffed by a razor-thin Tory majority that depended on unionist MPs, and that letting Sinn Féin come to the table would cost him unionist support and cause his government to fall. Morrison believes that claim was specious:

> The excuses have been given that it was his precarious politi-
> cal position, that he was dependent on the unionists to main-
> tain his majority, and while that was literally true, no one at the
> time believed that the Labour opposition would bring down
> his government in any way that could be attributed to unionist
> objections to things that were happening in Northern Ireland,
> no matter how that vote of confidence was couched. Labour was
> not going to be part of that kind of a vote because they always
> viewed it as a matter of bipartisanship, not as something that
> should be played for political advantage. Much as they were
> interested in getting into government, they were not interested
> in doing it on the say-so of the unionist parties.

Tony Blair, who succeeded Major as prime minister when his Labour Party trounced Major's Conservatives in 1997, confirms Morrison's analysis that Labour wouldn't have been a party to taking down Major's government over Northern Ireland. Citing the approach taken by his predecessor, when it was discovered that Major's government had been conducting direct conversations with the IRA despite their repeated claims to the contrary, Blair said, "John Smith deliberately decided not to go for the government over it, which was an act of great statesmanship, actually, because I'm not sure whether, if it had happened the other way around, Conservatives wouldn't have gone for us."

Blair candidly acknowledged that his party would have welcomed any opportunity to oust Major's government but stressed that Northern Ireland was off limits for that purpose: "I think we would have tried to bring them down any way we could, but not on anything attached to this issue."

Bill Clinton has an interesting take on Major's supporters' claim that he had to focus on protecting his position. In essence, he sees a lost opportunity:

> It's hard for me or anyone else to make a judgment about some-one else's politics, and the British system is complicated, but I think ironically that not doing more with the ceasefire probably hurt him politically, because what he thought, I believe, was, "Oh my God I did this and now I gotta be careful, we're going to have elections, we've been in a long time." But the truth is, once you've been in a long time, the only way you can stay in is if people think there's a new reason to be for you. So I don't think his political analysis was correct, but I think it was, from a conventional point of view, understandable.

In his analysis of Major's failure to capitalize on the ceasefire, Morrison reflects a sympathetic understanding of the unique challenges unionist politicians faced in doing politics effectively—and why they desperately needed Major to lead them, not to reinforce and pander to the reluctance they would naturally feel:

> From the early 1970s, when the British closed down the devolved government at Stormont, until very recently, there was no government or any authority worthy of the name exercised by politicians in Northern Ireland. They were elected to things, they served in positions, there were parties, and there were party leaders, but they had no power. Even their local councilors and governments had little or no power that wasn't superseded by the government at Westminster. The unionist politicians had no occasion to hammer anything out that mattered. They just had the occasion to hammer out their own obstinacy, their own clear view of right and wrong, and their superior views over those of their opponents. It was all about rhetorical battles and not at all about governmental ones. In that context, it would require an enormous shift for politicians to sit down and start negotiating.

It was always going to be slow and a learning experience, and the sooner it started, the better. It was going to be hard slogging to go from hot air to negotiation.

―――――

One remarkable feature of the peace process was that whenever a top figure was summoned by history to move things ahead in a bold and essential way, often at serious risk to his or her political or personal well-being, in every case except one the call was answered. The sad truth is that John Major did not answer history's call when his great moment—the long-demanded IRA ceasefire—came. He demonstrated over and over that he was unalterably locked into his preconditions, obstacles that made all-party talks impossible.

Major's unwillingness or inability to do what history demanded of him is particularly disappointing in light of the important positive aspects to his earlier involvement in Northern Ireland: He certainly de-Thatchered British policy by moving away from the Iron Lady's unyielding determination to use every bad development in Northern Ireland to demonstrate how tough she was, how it was all a simple matter of cops versus criminals, right versus wrong. In negotiating the Downing Street Declaration, Major displayed a willingness to engage with an Irish prime minister in a full-hearted way that no British prime minister had ever done, and the accord he and Reynolds reached undeniably helped move the peace process forward. But it was the IRA ceasefire—what Morrison has called the great watershed of the entire peace process, the crucial event that made all future progress possible—that presented Major with his greatest moment of opportunity, and he just wasn't able to seize it. In Morrison's poignant description, Major "could look through the door and know that there was something better on the other side, but he could never bring himself to actually walk through. So he wasn't really wrong. He kind of got it, and he did some brave things, but he never cashed the check. It was just not in him."

Nancy Soderberg, so bold in helping Clinton carry the process forward, feels that focusing on Major's failure to meet the challenge of the IRA ceasefire is unfair. She stresses that Major chose to become seriously involved in the search for peace, something British prime ministers hadn't previously done because it seemed to be such a no-win proposition. Major had the option of steering clear of the whole mess, but he decided to engage and made genuine strides. Conor O'Clery, the *Irish Times* Washington correspondent who closely observed the development of the peace process and the American role in it, shares that perspective:

> I wouldn't be too hard on John Major. He worked constructively with Reynolds on some issues. He went so far as to develop a good relationship with him. Remember that no British prime minister had ever sought to have a good relationship with the Taoiseach. Thatcher did it, but while holding her nose. I think, to his credit, he and Albert Reynolds sat down and talked on an equal basis about bringing the process forward. He may have failed to grasp the initiative as he might have, but given all the historical pressures on him and the atmosphere at the time where Sinn Féin was untouchable, it was a big ask.

Soderberg and O'Clery aren't alone in their sympathetic regard for Major. Bill Clinton, while discussing the value of Major's accomplishment in the face of considerable resistance from his own party, spontaneously interjected, with real affection: "He was low-key and all that, but I rather liked him." It was a testament to how far Major had come, when during negotiations building up to the Downing Street Declaration, an overheated John Hume accosted him in the bar in the House of Commons and said, "Gladstone failed, Lloyd George failed, and Churchill failed. If you succeed you will go down in history as the prime minister who brought peace to Ireland. Take the leap." When Major got well-and-truly stuck, unable to walk through Morrison's door, it was undeniably poignant.

But it is also undeniably true that by the summer of 1994, eighteen months after the Downing Street Declaration, the entire centuries-long history of the conflict had narrowed to a single issue: Major's long-standing insistence that the IRA declare an unconditional cease-fire before all-party talks could begin.

The focus on declaring a ceasefire had been so intense for so long that no one had really thought very much about this problem: What if the IRA delivers the ceasefire, but the British still won't convene all-party talks? Before the ceasefire, such an outcome seemed no more likely than the possibility of Gerry Adams refusing to go to New York for the peace conference after pressing so hard for a visa. Yet as the months ground on, that remote possibility hardened into an undeni-able truth: John Major would not or could not—who could possibly know which, let alone why?—convene all-party talks. Whether he understood that he was at serious risk of squandering the unprec-edented ceasefire is an abiding mystery that even his own autobiog-raphy does nothing to resolve.

Morrison looks back on that period with distress and exasperation:

> It was truly a surprise that John Major was so uninterested from the moment of ceasefire in grabbing the nettle and making something happen. He was trifling with the deal on offer and with world history, basically walking around the gas station with matches. His intransigence was totally backward looking.

Major's relentless demands for a ceasefire, followed by his paralysis when it happened, begs the question of why he ever called it a ceasefire, when what he really meant was surrender. In Morrison's mind, the answer lies in a failure of perception that has historically afflicted any number of British prime ministers: egregious underestimation of the opponent. Major felt free to call for a ceasefire when he meant sur-render because it was inconceivable to him that Sinn Féin and the IRA would ever be capable of anything but stupid, self-defeating choices. So when the ceasefire actually happened, he had no idea how to respond, no strategy to pursue, and nothing but words to fall back on.

As Morrison wrote on the twentieth anniversary of the ceasefire, "A ceasefire, the fervent hope of all sensible observers, threatened the end to the 'terrorist' label and all the prohibitions on republican political activity. Major knew the world had changed. He just never figured out how to change with it." Ironically, the man who condescendingly assumed the republicans would be prisoners of their own ideology, and therefore unable to stop the violence even when it was in their best interests to do so, was himself captive to an imperialist ideology that only with an IRA surrender could Sinn Féin get to the table—and he was caught utterly flatfooted when his opponents displayed the pragmatism, the political astuteness, and the flexibility to stop the violence and put the onus on Britain to respond. Major repeatedly cited instances in which he had, prior to the ceasefire, made mention of the various preconditions that he used to stymie all-party talks, but it got him nowhere. Simply put, he squandered the ceasefire. And his complaint in his autobiography that republicans spun the ceasefire, in his eyes a defeat for them, as a victory begs another question: Why didn't he immediately declare victory and graciously usher Sinn Féin to the table now that their benighted republican comrades had accepted the wisdom the British had so charitably offered for so long?

Major's inability to respond constructively stands in striking contrast to the way the loyalist paramilitaries responded to the ceasefire. On October 13, 1994, less than two months after the IRA declaration, they declared their own unconditional ceasefire, announced by none other than Gusty Spence, the avuncular ex-prisoner with the curved pipe that the Americans had met with in Dukes Hotel when they visited Belfast in 1993. Spence asked Bill Flynn, who had continued to forge connections with the unionist community, to join them when they told the world. The loyalists even asked him to look over the text of their announcement and offer suggestions. His only one was that they keep in their apology for the harm their violence had caused innocent victims. He told them he wished the IRA had done the same.

John Major praised the loyalist ceasefire, saying, "another very important part of the jigsaw has fallen into place." The BBC reported that "the British government believes talks between Northern Ireland officials and Sinn Féin could be under way by Christmas." But Major went on to signal that no one should expect anything to change very soon:

> What we need to do is to absorb what has happened, consider it, and then decide how we move forward. We will do that in our own time and our own way. . . . We must analyze precisely what is being said this morning, precisely what it may mean. Just a few months ago, people were saying we would make no progress at all. They said the Downing Street Declaration wouldn't work. We have taken it cautiously, we have taken it slowly. I believe one of the reasons that we have made the progress we are now beginning to see is precisely for that reason. So we don't intend to be pushed.

The words with which the loyalists announced their ceasefire were eloquent and direct, and the heartfelt apology for the loss of innocent lives lifted their statement to a higher realm. But words weren't the point: Action had been taken. Like the IRA, the loyalist paramilitaries stopped fighting. It's difficult to imagine a more powerful testament to the genuineness of the IRA ceasefire than the actions of the loyalists who for so long lived and died in IRA crosshairs.

CHAPTER TWELVE

Stalemate

The stalemate over John Major's unrelenting insistence that the ceasefire be "permanent" and that the IRA start decommissioning weapons in advance of all-party talks ground on through the rest of 1994 and all of 1995. Late in the summer of 1995, with the IRA ceasefire a year old, Morrison, O'Dowd, Flynn, and Feeney returned to Belfast to explore ways to break the stalemate. When a British official stressed that the unionist parties would refuse to participate in any all-party talks that included Sinn Féin unless decommissioning had begun, adding that it wouldn't do to have empty chairs at the negotiating table, Morrison replied that empty chairs were better than death and destruction.

When the Americans returned to New York, Feeney paid for a full-page ad in the *New York Times* that declared: "Mr. Major, you must act now. Convene all-inclusive talks or be judged on your failure to act." The Americans were under no illusions that the ad would influence Major; their hope was that it would push the US administration to lean harder on the British.

The administration may not have needed such a push: As it became increasingly apparent that the British wouldn't, or couldn't, take advantage of the historic opportunity the ceasefire offered, a remarkable series of decisive and far-reaching actions on Northern Ireland were taken in the United States in an effort to get to all-party peace talks before it was too late. It was clear that Clinton was determined to do whatever he could to capitalize on this unprecedented opportunity.

On December 1, 1994, Clinton took what would prove to be a key step toward peace with his appointment of retiring Senate majority leader George Mitchell as his economic envoy to Northern Ireland. Although this didn't precisely fulfill Clinton's campaign pledge to appoint a peace envoy, subsequent events would obliterate the distinction. In many respects, Clinton's appointment of Mitchell marked an important shift in the dynamic of the American involvement, because he made the appointment without a hard push from Morrison and the Irish Americans. This was Clinton taking full ownership of his Northern Ireland policy, the Clinton of whom Morrison said, "When he gets something, he really gets it, and he gets his arms completely around it."

Clinton's administration also made good on its commitment to allow Adams and Sinn Féin unfettered access to the United States. Adams soon embarked on an American tour that took him from Boston, where he met with Ted Kennedy; to Detroit, where he met with Rosa Parks; to Hollywood, where he was given a lavish birthday party; to New York, where Mayor Giuliani affirmed his approval of the visa; and then finally to Washington, where Vice President Al Gore told him by telephone that Sinn Féin was no longer classified as a banned organization and that American officials were now free to meet directly with its leaders. In December of 1994, Adams finally got to visit the White House, meeting with Gore and the National Security Council (NSC) staff that had been so influential in Clinton's visa decision.

Adams returned again in March of 1995 for the opening of the new Sinn Féin office in Washington, funded by Chuck Feeney. They grandly called it a diplomatic mission. At a reception, English journalist Peter Hitchens, an unrelenting critic of Adams who seemed determined to make his American visits as difficult as he possibly could, demanded to know whether the Sinn Féin mission would have a military attaché. Adams shot back that it was time for Hitchens to decommission himself.

On that same visit, Adams got to participate fully in the St. Patrick's Day celebrations for first time, both the House Speaker's St. Patrick's Day lunch and the White House party. At both events, handshakes between Clinton and Adams were choreographed in excruciating—one might even say ridiculous—detail.

Bruce Morrison had his own special moment with Clinton at that White House party. As the two old classmates shook hands, Clinton said, with intense feeling and good cheer, "Well Bruce, I delivered for you." From one politician to another, this was the most elevated and profound declaration Clinton could make. For all the cynicism that can be mustered about politics and politicians, delivering on a promise is their highest, noblest act. With these simple words, Clinton was claiming the full measure of the purpose and solemnity of his promises on Northern Ireland, and he was claiming the acknowledgment he knew he richly deserved for delivering. At the same time, the president was reflecting back at Morrison his sheer delight in what his classmate and his friends had gotten him into and in the progress made so far.

The British, of course, had plenty to say about actions the Clinton administration was taking, calling them "rash," "irresponsible," and a host of other pejoratives. Major dispatched Northern Ireland secretary Sir Patrick Mayhew to Washington for St. Patrick's Day 1995, and he called for an arms decommissioning process with three elements, the third of which restated Major's requirement of decommissioning before Sinn Féin could be included in negotiations. Mayhew's restatement of Major's long-standing precondition was made so firmly that it became known as "Washington 3" and remained the immovable obstacle to all-party peace talks. On later occasions, the British would claim that the United States had agreed that decommissioning should be a precondition to all-party talks, but each time they made that claim, Nancy Soderberg or another administration official would reaffirm that the only precondition the administration supported was that Sinn Féin agree to "seriously discuss" decommissioning and that they were satisfied with its commitment on that score. Indeed, Clinton was so satisfied that he decided to allow Sinn Féin to fund-raise in the United States—a step the British steadfastly opposed. The British response was one of enormous consternation, even though Sinn Féin had long been permitted to raise funds throughout the UK. Major's personal response was once again not to take Clinton's telephone calls for several days.

During that same period, a split in the Irish government became apparent. John Bruton, who became Taoiseach in December of 1994 after Albert Reynolds had to resign when an old scandal (having nothing to do with Northern Ireland) came to light, argued in favor of prior decommissioning, whereas Foreign Minister Dick Spring said it was unrealistic to expect the IRA to begin disarming before talks. In subsequent months, however, the gap between them had obviously narrowed considerably when Spring, reflecting what was now apparently the official Dublin position, said on a visit to the United States that the Washington 3 should be dropped so all-party talks could begin; soon after that, he declared at the UN that the precondition of prior decommissioning entirely ignored the psychology and motivation of the paramilitaries.

In May of 1995, the Clinton administration sponsored a major conference in Washington promoting investment in Northern Ireland. This was a major event on the road to peace, especially noteworthy because it was attended by many important unionist and loyalist leaders, a contingent that showed up in the United States in force for the first time.

To Morrison, that event signaled a profound shift in the peacemaking effort:

> When the Clinton administration sponsored its economic conference, the center of gravity for peace in Northern Ireland had moved from London to Washington. This included a dramatic change in the contacts between parties that previously never spoke: On the unionist side, on the loyalist side, and on the nationalist and republican side. In Washington there was space to meet those who were anathema to be met or talked to in

Northern Ireland itself. This creation of a new opening, a new venue, was part and parcel of what the Clinton administration had accomplished. They were facilitating a peace process with an American eye for what might work, opening the door at the White House and elsewhere in Washington for people to start to talk in realistic terms about changes on the ground in Northern Ireland. This conference wasn't happening in Dublin or London or Belfast but in Washington. It really marks the end of the old view that London would decide the outcome for Northern Ireland and made it clear that Washington would facilitate the peace process.

———

On June 1, 1995, Morrison was sworn in as chairman of the Federal Housing Finance Board. He was now officially part of the administration, but he intended to remain fully involved in his unofficial peacemaking activities, and he negotiated an agreement with the administration that would enable him to do so. Both Morrison and the administration found that the new situation took some getting used to. When Morrison said on television that London should move on its preconditions, Nancy Soderberg promptly called and firmly reminded him that he was now part of the administration and needed to be more careful in his public statements.

In July of 1995 Clinton took another huge step forward and announced that he would visit London, Belfast, and Dublin in late November. This wasn't entirely unexpected: The 1996 election was fast approaching, and a rousing welcome in a Northern Ireland enjoying the peace the paramilitary ceasefires had brought about would be a fine thing to see. But it was a brave commitment nevertheless, because the peace process was so stuck. If the British intransigence persisted, the situation could deteriorate so badly in the coming months that Clinton's visit would end up showcasing not a triumph but a mess, or, even worse, the visit might end up having to be scrapped altogether. Clinton's willingness to make that commitment in the face of such uncertainty—Britain had still given no sign of relenting on the demand for prior decommissioning, and Sinn Féin had finally abandoned as futile the endless "exploratory talks" the British said would eventually lead to all-party talks—was a powerful indicator of his determination to redouble his efforts to help bring about peace.

In the fall of 1995, Soderberg and National Security Advisor Tony Lake went to London to try to help untangle things. As Lake later recounted to Conor O'Clery, they were careful not to let the process turn into an American negotiation in which the parties would look to Washington for solutions instead of finding them for themselves. Lake stressed how important it was that the United States not tell the parties how things should come out, because "we honestly don't know."

One of the ideas getting attention during this discouraging period was a twin-track process, under which all-party political discussions would move forward concurrently with an independent commission evaluating the decommissioning issue and making recommendations. Economic envoy George Mitchell said he would be willing to chair such a commission if asked, and Lake and Soderberg both supported that approach, but Major and Sinn Féin both opposed it. Another idea came from unionist leader David Trimble, who advocated new elections in Northern Ireland as a confidence-building measure: A body would be created to conduct all-party talks, and participants would be selected in proportion to the votes they won. Lake and Soderberg felt that idea had merit as well, but the nationalist parties resented having to prove themselves yet again and dismissed the idea as another unionist tactic to delay all-party talks.

Major argued throughout the duration of the ceasefire, and long after he left office, that Britain repeatedly took meaningful action during this period, but the truth is that no actions he took ever came close to overcoming his words. During the many months in which the British pursued "exploratory talks" with Sinn Féin, there was never a moment when they displayed a willingness to set aside their precondition of prior decommissioning. They made great efforts to persuade the Irish and American governments to make the same demand, but they were never able to get them fully on board. Of the three Irish prime ministers to hold office during the peace process, John Bruton was the most amenable to the British position. But while his administration flirted with adopting it, ultimately they did not, if for no other reason than the fact that Bruton realized the IRA would never agree. As the Irish saw it, the British position created an insuperable barrier to the all-party talks that were essential to reaching a settlement.

Late in September, Clinton's advance team went to London to work out the details of his trip with British officials—where he would go, whom he would meet, where he would stay, what he would do— and encountered a wall of British resistance to pretty much everything. They cited old security concerns that might have made sense when the Troubles were at their worst, but that in the present circumstances seemed to be more about British determination to limit the impact of Clinton's visit. It was made particularly clear that they didn't want Clinton meeting with Gerry Adams; obviously a boost to his status and legitimacy was something they couldn't abide.

As the presidential visit drew closer, Clinton let it be known that he would be pleased to have all-party talks underway before he arrived. His team realized that not only was that unlikely, but that events beyond his control could make him and his policy look foolish—not an appealing prospect for a president facing an election in the coming year. But at the same time it was clear to Clinton and his team that the trip would almost certainly have a tremendously positive impact on the ground and would give his policy a huge boost. The positives carried the day: Clinton was going to Northern Ireland, no matter what.

At 10 P.M. on November 28, 1995, the eve of Bill Clinton's touchdown in London, Major and Bruton announced their agreement on a twin-track process that they said could lead to all-party talks. On one track would be an international commission headed by George Mitchell to study and provide recommendations on decommissioning, while on the other track political talks would move forward immediately. Both the British government and Sinn Féin had long resisted this approach, despite American support for the idea. During the late-night announcement, Major acknowledged with disarming candor that Clinton's impending visit had "concentrated the mind" and led to the agreement, but his insistence on preconditions caused his statement to balloon beyond anything that needed saying in that moment. Bruton's own statement punctured Major's balloon of words with an injection of reality: "It is the position of my government that a physical gesture decommissioning of arms in advance of talks, while undoubtedly desirable, is not an attainable objective."

Last-minute endorsement of the twin-track approach was the limit of Major's willingness to temper, in anticipation of Clinton's visit, his insistence on decommissioning. He gave no reason to believe that his stance would shift even if the commission recommended otherwise, and his frequent references to Washington 3 were discouraging. That concern would loom large in coming weeks, but now all eyes turned to Bill Clinton, very soon to arrive in London on the first leg of his Irish Peace Process tour.

CHAPTER THIRTEEN

Bill Clinton Comes
to the North

While the focus of the Irish part of Bill Clinton's journey—Belfast, Derry, and Dublin—was going to be one of celebration and hope, his business in London was reparative. The great alliance, the special relationship between the US and the UK, had been bruised and battered, both personally and politically, by Clinton's independent course on Northern Ireland.

As part of his repair work, Clinton addressed a joint session of both houses of Parliament, praising the great long-standing relationship between the two countries and their alliance in both World Wars. He acknowledged the recent rough patch, invoking the scorch marks still to be found on the White House from its burning by the British in the War of 1812, saying they reminded him of the importance of keeping the peace between their nations. He also announced that a powerful new navy destroyer would be named the *Winston Churchill*. Major reciprocated with a dinner at 10 Downing Street.

The next morning Clinton flew to Belfast, becoming the first sitting US president to ever visit Northern Ireland. The security apparatus accompanying him was massive, involving dozens of Secret Service agents and hundreds of police. Snipers manned the roofs, and helicopters patrolled overhead. A suggestion had been made that perhaps a lower-key entry into Belfast in a smaller military plane might make sense, but that had gone nowhere: This was a day for

Air Force One. Anne Edwards, Clinton's director of press advance, whose focus involved making sure images and events—they're called optics—supported and advanced the policy central to the trip, was already on the ground in Belfast. She recalls the moment the big plane bearing Bill and Hillary Clinton and the presidential party approached:

> We were trying to show them a different future was possible. That's what it did when that big, beautiful blue and white plane was floating out of the sky onto Belfast. This was a moment for the public to see that they themselves had changed enough that they could welcome Air Force One to their city. This was about them. You could almost feel the city perk up. They were all watching television—every minute of it was live, like space shots used to be in the old days. All of the Northern Irish around me, whatever their job—big shot correspondent or the person who was tidying the hotel—stopped to watch. You could feel the city take a breath when Air Force One was on final.

Clinton's first stop was Shankill Road, in the heart of loyalist Belfast. He went into a store next to where Frizzell's Fish Shop, the site of the horrific 1993 bombing, had stood and bought some fruit and flowers. This was a powerful signal that he cared about both sides in the conflict.

Next was the factory where the venerable Belfast firm of Mackie International manufactured textile equipment. Its workforce was 70 percent Protestant and 30 percent Catholic, and the factory itself sat right on a peace line between loyalist Shankill Road and republican Falls Road, with separate entrances for the two communities. It was a fitting place for Clinton's major Belfast speech.

Clinton's words at Mackie were his most stirring of the journey, but they weren't the most moving of the morning. Those came from the two children who introduced him: a ten-year-old Protestant boy named David Sterrett and an eight-year-old Catholic girl named Catherine Hamill. David said, with stark simplicity, that peace "means I can play in the park without worrying about getting shot." Catherine read from a letter she wrote to welcome the president: "My first daddy died in the Troubles. It was the saddest day of my life. I still think of him. Now it is nice and peaceful. I like having peace and quiet for a change instead of having people shooting and killing. My Christmas wish is that peace and love will last in Ireland forever."

In his speech, Clinton, tacitly invoking the IRA slogan "Our day will come," declared that the people of Northern Ireland "must say to those who still would use violence for political objectives: You are the past, your day is over. Violence has no place at the table of democracy and no role in the future of this land."

The awful history of the conflict and the current difficulties plaguing the peace process flared up when Clinton declared, "Those who show the courage to break with the past are entitled to their stake in the future" and a supporter of DUP leader Ian Paisley in the back shouted, "Never!" When Clinton added, "You must also be willing to say to those who renounce violence and who take their own risks for peace that they are entitled to be full participants in the democratic process," the heckler shouted it again. But on this day the audience was with Clinton, not the DUP man.

Next Clinton made the short trip to Falls Road, the heart of republican Belfast, and stopped in front of a beloved family-run bakery where the crowd greeted him. Gerry Adams emerged from the bakery, as if by splendid coincidence rather than painstakingly plotted choreography, with the traditional greeting, "*Céad míle fáilte.*" (In his book *My Life*, Clinton sticks to the story that the encounter was happenstance, nothing more, with his description of shaking hands with "a quickly growing crowd of citizens. One of them was Gerry Adams.") As Clinton and Adams shook hands, they chatted briefly; Clinton told the Irishman that he was reading his collection of stories about life on Falls Road. At that moment, Gerry Adams was truly front and center on the world stage.

But soon enough Clinton was off to his next stop and the great moment evaporated. Gerry Adams reverted in an instant from international player to local politician on the street. For Morrison the transformation was captured perfectly when an angry woman approached Adams in the wake of Clinton's departure and demanded that he do something about some injustice related to her job. There was clearly nothing Adams could say to assuage her distress, but she was not about to let go. She followed him down the street, as Morrison recalls, "like a barking dog." He was a local politician, she was a constituent who needed help, and that's all there was to it.

Clinton's departure from Falls Road left Morrison and O'Dowd with a feeling of wonder that their meeting nearly five years earlier in O'Dowd's Manhattan office had led to all this. The success of their plan was astonishing, and they were naturally thrilled by it. Morrison recalls:

> The handshake with Adams and Clinton was quite surreal. Of course it had to happen, we had insisted that it had to happen, yet until the moment it did happen, we weren't sure it would. It was the best thing Clinton could do. It was completely without risk to him in any political sense, and it made clear that he understood the path that he had chosen when he approved a visa for Gerry Adams. This is the most obvious of points on that path, but when it was happening, it was much more like a dream come true than it was a real event. It was a moment to say, "Well, look at that: The leader of the free world has come to the Falls Road and met Gerry Adams. We never thought we would get this far but, man, how much further do we have to go?"

It's fair to say that Morrison and his contingent were never in it for the glory, but this moment was truly glorious and they took it in with intense pleasure—until reality intruded. First, it was when Gerry Adams was hectored and tracked by his constituent, which brought everything down to earth. Then Adams gestured to Morrison and O'Dowd and said solemnly, "Come with me." He pulled them away from the presidential party and all the joyous goings-on for a secret meeting in the living room of a terrace house on nearby Kashmir Road, one of many streets in West Belfast commemorating past triumphs of the British Empire. Morrison remembers Adams's somber presentation:

> In his report on the state of the peace process, he said that the ceasefire was very much at risk and that while the president's visit would be a confidence builder and would certainly illustrate a long journey traveled, the British intransigence on moving the process forward was really dangerous. The message to us was, "This has been a great day and it's a great thing that Clinton is here, but don't be misled: We're at the very end of the ceasefire if this new process with Mitchell doesn't pull a rabbit out of the hat. The IRA is at the end of its patience."
>
> Gerry is unexpressive in his demeanor most of the time. He speaks like a professor, in a measured way; he very rarely shows agitation, even when his words are about things that agitate him. So his delivery of this news was matter-of-fact; someone who knew him less well could have misread this as just words. But it was quite clear that he was warning us there was imminent danger in terms of the whole edifice that we had helped construct, of which the ceasefire was a central plank—that it was about to come undone.

Yet even while the bad news was being delivered in that living room in West Belfast, Morrison and O'Dowd knew that crowds were continuing to greet Clinton with joy and hope. It was a jarring juxtaposition of simultaneous realities.

Clinton's triumphant procession through Belfast maintained the careful business of honoring both populations of Northern Ireland throughout the day. After speaking with Adams, he went to East Belfast for a visit and a handshake with Peter Robinson, deputy leader of Ian Paisley's DUP. After that he was off to Derry by helicopter to meet with John Hume, longtime nationalist advocate of nonviolence.

When the distressing meeting on Kashmir Road was done, Morrison and O'Dowd were supposed to be taken back to the presidential party by a driver who maybe had been IRA. The grim reality that had just been conveyed to them was briefly relieved by the low comedy of a nervous driver who seemed to make one wrong turn after another, finding himself increasingly ensnared in the enormous web of security surrounding Clinton. When they finally got within sight of the airport, which was still bristling with security even though the presidential party was far away, the frightened driver dumped them off at the far back, leaving them to fend for themselves, and sped off, desperate to get out of there as fast as he could. Morrison and O'Dowd trudged along the airport fence until they encountered a guard in uniform, RUC or the British army. The guard, highly skeptical of their claim of being part of the presidential party, had to be talked into walking them across the tarmac to the terminal, during which they were in a sort of custody, not to be released until their story checked out. When they finally made their way to the White House press bus, Clinton's communications director Mark Gearan vouched for them and the cop released them to his custody. After the guard left, Gearan couldn't resist cracking, "Lucky for you I didn't give you up."

The crowning event of the day was to be the tree lighting in the plaza in front of city hall. Both the location and the event were the product of meticulous advance planning as well as plain old good luck. Anne Edwards and her team had spotted the location during a visit to the Belfast city council on a dark night to find the right place for Clinton's speech. When they rounded a corner and came upon it, "our eyes lit up," she says. It was ideal: an open public space with the grand Victorian city hall as a backdrop. During the planning meeting, the British Foreign Office people were against it and a local person said the space was already committed for the lighting of the community Christmas tree by the Mighty Morphin Power Rangers. Edwards instantly envisioned Bill Clinton, not the Power Rangers, lighting the tree:

> My heart stopped and I remember saying slowly and just loud enough so the others heard it, "When do they light it?" Our

heads snapped and turned at the answer: "Well, they light it about the first of December, about that weekend." We didn't say anything—we knew we had it. We went in, we asked the council about the plaza, but they were just, "No." When we got home, it took a while. But we knew the Secret Service could figure it out. So we planned this event in front of the city hall that would be part of turning on the lights. The whole day would build to that.

Now the day was here. As night approached, the Americans had high hopes for the event but also had their worries. Recalls Anne Edwards:

We were confident that people would come, that there would be a respectable base. Here's what we didn't know: *throng*. I'd gone to my table, which was at the front windows of the Europa Hotel, and I'm looking out and it's dark but I'm seeing motion, and I look and I realize that it's a steady stream of people walking up to the checkpoint to go into the speech site about a block away. They're young, they're bringing strollers, they've got kids on their shoulders—they're coming, real people are coming. And it kept up.

I left and went over to the speech site. The stage had been set so it looked straight down the canyon of the shopping street straight in front of the city hall. The lights were bright. We were very close to event time. There were people everywhere, as far as the eye could see. And when you look at a crowd in Northern Ireland, you can't tell a Catholic from a Protestant.

The great Van Morrison, born and raised in Belfast, serenaded the crowd with his song "Days Like This," which had become an unofficial anthem of the hope and enthusiasm sweeping the city:

When everything falls into place like the flick of a switch,
Well my mama told me, there'll be days like this.

Then it was time for Clinton's address. In very personal terms, he spoke of what peace meant to Northern Ireland and what the reception he received meant to him:

> As I look down these beautiful streets, I think how wonderful it will be for people to do their holiday shopping without worry of searches or bombs, to visit loved ones on the other side of the border without the burden of checkpoints or roadblocks, to enjoy these magnificent Christmas lights without any fear of violence. Peace has brought real change to your lives.
>
> Across the ocean, the American people are rejoicing with you. We are joined to you by strong ties of community and commerce and culture. Over the years, men and women of both traditions have flourished in our country and helped America to flourish.
>
> Ladies and gentlemen, this day that Hillary and I have had here in Belfast and Derry and Londonderry County will long be with us as one of the most remarkable days of our lives.

After the tree lighting, Clinton spent the rest of the evening meeting one-on-one in carefully balanced twenty-minute segments with the full range of Northern Ireland's political leaders. That included Ian Paisley, no fan of the peace process, an encounter Clinton later recounted with a nice edge in his book: "Though he wouldn't shake hands with the Catholic leaders, he was only too happy to lecture me on the error of my ways. After a few minutes of this hectoring, I decided the Catholic leaders had gotten the better end of the deal."

Special attention was given to UUP leader David Trimble since Clinton had gone to visit his nationalist counterpart John Hume in Derry earlier in the day. Trimble got his twenty minutes with Clinton in the presidential limousine en route to the Europa Hotel. The Europa had been targeted so often in the years before the ceasefire that it became known as "Europe's most bombed hotel." Clinton's party made a special point of staying there in order to show the world how much Belfast had changed since the ceasefire.

Clinton spent the next day in Dublin amid huge ecstatic crowds, and then it was off to Germany to review troops headed to Bosnia, where Clinton told the soldiers, "The power of the United States goes far beyond military might. What you saw in Ireland, for example, had not a whit to do with military might. It was all about values."

Grumpy Paisley people aside, the response to Clinton's visit was uniformly positive. The overriding sense was one of accelerating celebration and hope. In his dispatch, veteran *New York Times* correspondent R. W. Apple quoted a Protestant woman: "I didn't think his presence would do much good, but he was absolutely first-class, and after listening to him, I think he will help people come together."

Morrison saw the day as a watershed moment for Clinton as president:

> That was an example of timing that was really critical, because it was a period of testing and transition for Clinton coming out of the '94 elections. I certainly noticed a kind of growth in stature that seemed to happen at the time, and the Ireland piece of it was key. It was a great psychological boost. There was a spring in his step. All of a sudden he was on the world stage and he was making this difference.

A particularly gracious note was struck by veteran *Washington Post* columnist Mary McGrory, an implacable opponent of Clinton's Northern Ireland policy, particularly his visa for Gerry Adams. Social encounters with Adams only increased her vehemence. Despite her depth of feeling—*contempt* is probably not too strong a word—McGrory elegantly ate crow in her column when she got back to Washington after witnessing the presidential visit to Belfast:

> If President Clinton had listened to the likes of me, he would never have had his Irish triumph. I was one of those who thought he was mad to let in Gerry Adams, the IRA propagandist. But he paid no attention to us. Adams was the key, and last week

Clinton brought genuine joy to Belfast, one of the planet's most cheerless sites.

With an about-face like that, is it any wonder that Clinton thought—and still thinks—that these were the best two days of his presidency?

CHAPTER FOURTEEN

George Mitchell
Offers a Way

After his two magical days in Northern Ireland, Clinton departed, and it was back to reality—not the full force of the Troubles, to be sure, but worrisome nevertheless—for those who called it home, especially those hard at work to put the violence firmly in the past. The ceasefire was shaky, with an IRA that felt it had done its part for a year and a half and gotten nothing in return.

There was simply no reason to believe anything new would be coming from John Major. His words, in fact, started to become even more inflammatory. In late December he approvingly described unionist refusal to meet with Sinn Féin by saying "You cannot negotiate for peace with an Armalite in your hand held at the negotiators' heads."

Any possibility of saving the ceasefire hinged on the report from the International Body on Decommissioning headed by George Mitchell, which was due in January. It would not only have to thread the needle brilliantly, but it would have to be so compelling that it would make even John Major see things differently.

The commission consisted of Mitchell, Canadian general John de Chastelain, and former Finnish prime minister Harri Holkeri. In preparing their report, they talked exhaustively with a wide array of experts, as well as virtually everyone in Northern Ireland who knew anything or had any stake in the outcome.

The report was released to the parties on January 23, 1996, and to the public the next day. Its core conclusion was that decommissioning should not be a precondition for all-party talks because there was no realistic prospect that any of the paramilitary forces—republican and loyalist alike—would ever agree to it. "In the real world of Northern Ireland, prior decommissioning simply was not a practical solution," Mitchell wrote later. "That was so clear that I wondered whether someone as astute as John Major ever really believed that we would simply endorse it." The report concluded that the way to move forward was for "some decommissioning to take place during the process of all-party negotiations, rather than before or after." The commission cushioned its solution in gentle diplomatic language, offering that "the parties should consider" such parallel decommissioning and adding, "Such an approach represents a compromise. If the peace process is to move forward, the current impasse must be overcome. While both sides have been adamant in their positions, both have repeatedly expressed the desire to move forward. This approach provides them that opportunity."

At the request of the British, made directly to Mitchell "by letter, by fax, by telephone, in person," the report, in its discussion of possible confidence-building measures, observed that "an elective process could contribute to the building of confidence." Because Major had told Mitchell that he would have to reject the report if it outright recommended parallel decommissioning, Mitchell's commission ultimately acceded to a British request, a late evening question "asked softly" by the British minister in Northern Ireland, that it be presented as a suggestion rather than a recommendation in order to "soften the impact of parallel decommissioning." As a skilled negotiator, Mitchell wanted to ease the way for Major to receive the report as positively as possible. And as an experienced politician, he had more than one reason for cutting Major some slack: "I was keenly aware that he had created the International Body on Decommissioning, with an American chairman, overriding critics in his own party. The last thing in the world I wanted to do was to embarrass him."

Any hope that the Mitchell report would save the ceasefire depended entirely on Major's response. He addressed Parliament on January 24, two days after receiving the report. His words were, as ever, plentiful—a deft yet maddening combination of distortion, avoidance, and obfuscation. He basically ignored the commission's central point that parallel decommissioning was the only realistic way forward, stressing the fact that the report's conclusion wasn't a "formal recommendation"—just as his minister had asked. "Although the body makes no formal recommendation on this point, it suggests an approach under which some decommissioning would take place during the process of all-party negotiations." As David McKittrick and David McVea succinctly put it in their superb book *Making Sense of the Troubles*, "Major rose in the Commons, thanked Mitchell for his report, and then in effect overturned it."

Then Major pivoted to the elections idea, which the British had also pressed the commission to mention, as if that had been its primary recommendation. "An elective process offers a viable alternative direct route to the confidence necessary to bring about all-party negotiations," the report said. "In that context, it is possible to imagine decommissioning and such negotiations being taken forward in parallel." In other words, new elections first, and then possibly—only *possibly*—all-party talks could follow without prior decommissioning.

Major's elections concept was a new version of the proposal offered months earlier by UUP leader David Trimble. But from Major, in late January 1996, it was too little, too late. Elections would take yet more time, and to an IRA already seventeen months out on a limb about which many of its members had deep reservations, Major's proposal was just another burst of words that communicated exactly one thing: There would be yet more delay before any possibility of all-party talks. Even John Hume, moderate though he was, was furious: "The government praises the report, then ignores it." He lambasted the elections proposal as a "delaying tactic," "utterly irresponsible," and "play[ing] politics with the lives of people."

To Gerry Adams, Major's response was nothing less than bad faith: "Mr. Major rejected the core of the Mitchell report, scuppered the twin-track approach and the February date for all-party talks, and in their place has produced a new precondition based on a unionist proposal."

There was no possibility that the prospect of future elections, about which both republicans and nationalists were deeply skeptical, could rescue the tottering ceasefire. Only a clear acceptance of the Mitchell report's primary recommendation for starting all-party talks and promptly taking up decommissioning could do that. And Major made it unmistakably clear that he would not take that step, a reality that rendered the closing flourish of his address to Parliament strange, insincere, or both: "I pledge that I will leave no stone unturned to deliver to the people of Northern Ireland, on a permanent basis, the precious privilege of peace that they have enjoyed for the past seventeen months." No stone, that is, except the one presented by an independent international commission as the only realistic and effective way forward. But as detached from reality as Major's comment was, he managed to top it in his autobiography: "The Mitchell report was a balanced and reasonable attempt to find a way through, and I accepted its recommendations in the statement to the House of Commons."

Mitchell later said that the members of the commission hadn't anticipated Major's reaction to the report. Although he saw Major's pivot to the elections idea as an adroit political move, the world at large—and especially the IRA—heard Major's answer to the recommendation of parallel decommissioning loud and clear: unavoidably, unalterably, unequivocally "No!" His elections idea barely registered, something Major himself would soon acknowledge.

Bill Clinton had gone home, George Mitchell and his co-chairmen had tried their best, and now John Major had spoken. It was hard to imagine that the ceasefire could last much longer.

CHAPTER FIFTEEN

After a Year and a Half, the IRA Loses Patience

The surveillance video opens on a tree. This is February in London, so the tree is bare. In the harsh glare of the streetlights, its trunk and branches arrest the eye. Orange is everywhere: not the familiar bright and warm hue but a cold, acrid orange of sodium vapor streetlights trailing down to South Quay, reflecting harshly on the road surface, and giving an unpleasant tinge to the dark sky above the hulking forms of the buildings at the bottom of the hill. The camera, apparently set up after the warning call came, is stationary, looking straight down toward South Quay Station, where the truck is parked. The Docklands and Canary Wharf, the high-end, mixed-use development that would give the attack its name, are nearby. The date—96-02-09—can be seen on the left side of the screen. In the upper right-hand corner, a clock shows the time to the second, and another time counter spins in increments even smaller than that. Traffic cones close off the street, and a bespectacled man clutching a metal briefcase crosses in front of the camera.

Unlike a typical surveillance video, this one has sound: first a male voice, then a female one, then a loud metallic buzzing. The picture jars, then the buzzing stops. A figure in the distance crosses the street, headed right toward South Quay. The picture becomes clear again, and then the explosion—a distant bang and an intense flash topped by a plume of smoke and dust bending to the right as if driven by a crosswind. Debris showers down onto the roadway. Lights go out. There is the sound of excited voices, wailing and crying. Then a second flash and a huge cloud sweeps across the street. Two figures running away from the blast are silhouetted against the cloud. Lights come back on in less than thirty seconds.

It began and ended in no time: A massive truck bomb exploded. Two men working at a newsstand nearby were killed, forty-three people were injured, and the damage sustained by the surrounding buildings cost more than 100 million pounds. After nearly eighteen months, the ceasefire was over.

———

The IRA was roundly denounced in London, Dublin, and Washington. Gerry Adams, who shortly before the blast told the White House that he was "hearing disturbing news" but gave no details, would not be welcome at 1600 Pennsylvania Avenue until the ceasefire was restored. Adams said later that he believed a more positive British response to the Mitchell commission proposal could have kept the ceasefire alive: "At least it would have given us something to work with."

Morrison weighed in, deploring the attack, as did Ted Kennedy and other prominent Irish Americans. Someone called Chuck Feeney at his San Francisco office to tell him about it, and when he hung up the phone, tears were rolling down his cheeks. Most people were discouraged but not surprised. George Mitchell had told David Frost in a televised interview just days before that he was afraid the cease-fire wouldn't last much longer, citing his understanding that the vote within IRA to authorize it had been close and that many were running out of patience. His words seemed so prescient that some were sure Mitchell had inside information; he staunchly denied it, writing later that it had just been a matter of "plain common sense. . . . The IRA had declared a ceasefire in August 1994 in the expectation that inclusive negotiations would begin immediately. Now, eighteen months later, there were no negotiations in sight."

There was every reason to fear that this violent end to the ceasefire would be so discouraging that Clinton would no longer be willing to stick his neck out in hopes of helping end the ancient warfare. But, miraculously, the eyes of the Americans on the front lines—Clinton, Soderberg, Morrison, O'Dowd, Feeney, Flynn, and Mitchell—never left the prize. In fact, the Americans doubled down on their commitment. Soderberg said later that the image of the thousands of hopeful faces she saw as she looked out from the stage in the Belfast plaza the night Clinton lit the Christmas tree made it impossible for her to walk away: "People just so wanted it, and the people were so far ahead of the politicians. The people who opposed us doing this in the first place would say, 'Okay, now you've got to cut these guys off.' But honestly we never seriously considered it, because you don't want those who are trying to destroy the peace process to win."

Morrison wasn't surprised that Soderberg kept the faith: "Once the 1995 trip to Belfast happened, she became a total convert. She saw what it was all about in very personal terms and never stopped working to implement it. It's very easy in the White House to lose touch and forget about why you got involved, but that was never the case with her."

Less than three weeks after the bombing, John Major met with his Irish counterpart John Bruton, and later the same day he told Parliament that the two had agreed on "a way forward." A "broadly acceptable elective process" would be devised to select participants in "all-party negotiations with a comprehensive agenda" that would start in early June—and include Sinn Féin if the ceasefire has been restored. Prior decommissioning wouldn't be a requirement for entering the talks, but Britain's preoccupation with decommissioning hadn't gone away. Major went on:

> At the beginning of the negotiations, in order to build confidence, all participants, including Sinn Féin if the ceasefire has been restored, will need to make clear their total and absolute commitment to the principles of democracy and nonviolence set

out in the Mitchell report and to address also at the beginning
of the negotiations Senator Mitchell's proposals on decommissioning of weapons.

These weren't new points: Major had mentioned them during
his late January speech before Parliament in response to the Mitchell
commission report. But then they'd been mostly lost in the smoke of
his roundabout rejection of the commission's central recommendation
of parallel decommissioning.

Even Major conceded that his elections proposal "has been mis-
understood widely." It was true that he had stressed the proposal
more clearly in his remarks after his speech in Parliament, but at that
point the sound bites and headlines had taken over—"Major puts the
report in the shredder" ran one in the *Irish Times*—and drowned out
everything else. That was no surprise to Morrison, because Major's
approach had been to say (however indirectly) "No" to Mitchell's astute
finessing of the decommissioning obstacle, instead of "Yes, but . . .,"
which would have offered a perfect segue to the elections idea to which
he was now such an ardent convert. The difference between those two
approaches may seem small and subtle, but it was crucial: It would
determine what the world—a world that included the IRA—would
hear as Major's answer to Mitchell's core proposal.

Major's disregard for such a basic principle of political communication felt to Morrison like something from the realm of personal
limitations and vulnerabilities. His defective sense of how to make his
elections proposal heard was exceeded by his even more defective
sense of the timing of the proposal. Unionist leader David Trimble had
been pushing the elections idea since the fall of 1995, and there had
been some significant American and Irish support for it. If Major
had taken it up at that time, the process would have played out in
the context of an ongoing ceasefire. Whatever complaints Sinn Féin
and others might have had about going through elections at Major's
command wouldn't have seemed so important if all-party talks really
were right around the corner. But in making the elections proposal

when he did, Major made it a virtual certainty that the idea would be seen by republicans and nationalists alike as just another stalling tactic in the seemingly inexhaustible British supply. Even worse, there was no realistic prospect at that point that elections would lead to prompt all-party talks, since no one—not the British, not the unionists, not the Irish Republic, not the Americans—would let Sinn Féin join the negotiations while the IRA was back at war. Yet without Sinn Féin—which, in Major's biting phrase, "has of course excluded itself"—any talks that started in June would have been incapable of producing an agreement that worked. George Mitchell said later that he was hopeful that Sinn Féin would come in eventually, "because I felt it would be necessary to have them there to get an agreement on the nationalist side."

As for the prospects of a new ceasefire, there was no possibility that an IRA—in which the ceasefire skeptics, who had been sure all along that the only thing the British understood was the bomb and the gun, now had the upper hand—would quickly agree to a new one. The real question was whether the IRA would ever take that leap again.

To make matters even more complicated, the situation of Sinn Féin itself changed after the Canary Wharf attack in a fundamental way that wasn't evident to Morrison then but has become increasingly clear with the passage of time. The attack was indeed a watershed moment, but not in the way the British interpreted it. As Morrison came to see it, before Canary Wharf, the central drama was about Sinn Féin finding a way to get into the negotiations; after it, the focus shifted to the others chasing after Sinn Féin to get them to join the talks, which would basically be fruitless without them, and about a supremely political Sinn Féin determined to extract every possible benefit in return for agreeing to come to the table. Morrison later made this analysis:

> After Canary Wharf the realization seemed to hit the British government that they really needed Sinn Féin and the IRA to come back into the process. The fact that they finally understood that was another example of how the Clinton big-tent approach had

taken over the process. There was a long time in which the British assumed they could do the deal without Sinn Féin and make it stick, and it became clear after Canary Wharf that they didn't believe that anymore. They were profligate with their opportunity, and now they scrambled to find a way back to a ceasefire and back to a road to negotiations.

But now the republicans saw the British pursuing them for negotiations, when just months before they couldn't seem to get the British to do anything. So the signal was quite clear that the balance had shifted. The lesson was, for all the talk about resisting violence, violence has gotten the attention of the British. That was hardly the lesson one would hope the British government wanted to teach.

I think the republicans concluded something else, and that was, if for no other reason than the required electoral calendar, this British government was in its last year. Since their experience with Major was that he would not do a deal, they became pretty convinced that they need not be in any rush: Nothing was going anywhere without them, and soon there would be a new government. This really was a holding pattern in which a new prime minister, a new day, wasn't that far away and was worth waiting for.

It was a perfect example of what Morrison calls "revolutionary patience," which had long been characteristic of Sinn Féin. Their view was the long view and their only calendar was their own calendar, no matter what the world said or demanded. "They didn't accept deadlines," Morrison says. "They viewed themselves as revolutionaries who would wait out those who made demands that they were not going to accept. Their stance was, 'It will come to us on our terms.'"

As Morrison saw it, British intransigence had given the upper hand to the IRA fighters who had opposed the ceasefire from the beginning. They blew up South Quay and with it the ceasefire itself. Now the British were promising all-party talks without the requirement of prior decommissioning. Despite Major's vehement protestations to the contrary, the IRA had undeniably "bombed its way to the conference table," and, even worse, the question of when and how Sinn Féin would join the discussion was now entirely in the hands of the IRA. Such an absurd situation exasperated Morrison to no end, while at the same time leaving him astonished at what the British had wrought: "The British didn't hold their cards; they threw them down, and the IRA hard-liners wound up in the catbird seat. They got to reset the bargain and got a better deal after the ceasefire. This would have been a republican masterstroke if they had planned it that way, but it was really the result of British blundering." The ghosts of the sixteen executed after the Rising couldn't have devised a more exquisite revenge.

———

It would be a long slog to a new ceasefire. Bill Clinton, ever determined, remained ready to do his part. How bold and pragmatic Clinton was willing to be came across to Morrison during the St. Patrick's Day Shamrock ceremony in the Roosevelt Room of the White House in March of 1996, shortly after the IRA bombed South Quay. In his remarks Clinton, while arguing for a new ceasefire, offered a startlingly candid analysis. When asked what he would say to those on the IRA ruling body to convince them to trust Major and the British, he answered bluntly: "You don't have to all of a sudden start trusting people. You just have to show up, start, and go to work."

Asked how confident he was that the IRA would listen, he responded:

> What's been done in the past hasn't worked. What's been done in the last couple of years has a chance of working. There's nothing to be lost here by taking a leap of faith. You know, everybody can always go back to behaving in the terrible way they once behaved—that's true of every human being in the world. If it's ultimately unsatisfying, if it leads to a dead end, what's to be lost in trying? Nothing, nothing. That's the argument I make: It's in everyone's self-interest to go forward. It is in no one's self-interest to keep their foot on the brakes of this process.

The extraordinary directness of Clinton's statement stunned Morrison, but it didn't seem to strike anyone else. Clinton was in truth describing precisely the essence of the ceasefire—fighters who decide a ceasefire isn't working out for them can always go back to the warfare—but it was remarkable for the president of the United States to lay it out so candidly. It was a revealing glimpse into how committed Clinton was to his Northern Ireland policy, how determined he was to have it succeed, and the risks he was willing to take to get it done. Morrison was genuinely startled:

> I thought what he said was true, but I was surprised to hear it uttered in public rather than whispered in private to Adams or something like that. So I wasn't talking about it to anyone else; I kind of kept it my little secret. I thought that broad reporting of that point would not have been helpful, that it would have brought forth a lot of criticism of Clinton going soft on terrorists. But it kind of went over people's heads or under people's noses or whatever. I didn't hear a gasp from the press corps. The only gasp I heard was my own.

———

In Northern Ireland, Major and Bruton went ahead with the plan for elections in May. John Hume reversed his angry opposition to the plan and said the SDLP would participate, which forced Sinn Féin to reevaluate its own opposition. Ultimately, after a fair amount of grumbling from Adams, Sinn Féin set aside its initial reluctance and participated fully. To those in the British government who thought Sinn Féin would do so badly at the polls that their legitimacy as a political force would be fatally compromised, this was surely good news. If it came out that way, Britain could revert to its insistence that peace could be made (on terms much more congenial to the British) between moderates who were unalterably opposed to the use of political violence—and there would be no need to even consider having Sinn Féin at the table.

But that's not how it worked out. Sinn Féin increased its share of support to 15.5 percent of the Northern Ireland electorate—more than a 50 percent gain—and drew closer to Hume's SDLP party, which got 21.4 percent. That outcome might have been a surprise to the British, who had routinely disparaged Gerry Adams as "Mr. Ten Percent," but it was no surprise to Morrison:

> It's hard to say what John Major would expect to happen in an election in Northern Ireland, but the one thing you can know is that the door-to-door, neighborhood-based politics of Sinn Féin would be completely unfamiliar to him. In the British Parliament, people represent districts that they don't live in, that they never lived in, that they don't have any connection to. The minister for Northern Ireland never has to set foot in Northern Ireland. There is a top-down structure in British politics that is the opposite of the grassroots politics Sinn Féin did so well.
>
> Another strength of Sinn Féin was its ability to tap emotion much more effectively than anybody else. They were just better at capturing the political emotions of the nationalist community than the SDLP, and that was going to be felt if you created elections that had high symbolic content.

Throughout the spring of 1996, Morrison met with the British, sometimes during elegant embassy dinners, to discuss how to get Sinn Féin into the talks. The British understood that he had special access to the thinking of Sinn Féin, but his ideas never got traction with the British, who told him they were seeking a "formula of words" to get the peace process on track again. Morrison was struck by that phrase "a formula of words"—certainly throughout the ceasefire John Major's only search seemed to have been for which words to deploy, as opposed to what action to take. It was painfully clear to Morrison that until the British accepted that the road to peace had to be paved with deeds and not words, the fighting wouldn't stop. Whether or not the British understood this reality was beside the point: Only when they accepted it and took action accordingly would peace be possible. As Morrison recalls,

> There was just a sense that decommissioning hadn't gone away and that they were going to pounce on the point again. Decommissioning was something that at the end of the day wasn't wrong; it just didn't fit the situation. It would have been good if it could have been achieved, but it couldn't and so you've got to find another road.
>
> The main point of my discussions was that when you get a new ceasefire, the reaction's going to have to be different, and the only way a different reaction would be trusted would be if the British response was essentially agreed to before the ceasefire happened. In other words, instead of the ceasefire being offered and a response coming, this will be a bargained-for ceasefire, it will be conditioned on having been promised certain things quite explicitly, rather than the expectation of a good-faith response, which was not their experience the first time.
>
> I never got far enough in those talks with the British, never got things I could take back to Sinn Féin and say, "Well if you did this, they would do that." They were pretty much mired in their "We'll have the elections and if they come back, they're going to have to deposit some of their arms at the door."

Morrison and many others, including top security experts he consulted, believed strongly that the British insistence on prior decommissioning was contrary to history, overblown in terms of its likely practical effect, and certainly not something that justified squandering the ceasefire. "Nobody ever decommissioned in Irish history," Morrison notes. "They just stopped. Beyond that, the security people we consulted made it clear that guns are so available in the world that decommissioning some guns didn't mean you couldn't get new ones."

Albert Reynolds had made a similar point directly to Major:

I explained to John Major that [when] my party went into power . . . they didn't hand over their guns to anybody. In fact, some of them brought their guns in their hip pockets going into the parliament. So I couldn't have any credibility in asking the leadership of Sinn Féin to hand over guns when our own party didn't and all the other partisan governments here didn't either.

Throughout this period in which so much hinged on a new IRA ceasefire, it wasn't clear that Major had any understanding of the situation from the republican point of view. He sometimes spoke as if Sinn Féin itself, regardless of what the IRA thought, could simply declare a new ceasefire and that would be that. Asked how Sinn Féin could reenter the peace process, Major answered this way:

Well the choice now is with Sinn Féin. We have set out, with the Irish government, the way that we believe matters should now proceed. There is an option for Sinn Féin. They can decide that they are going to opt into the democratic process, call a cease-fire, meet with the other parties, decide to meet the Mitchell principles, and deal with decommissioning, or they can decide to opt out of the democratic process.

Absent from Major's statement was the slightest recognition that the most Sinn Féin could ever do would be to persuade the IRA to restore the ceasefire. For all the British and unionist protests that Sinn Féin and the IRA were basically one and the same, there were plenty of professionals and knowledgeable authorities on their own side who were aware of the limits of Gerry Adams's ability to influence the decisions of the IRA. When George Mitchell and his co-commissioners on the International Body on Decommissioning asked RUC chief constable Hugh Annesley if Adams could persuade the IRA to decommission arms before all-party talks, Annesley said, "No, he couldn't do it even if he wanted to. He doesn't have that much control over them." His top assistants agreed, and Mitchell wrote later that that was the "clinching argument" against prior decommissioning. He also wrote that such truth-telling didn't go well for the messenger: During the commissioners' meeting with John Major, after they mentioned what they had learned from the RUC, a letter from Annesley was produced, obviously under pressure from above, "that modified and explained" what he'd told the commissioners, although he didn't change his conclusion. The episode made Mitchell feel bad for the chief constable: "He had been truthful with us, and now, because his opinion didn't fit with the government's policy, it became obvious that his honesty with us had gotten him into trouble with his superiors."

And still, Major either didn't recognize or didn't accept how difficult persuading the IRA to call another ceasefire would be in the face of their experiences after they called the first one. The IRA hardliners now had the advantage and they had plenty of operations to carry out, including an attack on a British military base in Germany and the detonation of a huge bomb in the center of Manchester in the English midlands. Major continued to maintain that in adhering to his demand for prior arms decommissioning or new elections, he was simply and sincerely seeking "confidence-building measures" that would make meaningful negotiations feasible, since without sufficient confidence, the unionists would never agree to negotiate directly with Sinn Féin. Morrison found himself extremely vexed by Major's complete refusal to recognize his own obligations as a leader to find—or perhaps create—the right moment and to act decisively, seizing the opportunity to help his supporters and his nation come to a better place, which everyone who had suffered for so long so richly deserved.

———

The talks among British-approved parties began, as Major had pledged, on schedule in June of 1996. Despite its electoral success, Sinn Féin was absent, because the IRA hadn't restored its ceasefire. George Mitchell presided over the talks, with de Chastelain and Holkeri returning as co-chairmen, and they accomplished as much as anyone could have. But there wasn't ever going to be an effective peace agreement while

Sinn Féin was on the sidelines. In the meantime, Mitchell and his co-chairman focused on what they saw as the essential task of just getting something going: "I do think it was important to get it started. The reality was that it was extremely difficult. It was more trying to get this thing going, trying to keep it going to make it a credible process."

There was also another outlet, not led by Mitchell, that was ostensibly available to the parties for further debate: the Northern Ireland Forum for Political Dialogue, the body to which those participating in the talks—and Sinn Féin as well—had been formally elected in May. Its sessions weren't promising. The unionists had a clear majority, which allowed them to dominate the proceedings and turn a purported forum for discussion into a unionist echo chamber. The sole voice of the nationalist community was that of moderate John Hume's SDLP, and they gamely went to the first session of the Forum. But Hume, who always seemed willing to go the extra mile for a conversation about the future of Northern Ireland, quickly registered his discouragement when he quit the Forum after a single session. He did stay with the slog of the Mitchell talks, although the rate of progress there was glacial.

In *Making Peace,* Mitchell's book about his role in the process, he summed up the first year and a half of negotiations with this cri de coeur:

> For hundreds and hundreds of hours I had listened to the same arguments, over and over again. Very little had been accomplished. It had taken two months to get an understanding on the rules to be followed once the negotiations began. Then it took another two months to get an agreement on a preliminary agenda. Then we had tried for fourteen more months to get an accord on a detailed final agenda. We couldn't even get that, and we were about to adjourn for the Christmas break.

Mitchell later spoke of the long road that got him to those talks:

I began by serving as President Clinton's economic advisor. When I went, it was to be for five months, until the May 1996 White House conference. As I described in the book, the night before [the conference], Clinton called me and I agreed to stay on for another six months. Then later that year Prime Minister Major and Irish prime minister John Bruton asked me to do this commission on the decommissioning of weapons. Then Major called me and said, "Your report is being used as the basis for the negotiations, so it's logical you should be chair."

I'm telling this to say that sort of one thing led to another. I became more and more involved, more and more immersed. I began to get to know people more, to spend more time there; I read more books—I read many, many books about the history of Ireland and Northern Ireland and so forth—and so you sort of get pulled in. And then it's hard not to have your emotions be engaged; you really want this thing to work. I think it's fair to say had I been asked to chair the negotiations at the very beginning, say just as soon as I left the Senate, I'm not sure I would have done it. By the time I was asked, it was by then a year and a half later and I'd become more deeply involved.

———

The state of war, along with the negotiations, ground on through the rest of 1996 and into 1997 with no indication that a new IRA ceasefire was on the horizon. John Major did demonstrate an understanding of the challenges facing the loyalist negotiators and the importance of having them at the table despite their violent affiliations: "With the end of the IRA ceasefire, loyalist paramilitaries were straining at the leash; it was essential to have their political representatives at the table if we were to keep them on-side and off terrorism," he wrote in his autobiography. It's a shame he wasn't able to muster the same understanding of the challenges facing Sinn Féin and the value to all sides in getting them to the table as well. If he had done so, there is every reason to believe the ceasefire would have held.

In the spring of 1997, the talks recessed for the British general election. Major's conservatives and Tony Blair's Labour Party were locked in a campaign that Labour was expected to win after eighteen years of Tory rule. The campaign was spirited but eerily silent on the war in Northern Ireland, with neither Major nor Blair discerning any political benefit to saying anything at all about it. Although Blair made it clear privately that he would take a new approach, he cautioned that as a campaign topic it wouldn't help his party win.

It was a landslide victory for Labour, which proved to be an essential step toward peace. Blair soon made it clear that a new ceasefire was essential, and if one came, the British response would be to include Sinn Féin in all-party talks quickly. He gave the IRA five weeks, after which time the "peace train" would leave without Sinn Féin.

Morrison stressed to the republicans that the opportunity had to be seized. He forcefully pressed his analysis that there would be a limit to Blair's willingness to expend his political capital on Northern Ireland: If the republicans couldn't bring themselves to take advantage of what he was offering, it wouldn't take long for his attention to shift to another urgent issue. How long Blair would put up with republican bickering and indecision was impossible to say. Unquestionably, the new ceasefire had to happen right away. But also unquestionable was the reality that pressuring the IRA to do something usually resulted only in stubborn delay.

In July of 1997, with the clock ticking on Blair's deadline, Morrison, his wife, and their young son were about to leave for Los Angeles, partly for a family vacation and partly for an immigration conference. In that sunny land of dreams at the edge of the Pacific Ocean, Northern Ireland would be far, far away. And then Sinn Féin called, saying they needed Morrison to come to Belfast right away and to keep it a secret. The precise purpose wasn't stated, but Morrison was fairly sure that it involved a new ceasefire.

After a quick family conference, they decided to fly to LA as scheduled, at which point Morrison would immediately fly to Belfast. His wife and son would start the California vacation without him, keeping his sudden departure, not to mention his destination, under wraps. Nancy Morrison, a highly practical person, knew she didn't want to face endless questions about where her husband was and what he was up to. Although she was tremendously supportive of his activities in the peace process and handled his many absences from home, long and short, with grace, she was becoming pleasantly accustomed to the lessening of the demands on his travel time as the British election took center stage. Her solution was to scoop up their four-year-old son, Drew, and head twenty-six miles out to sea to Santa Catalina Island to wait out his absence. Nobody on the island was going to ask her where her husband was.

For Morrison, the nine-hour flight to Belfast offered the possibility of more sleep than his usual flight from New York, but it wasn't going to be enough to compensate for passing through eight time zones. When his plane landed, Morrison, seriously jet-lagged and still with no information about what to expect, was whisked straight from the airport to a hotel and then, after a brief rest, to a meeting with Ted Howell. Howell was Sinn Féin's éminence grise: a theoretician, strategist, tactician, taker of the long view, and creator of the language necessary to get something done. Morrison describes him as Adams's "right-hand intellect"; he was like a chief of staff but much more so. When a problem was especially thorny, Adams would say, "Talk to Ted."

Howell was so rarely seen in public that a photograph taken through a window at night with a telephoto lens showing him with Adams was big news in its own right. Morrison and Howell had worked together previously, usually with others present. But this time it was just the two of them in a small room in Howell's home. Tea was poured, enjoyed briefly, and then it was time for Howell, in many respects the key architect of the political course Sinn Féin had begun more than ten years earlier, and Morrison, the key architect of the political strategy behind the new American policy on Northern Ireland, now in its fifth year, to get down to work.

CHAPTER SIXTEEN

All-Party Talks at Last, Good Friday Ahead

Tea enjoyed, small talk—not the forte of either man—kept to a minimum, Bruce Morrison and Ted Howell were hard at work in the small room in Howell's house. It was immediately clear to Morrison that the IRA was ready and willing to declare a new ceasefire. Now the two men were putting together a list of the guarantees and commitments needed from the White House in support of that step, which Morrison would take to Washington.

After a full day's work, the list was ready, and Morrison was taken straight back to the hotel for some sleep before a morning flight back to California. When he touched down at LAX, he had been gone for all of forty-two hours. In Los Angeles there was the last of the immigration conference and a little more family vacation, including a visit to the La Brea Tar Pits on Wilshire Boulevard—a fine metaphor for the perils of getting stuck in the past.

Before leaving LA, Morrison e-mailed the list to the White House and scheduled a visit with James Steinberg, Nancy Soderberg's successor at the National Security Council, to discuss it. In Washington they went over the list and quickly got it approved. Morrison told Sinn Féin, and soon after, on July 19, 1997, the IRA declared the new ceasefire.

———

New British prime minister Tony Blair responded to the IRA's latest declaration with impressive decisiveness. He wanted ninety days for the ceasefire to show itself to be the real thing, and he said that if it held, the peace talks, with Sinn Féin at the table at last, would resume in mid-September. There was no more talk from the British about the preconditions that the ceasefire be "permanent" or that decommissioning of weapons begin in advance of the talks. Blair wasn't going to bury the new ceasefire in words as his predecessor had done.

The ceasefire held, and, as promised, Sinn Féin was brought into the talks in September. For this critical new phase of the peace process—September 1997 until April 1998—matters were at last in the hands of those who lived in the north: nationalists, unionists, loyalists, and republicans. The leaders of the governments of the United Kingdom and the Irish Republic, the two sovereignties with the authority to make official agreements, were intensely involved and showed themselves willing to negotiate and do whatever was necessary to put together a good agreement that the Northern Ireland representatives would support and the voters in Northern Ireland and the Republic would approve by referendum. The Irish Americans who had done so much to bring the United States into the process watched from a distance as it played out.

When Morrison and others from his group went to Northern Ireland during the talks, it was, as he put it, as "cheerleaders and kibbitzers." What they saw in Belfast was that real all-party peace talks capable of bringing about an end to the centuries of warfare were well and truly under way at last. The people at the table were direct representatives of those who had been fighting for all those years, and they had plenty to get off their chests before they would be able to get down to the business of negotiating a deal and setting the course to the creation of a new society that accommodated both populations. Experiences and feelings were extreme, and the personal challenges participants from each side faced in dealing with the other were immense. Yet a willingness to proceed with hope despite the overwhelming losses suffered shone through miraculously in statements by participants from each side. Loyalist Gary McMichael explained it this way:

> It's very, very difficult for me, because they not only killed my father but also my best friend, and three years ago they tried to kill me. That obviously makes it difficult to even be in the room with representatives of those people, never mind engage in any form of negotiation with them. But it's actually that suffering that makes us take the line that we do and makes us go that extra mile to try and remove the threat against the community forever. That means we have to tackle republicanism, because we know that if we walk away from this process, there is going to be another stage of conflict, that others will have to go through what we've gone through.

Republican Alex Maskey expressed it in virtually the same way:

> I got a sawn-off shotgun blast in the stomach. I lost half a kidney, half my bowel, half my stomach, and I still have shrapnel inside me. I also had my house petrol-bombed by loyalists. I had to drag my kids out of bed and down a burning hallway. That was very traumatic for them. All too often people talk as if only one side has a monopoly on suffering. I'm trying to get on with people who tried to murder me, and that's because I want to make sure others don't have to endure the suffering that we have. We now have an opportunity to break the logjam.

George Mitchell's years of experience as majority leader of the US Senate, presiding over the endless bloviating that can afflict that chamber, proved to have been the perfect training ground for presiding over months and months of such expressions of deep feelings, accompanied, as is inevitable with imperfect human beings, by the posturing, parsing, bickering, dithering, and everything else that can make talks go on forever—especially with the Irish and British, truly great masters of those arts. Although in some respects this was the post-American, post-Clinton phase, in a deeper sense this phase was, as Morrison saw it, quintessentially American, a quality crucial to its success. Mitchell was the embodiment of that. In contrast to the hide-bound, class-based British way, this was the American way: Everybody speaks, nobody has to keep in his place, and tomorrow is a new day with potential not limited by class or position in society.

Morrison mentions another American aspect:

> Inclusiveness is inherently a goal—not always an achievement, but a goal—in the American political process. Marginalizing people as a way of dealing with them is just not how our politics works. The British are very class-based and very much, "we will sort it out at the levels of the people who matter, and those other people will just have to deal with it." There was a real culture shock in what Clinton did. The big tent was contrary to all of their theory of management of problems.

Mitchell found Morrison's description of that American quality to be "pretty accurate" and elaborated on the theme, emphasizing that while the talks were American in style, the agreement, if and when one was reached, would be all Northern Ireland:

> Here's what I had in mind: I knew that they didn't speak with each other. Or I guess it would be more precise to say they all spoke but they didn't listen to the other. So I also knew that it was going to be very difficult, and I wanted to create a sense of confidence that everybody would have his or her say, that nobody would be excluded or left out or unable to speak their piece. I couldn't guarantee them that the other side would listen, but I worked very hard at that privately, to say to people, you really gotta sit and listen, because they listened to you.

I said to them on the first day that I don't come here with an American agreement that I'm going to try to persuade you to accept. There's no Clinton agreement, there's no Mitchell agreement. I said, "Any agreement you reach will be yours," because I thought it important that they feel a sense of ownership in the process. In fact, I said to them, "Look, when this is over, I'm going home."

I was extremely careful two years later when it came time to draft the agreement to make certain that it was in their words, and I recall very clearly that when I sent around a covering note containing the very final version, I reminded them of my comment on the first day. I said, "Every word in this agreement has been spoken or written by a delegate from Northern Ireland."

Billy Hutchison, a loyalist paramilitary man who became a politician and a Good Friday negotiator—he was one of the four UVF men who met with Morrison, O'Dowd, Flynn, and Feeney at the Dukes Hotel in 1993—takes the theme even further:

George is very American. We all knew about George's love for baseball and that he wanted to be the commissioner. He always gave me the impression when he was chairing these things that he was very serious as an American politician. He loved that serious bit, but he also liked to do the razzmatazz, so I could see why he wanted to be a commissioner of baseball.

George started work early in the morning, and he continued at night, and he didn't understand that we like breaks. He just managed the whole thing—we worked hard, but he also gave us breaks and time to think. These were all very American things to us. Whenever they talked about "breakout sessions"—there were a number of ex-prisoners there—we were starting to think we were breaking out of jail.

When he was doing his analysis or stuff like that, it was as if he was using some sort of business manual from IBM, you know, this notion of having the breakout and this notion of its time to evaluate. He came across as very American, which was totally new to us.

Morrison may have left the playing field by this point, but the depth and breadth of his understanding of what was happening at Stormont makes him an ideal analyst of Mitchell's remarkable accomplishment in helping the parties make their way to the Good Friday Agreement.

I'd known George as a colleague since the 1980s. He was always the most gracious of people, always the consummate gentleman who was low on rhetoric and strong on focus and substance. Many expected him to be Bill Clinton's first appointment to the Supreme Court, but he declined in favor of staying in the Senate and working on healthcare reform. So sticking with a project and focusing on a result is something that was George Mitchell's calling card.

He was a very astute choice for Northern Ireland. He didn't come with the kind of baggage that some of us certainly had. He had connections to Ireland but was more a person of great experience in handling difficult negotiations and dealing with endless debate.

For most of the talks, the debate seemed to be mostly about nothing; they were long on talking and short on proposals. George experienced a certain level of frustration, but in some remarkable way, he let people talk to the point that they got everything they could possibly say off their chests. George exhibited this extraordinary patience in letting people kind of talk themselves out.

Then he made his decision to set a deadline. At the time, like most deadlines, you never knew how real it was, but George was adamant that he was going home if this wasn't a success by Good Friday. We'll never know if he actually would have, but he certainly convinced the people listening to him that he was serious. After all that time, George really came to sense his audience there and to have built a level of credibility. It wasn't given to him; he earned it for himself. That allowed him to tell people, "Enough already, I'm not going to sit here for the rest of my life. If you can't finish, then I'm finished."

People took it seriously, and they did what they hadn't done up until then: They got down to cases and they started negotiating. They started doing what politicians in Northern Ireland hadn't done for decades, which was to make substantive decisions about what they could agree to.

As Mitchell's Good Friday deadline drew close, Morrison, like much of the rest of the world, followed what he called "the cliffhanger" on television. There was no hint that Mitchell would relent on his deadline, and there were encouraging signs of progress. Tony Blair and Ireland's Taoiseach Bertie Ahern, who had taken office shortly after Blair became prime minister, were putting together a draft of an agreement that they thought all sides could support. It was their task because they would be the ones to sign a binding agreement on behalf of their respective countries. Their draft went to Mitchell the Sunday night before Good Friday. It was handed over with the proviso, especially important to the Irish, that, except for the areas of cross-border institutions still being negotiated, nothing could be changed—not a single word or punctuation mark.

When Mitchell read it, he was sure the unionists would never agree to it, but the no-alteration restriction boxed him in. Mitchell wrote later of how troubled and anxious this left him. Time was running out. He considered ordering an adjournment but knew it would eat up too much time. So he did what negotiators, diplomats, and politicians do when they want to resolve an impasse: He and his partners de Chastelain and Holkeri talked to everyone.

After working through the night, Mitchell, de Chastelain, and Holkeri reviewed their options. Monday morning was fast approaching. The possibility of doing a major redraft themselves was a nonstarter: It would take several days. They decided they had to accept the no-change rule and told the parties Monday morning that they would get the Blair-Ahern draft to everyone by midnight. But as the negotiators worked their way through the remaining issues all of Monday, it became obvious that the resolution of the cross-border provisions known as Strand Two, which would provide direct involvement of the Republic of Ireland in the affairs of Northern Ireland, was far from a loose end. Predictably, the nationalists, who welcomed more involvement by the Republic, wanted more areas of cross-border involvement; the unionists wanted fewer and, therefore, less involvement by the Irish government. Strand Two was a potential deal breaker for each side.

The negotiators finally got their markup of the Blair-Ahern draft to Mitchell shortly before midnight Monday. Mitchell and his co-chairmen knew once again that the unionists would never accept it, but they had promised that the full draft would be given to everyone by midnight. In a decision Mitchell quickly came to regret, they decided to keep that promise and out it went, festooned with desperate reminders that it was a draft only, not a final document to be accepted or rejected. In the after-midnight meeting with party leaders, Mitchell literally begged them not to leak the draft. They agreed, and it was never leaked, which avoided the public firestorm that could very well have made agreement impossible. They still had room to maneuver and a little time left. But not much: Good Friday was just seventy-two hours away.

Although the draft itself wasn't leaked, the unionists and loyalists minced no words in making their opposition clear. Mitchell knew that their reaction would be negative, but he "soon learned that I had underestimated how negative the reaction would be. The process now spun into a new crisis."

It was already Tuesday morning, and the Good Friday deadline would hit at midnight Thursday. UUP leader David Trimble told Blair that Strand Two would have to be changed fundamentally and that if there was no willingness to consider doing so, "we would prefer not to get involved in negotiation and to say, well, that's it."

Mitchell, de Chastelain, and Holkeri met separately with the representatives of the British and the Irish governments and laid it on the line. Mitchell said, "It's the unanimous judgment of the independent chairmen that the prime ministers have to agree to renegotiate, in good faith, the Strand Two section. Otherwise these talks are over. We don't think Trimble is bluffing. He can't live with this."

Tony Blair flew to Belfast Tuesday evening. Before leaving London he said, "I feel the hand of history upon our shoulders." Mitchell admired Blair's willingness to take the gamble of personally involving himself in the final negotiations when the outcome was so much in doubt, later writing that, "most political consultants would have told him to stay away."

Blair made plans to meet Bertie Ahern the next morning in Belfast. Ahern, whose mother had died suddenly just days before, left Dublin before sunrise Wednesday morning. At breakfast he gave Blair the welcome news that the Irish government would renegotiate Strand Two. After hurrying to meetings at Stormont, he left Belfast and got back to Dublin for his mother's funeral at noon; then he flew back to Belfast late that same afternoon for a series of meetings that ran into the early morning hours. Mitchell met with Ahern at 2 A.M. on Thursday, later writing of him with sympathy and awe: "I don't recall ever having seen a person as exhausted. I also had never seen a person more determined."

Blair and Ahern continued their negotiations throughout Thursday. They were making real progress, but Mitchell's deadline was just hours away. He had made it clear to both prime ministers that he was willing to keep the talks going after midnight with one proviso: "There's not going to be a break—not for a week, not for a day, not for an hour," he said. "We're here until we finish. We'll either get an agreement or we'll fail to get an agreement. Then we'll all go out together and explain to the press and the waiting world how we succeeded or why we failed.

It was a little like the way American football works: If a play is in motion when the clock runs out, the game continues until the play ends. As long as the parties stayed in motion, Mitchell was willing to keep it going.

Late Thursday night Ian Paisley and his DUP followers, who had long ago pulled out of the negotiations but didn't like what they were hearing about what was going on at Stormont, broke through the main gate and stormed up the mall toward the parliament building, flags flying, in what George Mitchell later described as "a last-ditch effort to block an agreement." They raised a ruckus and finally said they'd leave if they could hold a press conference. The British agreed. Paisley began with gusto, denouncing the talks and both governments. He called David Trimble a traitor. This was vintage Paisley, but suddenly it all changed: Other loyalists committed to the negotiations shouted him down with chants of "Go home!" and accusations that he was the one who'd run away. "We should never have listened to you, Paisley," shouted one. "We're not going to prison for you anymore!" George Mitchell later summed it up as "a sad spectacle." Although in the years to come Paisley would lead the DUP to become the dominant unionist party and show himself to be capable of remarkable surprises, that night he and his supporters eventually left Stormont to the negotiators.

With the Paisley distraction done, it was back to business as midnight approached. Sinn Féin still had not accepted the agreement, and Ahern decided he had to take action: to "sit down with Sinn Féin, have all the issues that concern them on the table, and negotiate this out, however long it takes." He got his sit-down, but when Sinn Féin pulled out a list of seventy-eight items they wanted clarified or resolved, he knew it was going to be a long night.

After hours and hours in which, as Ahern later recalled it, "I painfully went through every single one of those with them," a sense was building that Sinn Féin was getting there, although a persistent stumbling block was the release of prisoners who had been convicted in connection with the fighting. Sinn Féin wanted them released as soon as possible; the British said release in three years was their limit. Sinn Féin pounded away, and Blair finally agreed to two years but would go no lower. Sinn Féin argued vehemently for release in one year. Finally, at about six in the morning, Belfast time, Blair called Bill Clinton to ask for his help. It was well past midnight, Washington time, but Clinton was still up, following the events closely. He later recalled the conversation: "Tony Blair said they were getting close and George

Mitchell was over there hammering away. He said, 'We're close, but we can't get there.'"

Clinton agreed to speak to Adams, who told him the prisoner release issue came down to this: "When the war is over, the prisoners come home." Clinton, as only he could, went to work:

> I said, "Gerry, you gotta understand this is a nightmare for Blair, because if there's any act of violence after any one of these guys gets out, he'll be accused of basically being made a dupe for murderers. And so it's hard for him, and the longer he gets to wait, the more he can point to acts of good faith which justify this clemency."
>
> So we talked about it, and I explained to him what those kind of issues looked like on the other side of the table. It's a very difficult issue if you see people who are in prison as terrorists rather than freedom fighters—this really all depends on what your view is. It's the same exact problem we have in the Middle East every time we have to try to make another incremental step there. So I knew it was tough for Blair, but I knew it was tough for Gerry, too.

After that conversation, Adams and others he described as "very, very close colleagues" weighed everything up and decided to accept the agreement as it stood.

Now it was all down to David Trimble and the UUP. They had huge reservations, especially over arms decommissioning and Sinn Féin participation in the new government before decommissioning was underway.

Blair met with Trimble mid-afternoon on Friday to hear him out. Blair later gave this account:

> We had been going at it for days. Everyone was very tired, most of us had had about two, three hours of sleep in the last few days and no sleep whatever the night before. I remember at a certain point in the meeting when I really thought they were at the point of leaving, I really was concerned at one point that they would

just get up and walk out. I remember actually getting up and saying to them, "For goodness sake, calm down, we will sort this out. There is a way through, there has got to be. We haven't come this far to fail now."

Blair gave the UUP strong assurances that his government would support their positions as life under the agreement unfolded, and he agreed to put it in writing via a side letter. Trimble and his lieutenants appeared receptive, and Blair and his staff quickly drafted it. As soon as it was done, about four o'clock, Blair's chief of staff Jonathan Powell took it straight to Trimble. Trimble held the letter so he and his deputy John Taylor could read it together. When they got to the end, Taylor said, "Well, that's fine, we can run with that."

Trimble was also boosted by much-needed support from other UUP leaders, including Reg Empey and Ken Maginnis. For Empey, demonstrating the ability to negotiate and conclude a reasonable agreement was crucial: "My argument was simple: If this all collapses, do we not prove that Northern Ireland is a failed political entity?"

To Maginnis, it was a matter of meeting the moment:

> I remember pointing out that if we walked away from the agreement we couldn't come back tomorrow morning—we were actually turning our back on a defining moment in history.
>
> People knew that we hadn't got as much of our wish list as we would want. They knew that if we walked away we would be surrendering things that we did want. So there was this balancing act. Eventually we took a quiet moment again, we looked through it, and I remember saying to David, "Well, I'll accept it." And he looked round and he said, "I'm going to accept it."

At 4:45 Trimble called Mitchell and said the words he had been waiting all day—maybe all year—to hear: "We're ready to do the business."

Within fifteen minutes Mitchell had everyone gathered together for the plenary session that would take the vote and tell the world.

When the vote was done, Mitchell said, "I am pleased to announce that the two governments and the political parties in Northern Ireland have reached agreement."

The Good Friday Agreement was done. On April 10, 1998, the long war was over.

———

Just as Morrison had a unique understanding of the process Mitchell oversaw, he had a solid grasp of the final agreement itself, both what it was and what it was not:

> It was a watershed agreement. On the fundamentals, it under-pinned the ceasefire, so there was no sense that there was any going back. It wasn't the agreement to end all agreements: It was the agreement to create further agreements, a very politically astute resolution. When something couldn't be agreed [on] right then, instead of saying that's a deal breaker, it became, "Well, who should decide? Let's put that into this commission or that commission and let them decide. Let's get down to the core."
>
> The core was about the principle of consent and about creating a structure of governance that was protective of minor-ity rights, a referendum process North and South, cross-border, interisland, intercommunity kinds of structures, which could grow in strength over time as these other processes resolved the out-standing questions.
>
> Most of it was process, in some sense deferring decisions by delegating them. All of these were new processes that would have to be negotiated. The Good Friday Agreement came at the end of the negotiations—and it was the beginning of new rounds of negotiations.
>
> But the most essential wasn't the details of any of that. The most essential was feeling that a deal had been done and that all the people in the big tent were part of that agreement. You can't overstate George's accomplishment in helping the parties get there.

In the wake of this remarkable outcome, Morrison enjoys recalling that Mitchell initially came into the process as Clinton's economic
envoy, not the peace envoy he had promised during the 1992 campaign. A number of Irish American activists remained frustrated
that Clinton never appointed Mitchell or anyone else as his officially
designated peace envoy, even as Mitchell became more and more
involved as economic envoy, head of the international commission on
arms decommissioning, and overseer of the peace talks themselves.
Morrison could only respond that in Mitchell, Bill Clinton had delivered nothing less than "the peace envoy on steroids."

CHAPTER SEVENTEEN

Finishing Up, Holding It Together, and Starting Out

B ruce Morrison, whose adventures in Northern Ireland began in the ashes of his election defeat nearly a decade earlier, was back on the campaign trail in the spring of 1998, this time not as a candidate but as an observer of the referendum process that was the first order of business under the Good Friday Agreement. There were to be two separate votes, both on May 22, 1998, just six weeks after the peace agreement was signed at Stormont. Northern Ireland would vote on the agreement itself, since this would create its new governmental structure. The Irish Republic would vote on whether to amend its constitution to drop its claim that the six counties were part of the Republic, irrespective of the wishes of their inhabitants.

Morrison was well aware of the crosscurrents and sensitivities involved in the complex groupings and subgroupings that would be voting; he spoke with the discretion and restraint befitting a foreigner who would not himself be voting. In discussions and interviews, he stressed the moderate, respectful, and incremental nature of the peace agreement: Nobody was surrendering, and every voice and viewpoint was respected. He had a simple message: "If this passes, everybody has a vote. If it loses, nobody has a vote."

Describing his visit during the referendum campaign years later, Morrison said:

> I wasn't there to campaign; that would have been totally inappropriate. It was not a decision for Americans, it was a decision for the people of Northern Ireland. What Americans had fought for was the framework so that the people of Northern Ireland could in a peaceful way advocate their points of view and compromise and move forward. So this was the ultimate test of that proposition, and I was there to observe and celebrate that achievement. It was pretty amazing, if you take the fact that in 1992, this was seen as a largely hopeless situation in which American politicians tended to talk much more than act, that we'd got ourselves a president who did a lot more acting than talking, who created the environment in which this change could occur and in which the decision was made that there was a political solution to these problems and that the war was over.

He still marvels that the referendum ever came to be, with each side managing to surmount long-held bedrock convictions:

> The fact that one can get to that kind of vote is a triumph of practical politics. I think unionists felt they put themselves much at risk by giving what once had been a one-party, one-ethnicity state over to a local governmental structure that in their own perception was moving away from them, moving toward Irish rather than British as its identity, and put themselves at risk to consent because that consent could go against them over time. At the same time, republicans gave up, for the time being, their position that you can't have partitionist institutions because they represent illegitimacy: They're a product of the conquest of Ireland, not the self-determination of the Irish people.

Then there were the all-important questions of who would vote and on what:

> What is the unit of self-determination? The British Isles? The island of Ireland? The Republic of Ireland? The United Kingdom? Just Great Britain? Wherever you draw the line determines the outcome in a certain way.
>
> It was pretty clear that the peace agreement was going to win, but it was also pretty clear that it depended on very strong nationalist turnout and there being enough unionists of goodwill to push it over the half—and that's about what it was. So the campaign for the yes was really a nationalist campaign, and that's what you saw when you were there: The main energy came more from the community segment, the Inez McCormack segment—the one part of Northern Ireland where women were really important and where cross-community work really went on, where people do things in a nonsectarian way—than from the political segment, which was always heavily sectarian.

In the north, election turnout was huge, over 80 percent, and when the votes were counted, the Good Friday Agreement won over 70 percent of the vote. Post-election polling indicated that well over 90 percent of Catholics voted yes and about half of Protestant voters, perhaps a slight majority, did the same. In the Republic of Ireland, nearly 95 percent of the voters approved the amendments to their constitution. If there was any doubt about whether the Northern Ireland Catholics as a group, nationalists and republicans, not to mention Irish citizens of the Republic, were willing to vote on the basis of their desire for a fair shake, an end to the violence, and a political way forward, instead of sacred tenets of republican ideology—principally, that Ireland is one nation, thirty-two counties, not twenty-six—a yes vote above 90 percent made their willingness clear beyond any question.

For Morrison, the referendum reflected Sinn Féin's profound shift under Gerry Adams:

> The strong republican and nationalist support for the agreement really is a testament to Adams's pragmatic politics. He wouldn't say it was the goal, but a stage in the evolution of Irish unity. I guess my observation is that Adams and Sinn Féin as political thinkers accepted compromise as the heart of politics and not the heart of revolution. This event was really the demonstration that they had made the switch in the years from '86 to '97, they had accepted that the way forward was going to be political, and that political institutions gave them the opportunity to persuade in a way that violence didn't.

With the peace agreement ratified by the people affected, the next stage was the establishment of new civic life and the creation of a new governmental structure. Morrison stressed the basic nature of the peace agreement: It was really an agreement to reach future agreements to create processes and institutions that would establish a government and a society to accommodate both populations. Key among the matters of early focus was the creation of a new police service to replace the Royal Ulster Constabulary and its long history of discrimination against Catholics. Policing had been a source of great contention and conflict throughout the Troubles; the unifying principle for getting it right, articulated by Gerry O'Hara, Morrison's Sinn Féin host in Derry in 1987 and who became a member of the Northern Ireland Policing Board—a nineteen-member body with the power to hire and fire the chief constable and other top leadership—was that "both communities have a basic interest in receiving effective police services."

————

With the Good Friday Agreement now ratified by the voters, Morrison found himself a bit bereft. The people of Northern Ireland were on their own, and he felt like a doting parent who has just sent his child off to college with high hopes and more than a few worries.

And sadly, there was plenty to worry about in the summer of 1998. In mid-August, less than three months after the referendum, Northern Ireland's new world of peace and democratic institutions was violently thrust back into the terrible old world of death and destruction, with an act of terror so awful that it had the potential to destroy everything that had been gained.

It was in the market town of Omagh in County Tyrone, a little after three on a busy Saturday afternoon. A republican splinter group calling itself the Real IRA detonated a 500-pound car bomb on a street filled with shoppers and tourists. Twenty-one were killed outright, and eight more died in ambulances or in the hospital. Six children and six teenagers were killed, as was a woman pregnant with twins. More than 220 were injured, many grievously. A woman who lost her sixteen-year-old son and suffered injuries herself described hearing an "unearthly bang," followed by "an eeriness, a darkness that had just come over the place"—and then the screams.

No bomb, no attack of any kind, had killed more people—Protestants, Catholics, foreigners—throughout the entire three decades of the Troubles. The feeble explanation by the splinter group that their intended target had been the courthouse farther up the street and that they had called in a warning in time for people to be moved to safety—something a still-seething Bill Clinton would denounce as "crap" over fifteen years later—only compounded the outrage, especially when it became clear that that the "warning" had been careless and stupid in the extreme—deliberately so, many believed—and actually led the police to herd people *toward* the bomb instead of away from it.

The young and still fragile world of Northern Ireland at peace was now at the mercy of answers to questions that no one wanted to face again so soon: Who did this? Who supports them? Can hope survive such a blow?

Morrison was outraged and worried. "Omagh was early on and I was very frightened. It set off all kinds of alarm bells. I mean it really did call the question of which side the republicans were going to be on." In other words, would Sinn Féin break with the past and condemn the attack?

The answer came swiftly and forcefully. Gerry Adams minced no words, declaring, "I am totally horrified by this action. I condemn it without any equivocation whatsoever." He later elaborated in movingly human terms: "This action was wrong. I hope that the people involved will reflect on the enormity of what they have done. I would like whoever is responsible to accept that responsibility in a public statement, and I want them to cease. I want them to stop."

Sinn Féin deputy leader Martin McGuinness spoke out with equal force: "This appalling act was carried out by those opposed to the peace process. It is designed to wreck the process, and everyone should work to ensure the peace process continues." McGuinness spoke movingly of how the tragedy, coming with supreme irony in the first summer of the Northern Ireland's widely agreed on shift from war to politics, was so murderous to both populations: "All of them were suffering together. I think all of them were asking the question 'Why?' because so many of them had great expectations, great hopes for the future."

For Morrison, the great development after Omagh was that historic shift from Sinn Féin:

> It was the first real occasion in which republicans condemned violence perpetrated by other republicans. That had never happened, and the condemnation that came was really a turning of the page, although it came at a very high price. The condemnation marked the fundamental change that Sinn Féin would no longer excuse violence in the name of the republican cause. They had now joined the side of the opponents of the use of force to settle political questions in Northern Ireland. That conversion, which was later followed by actual decommissioning by the IRA and essentially a stand-down of the IRA as the army of the republican movement, is the completion of the journey from 1986, from "the Armalite and the ballot box" to "put down the Armalite and trust the ballot box."

While Sinn Féin was in many respects the most crucial voice to be heard, it wasn't the only one. SDLP leader John Hume called the bombers "undiluted fascists." Taoiseach Bertie Ahern called it "a ghastly act . . . the most evil deed in years." Tony Blair said it was "an appalling act of savagery," and Bill Clinton called it "butchery." Queen Elizabeth sent her condolences, as did the Pope. Just days after the attack, Prince Charles went to Omagh, spoke of his own feelings when his great uncle Lord Mountbatten was murdered by an IRA bomb, and said, "Let us pray this time that it will be the end to all the horrors that poor Ireland has suffered."

Saturday, August 22, one week after the massacre, was designated a Day of Reflection. Tens of thousands came to Omagh, a town of 25,000. As many as 60,000 people, including nearly every top leader from Northern Ireland, the Republic of Ireland, and the UK, filled the downtown for a service held on the steps of the courthouse the killers had claimed was the target of the bombing. The names of the dead were read aloud, a moment of silence was observed at the exact moment of the attack, baskets of flowers were taken to the hospitals caring for the injured, and two children, a Catholic and a Protestant, gave a prayer of hope. As the crowd began to disperse, many exchanged the Sign of Peace, shaking hands and saying, "The peace of the Lord be with you."

Bill and Hillary Clinton, along with Tony and Cherie Blair, visited a week later. In its account of the visit, headlined, "Most Powerful Man on the Planet Weeps as He Visits Omagh," *The Independent* noted Bill Clinton's sadness and the local reaction to it: "'He had tears in his eyes,' said Brenda O'Leary, one of the nurses. 'I know he's a politician, but they were genuine.' 'Look, he's taken the time and the thought to see us here,' said Kelvin O'Rourke, who works in a shop upon the stricken High Street. 'Who cares why he's doing it?'"

In the end, the combination of precedent-shattering republican condemnation of the bombing, the powerful and sympathetic expressions of world opinion, and the enormous crowd that came to Omagh added up to an overwhelming determination not to let violent fanatics hijack the peace that so many had worked so hard to win. This was enough to keep the process on track. Not even the Omagh bomb could wreck the peace.

————

As the summer of 1998 ended and autumn followed, the judgment of the world, like that of the voters of the island of Ireland, was that the peace settlement in Northern Ireland was good. Formal recognition followed: The Nobel Peace Prize was awarded to John Hume and David Trimble at the end of 1998.

The award to Hume was easy to understand, even though it could be argued that his own preferred path was not ultimately the way to peace. But it was nevertheless an award he richly deserved, going back to his civil rights days and up through his collaborations with Gerry Adams and his crucial support for the Adams visa, which was in many respects against his own political interests, but was still the essential thing to move the peace process forward. Morrison saw it this way:

> For Hume it was the affirmation of a lifetime of fighting for pretty much all the same things that Sinn Féin was fighting for, but forswearing violence and accepting the limitations that went with that, and yet recognizing that the republicans had a place, an important role, and putting his own career at risk in various ways to recognize and cooperate with that to the extent he could. And so it was an award for a lifetime, a lifetime of taking the peaceful road. It was completely earned.

For Trimble, the award was basically for his answering the call when history tapped him on the shoulder on Good Friday. He had no particularly distinguished history as a long-term seeker of peace, yet he rose to his moment and, like many who answered the call during the peace process, he had plenty to lose in voting yes to the agreement. Indeed, for him, the Nobel Prize was a decidedly mixed blessing. Ultimately it contributed to the destruction of his political effectiveness in the unionist community: In Morrison's phrase, it was seen by many unionists as "a prize for a sellout." To Morrison, Trimble's response to the award was sad:

> The sadness was really that Trimble almost apologized for getting the award. He was not proud of it. The prize to Trimble demonstrated his limitations, because a better leader would have seen it as international affirmation for a hard job well done. Instead, he retreated into the traditional unionist position of "We don't care what the world thinks, we only care about what we think." That perspective has held the unionists back a lot, and I think that from the time he made the decision not to claim the high ground, he slowly became politically irrelevant.

In not much time, the new Nobel laureate became Lord Trimble and retired from the playing field.

There was no award for Gerry Adams, arguably the most groundbreaking politician of all, the one who had led the republicans' long journey from war to politics. Morrison offers this overall analysis:

> At a later time the peace prize could conceivably have gone to four individuals: to Hume and Trimble but also to Adams and Paisley. Certainly Adams was essential to the process, and Paisley, while he failed to contribute through much of the period, at the critical moment years later made the move that solidified the actual solution on the ground by giving viability to the government at Stormont. But that wasn't going to happen in 1998.
>
> The decision was quite reasonable: Adams would have been adding a second nationalist and would have called out for balance on the unionist side, and there really was nobody there. Adams's self-definition was to be an outsider, to be the revolutionary, and Hume's self-definition was to be at the center of moderate politics, to solve problems. Somebody like Adams doesn't expect to be revered. He's sort of chosen a role that is going to be denounced for being extreme.

As for the contributions of the new British prime minister, the new Taoiseach, and the American president who did so much to help the parties break free from the long-standing dynamic that had kept everything stuck for so many years, Morrison says, "They could have given this prize to Clinton, Blair, and Ahern, but that would've been a bad idea, because while they were the facilitators, the people who had to make the hard decisions were the ones on the ground in Northern Ireland."

Similarly, there was no Nobel Prize for George Mitchell, perhaps the ultimate facilitator, but at the White House St. Patrick's Day celebration in 1999, Clinton awarded him the Presidential Medal of Freedom, the nation's highest civilian award. Thomas Foley, the former Speaker of the House of Representatives who had been so steadfast in supporting the British position on Northern Ireland and opposing any participation by Sinn Féin or the issuance of a visa to Gerry Adams—a total Anglophile despite his Irish heritage—was knighted by the Queen. But because he wasn't a British citizen, he wasn't entitled to be called Sir Thomas.

Also in 1998, Conor O'Clery, Washington correspondent for the *Irish Times*, published his account of Bill Clinton's new American policy on Northern Ireland. In Ireland, the book was called *The Greening of the White House*, and in the United States, *Daring Diplomacy*. The book, which covered events into 1996, proved revelatory for Clinton. He loved it and invited O'Clery and his wife to visit him in the Oval Office. He told O'Clery, "I've known Bruce Morrison since law school and I had no idea he was doing all this." Morrison was particularly impressed by the delight Clinton took in what he and the others had done unofficially. As Morrison put it, "The world's most powerful leader didn't say, 'How dare they!' Instead it was, 'How great!'"

———

In the fall of 1998, Morrison returned to Belfast. He had been invited as director of the Federal Housing Finance Board to participate in a

Habitat for Humanity project. He found himself hammering nails at Glencairn, the same loyalist housing estate beyond Shankill Road that he had visited six years earlier, after he and Niall O'Dowd decided that Bill Clinton was the horse to ride on the road to peace.

As he hammered away, he noticed an older man, grizzled, not much hair, not many teeth, standing by the edge of the work site. Morrison realized this was the unforgettable fellow of many grievances whose long cigarette ash had so mesmerized him on his very first visit to Glencairn all those years ago. He put down his hammer and walked over. The man asked, "Do you remember me?"

Morrison looked again for an instant and answered, "Of course I remember you. How are you?"

While the man didn't seem surprised to find the American back in Belfast hammering nails, he did seem a bit flustered and uncharacteristically reticent, not so comfortable putting himself forward even that much. The encounter ended nearly as quickly as it began. The man pulled back, but as he slipped away, he left Morrison with a perfect benediction: "Ya done alright."

EPILOGUE

The mail arrived late in the afternoon, as usual. Her son, who had turned nine in May, got back from day camp, had his snack, and went up to in his room. She gathered up the mail and took it out to the deck, as she had recently started doing; this was something she never mentioned to her son and didn't think her husband knew about.

She set the mail on the table and sat down. Evening might be approaching, but this July afternoon was still too hot. Summer days were steamy around Washington DC, and this was the hottest part of the day. As she began to open the mail, she paid particular attention to any envelope without a return address, just as the people who sent the warning had recommended, although, oddly, their own envelope hadn't had one. She opened each piece carefully and attentively but didn't cringe or brace herself. When she was done, she went inside—the air-conditioning was a relief—and set some of the mail on the dining room table. She took the rest to her husband's office and left it on his desk. This business of opening the mail on the deck felt a bit foolish, but she still thought it was the right thing to do. If there was a letter bomb and it went off, her son should be safe inside and upstairs.

Nancy Morrison found herself following this routine after her husband Bruce received a letter in the summer of 2001 informing him that his name was on a list of alleged IRA activists and sympathizers marked for death by remnants of loyalist paramilitaries. The letter said that the danger would be greatest when he traveled to Northern

Ireland, but it also said that any attack in the United States would most likely be through the mail.

As the weeks passed and not a single piece of mail seemed suspicious, she decided it was no longer necessary to open the mail out on the deck. But looking back, she didn't regret having been so cautious. Soon enough Washington would be reeling from 9/11 and the anthrax attacks. In this changed America, the loyalist death list came to seem remote and somewhat abstract. Northern Ireland might be in the thick of the difficult and drawn-out process of implementing the Good Friday Agreement, but Americans were now focused on danger on the home front.

One American who continued to keep a watchful eye on developments in Northern Ireland was, of course, Bruce Morrison. He returned to Belfast, as well as Dublin and London, many times in the years following the 1998 agreement. Late in 2001, he went to 10 Downing Street in London, where the prime minister lives and works, to meet with Tony Blair's chief of staff Jonathan Powell about a range of issues on Northern Ireland, including, as always, arms decommissioning. While Morrison was waiting in the small area in the small place that is Number 10—a fraction of the size of the West Wing of the White House—Tony Blair walked by; he and Morrison greeted each other and spoke briefly about Northern Ireland. Morrison was impressed with Blair: He had a comprehensive knowledge of the situation and an instant ability to discuss it in depth, even though he certainly hadn't been briefed for their chance meeting. It was clear to Morrison that Blair was determined to stay on top of things and do everything necessary to successfully conclude the post–Good Friday processes. Morrison was happy to see that Blair had fully taken the torch from Bill Clinton and that the peace process was in such good hands.

———

From the perspective of more than fifteen years of post–Good Friday life, fundamental change and important progress are apparent, although much of it seemed dripping slow as it was unfolding. It has been a winding road to the higher ground that Good Friday brought within reach, with dips and turns, but the clear direction has been upward.

In June of 1998, soon after the Northern Ireland referendum ratified the Good Friday Agreement, elections were held for the new assembly. The moderate parties—the unionist UUP and the nationalist SDLP—continued as the leaders from their respective communities, although it wasn't until December of 1999 that the powers of government, held for so many years by the British, devolved to Northern Ireland. But just weeks later, in February, the unionist parties, citing more delay in decommissioning, refused to take office with Sinn Féin. That made it impossible for the devolved government to function, and the British government retook control. But the following May, after the IRA pledged to put its weapons "beyond use," the British once again restored governing power to Northern Ireland, although the political atmosphere would remain charged by the efforts of the UUP to be seen as tough on the republicans in an effort to keep its harder-line DUP unionist rival at bay.

All this back-and-forth reflected the basic reality that, as a self-governing political enterprise charged with operating for the benefit of both of its populations, Northern Ireland was a neophyte. It was attempting to do what it never had to do, nor sought to do, prior to the Good Friday Agreement. Northern Ireland had been directly governed by London for more than twenty-five years. Unionist politicians had come of age with little more to do than tell each other how awful the republicans were. The result was that those who were now in the business of governing had sparse experience with real negotiations and real deal-making on their own, with no George Mitchell at the helm.

Complicating matters further was the elaborate system of checks and balances built into the governing system that was, of necessity, part of the Good Friday Agreement. Each side knew how easily the minority could be overwhelmed by an unchecked majority. The Catholics knew it because that had been their lot in Northern Ireland from the beginning. The Protestants knew it because they were well aware of how they'd treated the Catholics—and, as they contemplated a Northern Ireland in which population changes could leave them in the minority, they worried they would be treated the same way. So when the agreement was made, each side demanded what would in effect be a veto. The result was a system so sclerotic that it makes American political gridlock seem like not much more than a speed bump.

And yet, despite these formidable obstacles, the Northern Ireland that emerged has made very real progress since that historic accord.

In 1998, a commission led by Christopher Patten, the former governor of Hong Kong, was established to make recommendations for changes in Northern Ireland's policing and justice systems—one of the central grievances that had fueled the Troubles. The commission issued its report in 1999, but there was no agreement on implementing its recommendations. Policing and justice issues would remain unresolved for several more years.

Also in 1998, the British created a Parades Commission with the power to reroute parades that were a regular source of sectarian conflict. Unionist parades held every July 12 celebrating the victory of the Protestant King William at Boyne in 1690, in which they insisted on marching through Catholic neighborhoods that didn't want them there, especially at night, had been particularly troublesome. Morrison says that in time the commission became a real success, but he stresses the importance of full respect for its authority from all quarters. When Britain's secretary of state for Northern Ireland, Theresa Villiers, spoke of creating a special process for particularly controversial Orange parades through Catholic areas of the Ardoyne region of North Belfast, Morrison felt strongly that the better approach would have been for the British to ask how they could help the commission that was already in place do its work.

In 2001, there was a disturbing preview of the challenges inherent in addressing the deep separation between Northern Ireland's two populations—a segregation that has in some respects become more pronounced since the Good Friday Agreement. Holy Cross, a

Catholic primary school for girls in the Ardoyne region, found itself in the midst of a loyalist neighborhood following population shifts that were themselves the cause of controversy and hard feelings involving claims that many had been run out of places where they had lived for years. Morning after morning, the front entrance of the school became the scene of frightening, sometimes violent, demonstrations. It looked like the school integration conflicts in the American South in the years following *Brown v. Board of Education.*

The Holy Cross demonstrations continued for months and into the following year. It was highly traumatic for the children, many of whom were quite young, and the loyalist community couldn't have looked worse. "I am ashamed to be associated with these people," said David Ervine, a great loyalist political leader. "The protest is wrong."

———

In October of 2002, more conflicts, including arrests related to an alleged IRA spy ring in the assembly, and unionist threats to quit the government unless Sinn Féin was expelled, led to the imposition, yet again, of direct rule from London. (The alleged spy ring was later found to be a concoction by a mole in the pay of the British; all charges were dropped.)

Decommissioning and related issues dragged on, but actually great progress was being made, largely due to the dogged efforts of Canadian general John de Chastelain, who had been co-chairman of both commissions headed by George Mitchell. In 2005, de Chastelain reported that the IRA armaments had been fully put "beyond use." It was in time learned that this had been done primarily by putting disassembled weapons into barrels that were then filled with concrete and buried under more concrete. The IRA agreed to permit the observation of this process by two clergymen—one Catholic and one Protestant— but would not allow any photographs or video, which they felt would make it look as if they had surrendered. No surrender and no turnover of arms had always been overriding principles for the IRA, and they were able to decommission with those principles intact. Additionally, by keeping the process under their own control and completing it in their own time, they made the limits of Sinn Féin's influence over the IRA clear. This would improve Sinn Féin's prospects in coming elections and ultimately help give the DUP a way to make a power-sharing agreement with them.

In the summer of 2005, the IRA issued a formal stand-down order to all of its members, officially ceasing to operate as a paramilitary force. It announced that it would henceforth rely exclusively on politics to pursue its goals.

The IRA stand-down was a huge and hopeful step, but progress on other fronts continued to be stymied. In 2006, representatives of the political parties met with the British and Irish governments at St. Andrews in Scotland in an attempt to hammer out a plan that would allow things to move ahead. The result was the St. Andrews Agreement, which included several key provisions: The Northern Ireland Assembly would be restored, the new police service recommendations by the Patten commission would be accepted by Sinn Féin, and the DUP would agree to share executive power with the republicans.

This last element was carried out in magnificent fashion when the DUP and Sinn Féin became the two top parties in Northern Ireland following the 2007 elections. Ian Paisley—that firebrand, Dr. No—became the first minister, and Martin McGuinness, the former IRA commander, became the deputy first minister. Both men worked so well and so affably together that they came to be called the Chuckle Brothers. Before long, their relationship deepened into one of genuine respect and affection. McGuinness said that his secret was to act toward Paisley as he acted toward his own grandfather. Dr. No had become the key to the success of the Good Friday Agreement he had so intensely opposed.

Another important step forward came in 2010, when the Saville Commission issued its findings on the 1972 Bloody Sunday tragedy in Derry. Previously, official inquiry had been limited to a British whitewash just weeks after the shootings. In early 1998, more than twenty-five years later, a new investigation led by Lord Saville, a prominent and widely respected jurist, was ordered to reexamine the episode. After years of extensive testimony and detailed investigation, the commission found that the British army had indeed killed fourteen unarmed demonstrators without justification. British prime minister David Cameron apologized in Parliament the same day the report was issued.

Also in 2010, the British turned control of the Northern Ireland police and justice systems over to the government of Northern Ireland. At long last, these systems were under control of a Northern Ireland in which both populations had major voices.

There have also been encouraging developments on the symbolic front. Queen Elizabeth visited Ireland in 2011 and laid a wreath to the fallen republicans at the Garden of Remembrance in Dublin. In 2012, she and Martin McGuinness shared a handshake in Belfast that was front page news around the world. The queen's outfit that day was a vivid fresh green—a fascinating choice for the occasion. But despite its obvious symbolism, the outfit seemed to pass without comment. Journalist David McKittrick later said that in Belfast, the queen is beyond criticism in such matters.

In 2014, McGuinness was invited to a state dinner at Windsor Castle in honor of Irish president Michael Higgins. He, of course, was not beyond criticism, and he took heat from both sides: Unionists said that inviting an IRA man was a disgrace, and some republicans accused him of selling out. But he looked elegant in his white tie and tails and had a fine time.

Not all symbolic issues developed in a positive way. In 2011, the nationalist parties won more seats on the Belfast city council than the long-dominant unionists, although they didn't win a majority. The nationalists wanted to stop flying the Union Jack over city hall but didn't have the votes. In late 2012, they supported a compromise by the small Alliance Party that would allow the flag to fly for the eighteen days of the year that it was being flown over Westminster. Unsurprisingly, the unionists, who had been flying it daily since 1906, were angry, and tumultuous demonstrations followed, continuing throughout 2013 and into 2014. An effort to broker a resolution was made by George Bush's envoy to Northern Ireland, Richard Haass, who had originally been an opponent of Clinton's involvement in Northern Ireland. Haass's involvement in the flag dispute helped but fell short of fully resolving it. Morrison felt that a more vigorous practical-politics approach—expanding the scope of issues beyond the symbolic to include practical things that would give those on each side something important to them—would have yielded better results.

Despite considerable overall progress, the cold hand of the Troubles was never far away. Many argued that Gerry Adams, who had always denied being a member of the IRA, should be held accountable for orders some believe he gave as an alleged IRA commander. Efforts to expose as fraudulent Adams's claim that he was a politician seeking peaceful resolution of issues became something of a cottage industry on both sides of the Atlantic. In 2014, he was detained by the police in connection with the IRA murder of a mother of ten whose body had been discovered buried on a beach. He was released within days and never charged; in 2015, prosecutors decided that they wouldn't prosecute him because there wasn't sufficient evidence.

Also in 2015, while the Northern Ireland government was struggling with a difficult fight over welfare cuts planned by the UK, two former IRA operatives were murdered in separate shootings, most likely by former IRA men. The second victim was a suspect in the first murder. The killings appeared to stem from criminal activity, not paramilitary violence. Sinn Féin and politicians of all stripes immediately denounced the murders; Martin McGuinness said the killers were "low-life criminals." Nevertheless, unionists raised concerns that the IRA might still be operating as a paramilitary force. They thought that an ambiguous statement from the police that the IRA "was not on a war footing" implied that it might still be involved in violent activity.

Many unionists wanted Britain to take over governing power once again and when they said no, DUP and UUP resignations followed.

First Minister Peter Robinson avoided a complete breakdown by keeping his party's participation in the power-sharing government alive in what *The Guardian* called "zombie form." The British agreed to appoint an independent commission to investigate whether the IRA was operating as a paramilitary force.

Drawing on the resources of MI5 and the Northern Ireland police and citing "confidence in our judgments," the commission concluded that the IRA and other paramilitary groups were "committed to peaceful means to achieve political objectives." They said that the paramilitary structures that remained actually aided the transition from warfare to politics and were a way to maintain more control over individual members. They cited the danger of republican splinter groups and general criminal activity for personal gain but said that IRA return to large-scale conflict "is well beyond recall." That was good enough for the DUP and its ministers returned to their posts.

———

While the substantial and generally steady progress since the Good Friday Agreement is an accurate measure of how far Northern Ireland has come, it is also an accurate measure of how far it still has to go. At some point the peace lines—high walls separating Protestant and Catholic neighborhoods—need to come down. Politicians have to find ways to attract votes from both communities based on shared concerns. Overcoming the segregation resulting from the sectarian divide is the enormous issue that the Good Friday Agreement did not—and surely could not—resolve. But in the generally improving situation in which the aspirations of the Good Friday Agreement are becoming more and more realized, the political focus is becoming more on solving practical problems and less on identity and symbolic issues. Identity, of course, is always in the picture and can flare up at any time, but the movement away from the symbolic issues to which Northern Ireland has for so long been drawn suggests that, in time, tackling the huge problem of a fundamentally segregated society will be within reach. Morrison says that's the next frontier for Northern Ireland.

It is likely, though, that these changes will not come quickly, especially since the children of each community are for the most part educated only with their own: Catholics almost all in parochial schools; Protestants almost all in the public school system. Efforts have been made to change that, but a reasonably integrated education system is not on the near horizon. Hopefully the time will come when leaders and voters understand the price children are paying for this sectarian division. As these children mature, they will struggle to make their way in a world that is increasingly diverse. It's one thing to want to stay close to your roots, but quite another to grow up unequipped to deal with people from different backgrounds.

In the meantime, Northern Ireland, like many places in the world, may for a time have to muddle through as an essentially segregated society. But as its people well know, muddling through isn't the worst option. The way forward, of course, remains the same one that brought things this far: a vigorous political process in which *everyone* has a voice. Leaders on both sides must commit to negotiating and hashing out deals to meet their constituents' practical needs and to address the problems holding the society back. Morrison sums it up perfectly: "It's all about process. The process is to get up every day, don't kill each other, keep negotiating, and at the end of the day find yourself further along."

———

In the years following the Good Friday Agreement, several noteworthy figures passed from the scene. The most consequential death was that of David Ervine, who suffered a heart attack and a stroke in early January 2007 and died two days later, at the age of fifty-three. Tributes poured in from every direction. Green Party leader Trevor Sargent said, "His death leaves a major vacuum in terms of the quality of political representatives in Northern Ireland." Morrison had always made it a point to meet with Ervine whenever he went to Belfast, regarding him as a dependable barometer of what was really going on. Whenever Ervine seemed discouraged, Morrison found himself getting discouraged as well.

A sense of what Ervine might have been able to help bring about by way of politics that would cut across sectarian lines can be gleaned from his words at a conference in 1994:

> The politics of division see thousands of people dead, most of them working class, and headstones on the graves of young men. We had been fools: Let's not be fools any longer. All elements must be comfortable within Northern Ireland. We have got to extend the hand of friendship, we have got to take the peace lines down brick by brick, and somehow or other we have got to introduce class politics. You can't eat a flag.

A great void in the politics of Northern Ireland is that while the urban working-class Catholics have a strong and effective political voice in Sinn Féin, the urban working-class Protestants have nothing comparable because the top unionist parties are geared principally toward those who are middle-class and up, living mostly in rural and suburban areas. Ervine was a political leader of real scope, profound goodness, and great gifts, and it isn't hard to imagine that resolution of the toughest issues would be closer if he hadn't died so soon.

In August of 2014, Albert Reynolds, the Taoiseach who did so much to lay the foundation for the peace process, died after a long battle with Alzheimer's. John Major attended the funeral, and when the priest thanked him for coming, he replied simply and perfectly, "Where else would I be on this day?"

Just a few weeks later, Ian Paisley died at eighty-eight. The sadness of Martin McGuinness, Paisley's improbable partner in government, was palpable. Paisley's family invited McGuinness as a family friend to visit Paisley at home during his last illness, as well as to the private family service after he died. The Sinn Féin man was the only political figure invited.

In April of 2015, Jimmy Creighton, the loyalist community organizer whose name Morrison didn't catch, the man with the unforgettable cigarette ash early in 1992 and the perfect benediction for Morrison late in 1998, died suddenly in Glencairn.

A central question asked persistently about Northern Ireland, with varying levels of anxiety, is whether or not the peace will last. Although it seems highly likely that it will—there is simply no substantial constituency for a return to warfare—worrisome possibilities can be imagined. If the government were to become so stuck that nothing of importance could be dealt with or if through either relentless majority domination of the political process or takeover of government by the British, the nationalist community came to despair that it had been stripped of any effective voice, the peace could be vulnerable to the voices of hard men arguing that the idea of a political way forward was, and remains, nothing but a fantasy. Yet even if such a situation were to develop, the likelihood of a return to warfare seems remote, because there are solid answers rooted in important changes that have been institutionalized in Northern Ireland today—particularly the reform of the policing and criminal justice systems, as well as the creation of a basic foundation of equal rights and opportunity.

But nested within that worrisome though unlikely scenario is a crucial point: The Good Friday Agreement is inherently vulnerable, and it will continue to be so as long as Northern Ireland remains so intensely segregated and politically divided. It requires unflagging attention and protection.

What has been accomplished in Northern Ireland is one of humankind's great political creations. Its essence is process—complicated, messy, shifting, uncertain, imperfect, and vital process, like democracy itself, like life itself. If the creation that arose from the peace process had been a concrete object—iconic works of art like Michelangelo's *David* or van Gogh's *Starry Night* come to mind—it would be regarded as a one of the great masterpieces, something to be treasured and, because of its inherent fragility, protected and always handled with great care.

That creation is now in the hands of the people of Northern Ireland; they, along with the UK, of which Northern Ireland is a part, and the Republic of Ireland, of which it may one day become a part, are its trustees. It is an indispensable part of the heritage and abiding greatness of Northern Ireland, as essential as its great legacy of ship building, engineering, and linen making, as well as its magnificent landscape and stunning coastline. While there is good reason to believe that the trustees of this remarkable creation will meet their responsibilities, it is crucially important for all who helped, including the American friends of the process, to attend to it, protect it, and help it evolve and develop to better meet the needs of the people by whom, and for whom, it was created.

CAST OF CHARACTERS

Johnny "Mad Dog" Adair

Adair, a fierce loyalist and head of the West Belfast Brigade of the Ulster Defence Association (UDA), had a reputation for viciousness—and was known for his unabashed boasting about it—that set him apart in a decidedly violent crowd of loyalist paramilitary men. He claimed to have killed at least 20 Catholics.

Gerry Adams

The Belfast native headed the Sinn Féin party and worked with great political skill to move the IRA away from armed struggle and toward politics. Many had doubts about him, but Adams was central to winning the peace. He now sits in the Irish parliament.

Bertie Ahern

Ahern became prime minister of Ireland in 1997, shortly before all-party negotiations began. He played a crucial role in bringing about the Good Friday Agreement.

Tony Blair

Blair's election as prime minister of the UK in May of 1997 opened the way to all-party talks. The IRA declared a new ceasefire that July, and Sinn Féin was at the negotiating table that September. In the final stages of the negotiations that led to the Good Friday Agreement, Blair threw himself with total commitment into the effort. He tirelessly oversaw the post–Good Friday processes that gave substance to the Good Friday Agreement.

John Bruton

Bruton was the Irish prime minister in the period after the 1994 cease-fire and before the 1997 all-party negotiations. He was generally more open to the British viewpoint than his predecessor Albert Reynolds or his successor Bertie Ahern. At critical points, however, he spoke bluntly and truthfully about the futility of the British position that made arms decommissioning a precondition of all-party talks.

Joseph Cahill

An elderly IRA hard man with an extensive record of violence and gun-running, Cahill was nonetheless granted a US visa in order to explain the 1994 IRA ceasefire to its hardcore supporters in Irish America.

Warren Christopher

As Bill Clinton's secretary of state from 1993 to 1997, Christopher vehemently opposed issuance of a US visa to Gerry Adams. When Clinton called him to say he had decided to issue the visa, Christopher tried for half an hour to talk him out of it.

Bill Clinton

President of the United States from 1993 until 2001. When he was an Arkansas governor running for president, his Irish American supporters got him to promise a new American policy on Northern Ireland that was independent of Britain's. The political conditions created by Bruce Morrison and others helped Clinton make good on those promises, and in time his determination to help bring peace exceeded their wildest hopes. His role in the peace process became one of his proudest accomplishments.

Jimmy Creighton

Morrison encountered this loyalist activist twice at the Belfast housing estate Glencairn: first in 1992 when he heard Creighton holding forth at a community meeting and again in 1998 when Creighton offered Morrison his judgment on his performance in the peace process.

Anne Edwards

As Bill Clinton's director of press advance, her job was to make the images and events of his 1995 visit to Northern Ireland visually compelling and supportive of the American policy Clinton was there to advance.

Reg Empey

He was an Ulster Unionist Party official who helped party leader David Trimble accept the final draft of the Good Friday Agreement.

David Ervine

Ervine was a former UVF man who came to believe while in prison that loyalists should practice politics instead of warfare. He was part of the group that met in secret with Morrison and the other Americans in 1993 and changed their view of the loyalist community. Ervine became a leader of the Progressive Unionist Party (PUP) and he was an enormously gifted loyalist political leader until his death in 2007 at the age of 53.

Chuck Feeney

Feeney, a brilliant and hard-nosed entrepreneur, became one of the richest men in the world and then gave nearly all of his fortune away. After the horrific IRA bombing in Enniskillen in 1987, he became determined to do anything he could to help end the violence. He was part of the team of unofficial peacemakers who went to Northern Ireland in 1993, and he lent crucial financial support to many aspects of the peace process.

Ray Flynn

The former Boston mayor and Irish Americans for Clinton-Gore co-chairman promised Niall O'Dowd that he'd lead an American delegation to Northern Ireland in the spring of 1993, a time when Morrison was unavailable. When he begged off at the last minute and the trip had to be cancelled, it threatened the credibility of the new American role.

William Flynn

As CEO of the insurance giant Mutual of America, Flynn was the very model of the fully arrived, establishment-certified Irish American business success. He was a major participant in the Irish American push for peace and a member of the small team of unofficial peace-makers who went to Northern Ireland in 1993. Flynn was Irish to the bone and a devout Roman Catholic, but he was able to forge important relationships with both the unionist and loyalist communities.

Thomas Foley

The Speaker of the House of Representatives from 1989 to 1995 was Irish American, but he was no friend of the republican cause. He abhorred the IRA and any individuals or organizations that seemed to have the remotest sympathy for their cause.

Martin Galvin

Galvin was an uncompromising longtime Noraid activist. When Bill Clinton appeared at the Irish American forum just before the crucial 1992 New York Democratic Primary, it was Galvin who asked the hottest question: Would he give Gerry Adams a US visa?

Ted Howell

Howell, who resolutely avoided public attention, was the Sinn Féin theoretician and strategist Morrison described as "Gerry Adams's right-hand brain." He was a major architect of Sinn Féin's creation of a political path for the achievement of republican objectives.

John Hume

Hume was the leader of the moderate nationalist SDLP party and a key figure in the civil rights demonstrations that preceded the Troubles. His influence on American policy on Northern Ireland was enor-mous. His moderate nationalist stance, especially his condemnation of violence, gave him enormous influence over the opinions of the mainstream Irish American political establishment. Hume always did what he thought was right for the peace process even when he knew it would hurt him politically, as when he supported the US visa for Adams. In 1998, Hume was awarded the Nobel Peace Prize.

Billy Hutchinson

Hutchinson was a former UVF man who came to believe while in prison that loyalists should practice politics instead of warfare. He was part of the group that met in secret with Morrison and the other Americans in 1993 and changed their view of the loyalist community. He became a leader of the Progressive Unionist Party (PUP) and a member of the Belfast City Council.

Christopher Hyland

As director of outreach to ethnic groups for the 1992 Clinton campaign, Hyland connected with Niall O'Dowd to get Irish Americans behind Clinton. He was a tireless advocate within Clinton's campaign for him to create a new American policy on Northern Ireland.

Ted Kennedy

Kennedy served in the US Senate from 1962 to 2009. He was its preeminent Irish American, and his views on Northern Ireland were by far the most influential. When he decided to support an American visa for Gerry Adams, despite concerns, he did it with the full force of his inimitable voice and heart, which greatly helped move the peace process forward.

Tony Lake

As Bill Clinton's national security advisor from 1993 to 1997, Lake oversaw and provided crucial support for Clinton's new American policy on Northern Ireland.

Richard Lawlor

Lawlor, a Connecticut lawyer, was national vice-chairman of Noraid. When he and Morrison met, Morrison felt that Lawlor made a strong case about the problems in Northern Ireland involving major human rights issues.

Ken Maginnis

He was an Ulster Unionist Party official who helped party leader David Trimble accept the final draft the Good Friday Agreement.

John Major

Major succeeded Margaret Thatcher as Tory prime minister of the UK in 1990. He softened her hardline stance on Northern Ireland and joined with Irish prime minister Albert Reynolds in the 1993 Downing Street Declaration, which relinquished any British claim to Northern Ireland and pledged that its future would be decided by those who lived there. But when the IRA ceasefire finally came in 1994, Major kept imposing preconditions that kept Sinn Féin out of the peace negotiations. He rejected George Mitchell's deft compromise plan for starting all-party talks, and soon after that, in early 1996, the IRA ended its long ceasefire. In 1997 Major was defeated by Tony Blair, who would go on to be crucial to the success of the peace process.

Sir Patrick Mayhew

Mayhew was the secretary of state for Northern Ireland from 1992 to 1997. He cordially greeted the American team led by Morrison when they visited him at Stormont in 1993, but he told them bluntly that he didn't like their peace envoy idea, which was a cornerstone of Clinton's new American policy. In 1995, he was sent to Washington to persuade the Americans of the rightness of the decommissioning precondition. His statement on that point became known as "Washington 3."

Inez McCormack

McCormack was a Northern Ireland Protestant activist who possessed a bottomless supply of commitment, energy, and good humor in her fight for an end to the violence and for fair treatment of the Irish minority. In the male-dominated world of labor union leadership, she became the first female head of the Irish Congress of Trade Unions in 1999.

Mike McCurry

McCurry was an experienced Democratic operative who became spokesman for the Clinton State Department and then Bill Clinton's press secretary. He saw how Morrison and others worked to bring Clinton into the Northern Ireland issue and he understood why it appealed to him when Morrison laid it out.

Christopher McGimpsey

McGimpsey called himself "a more left-wing unionist." As a Belfast councilor in the Ulster Unionist Party, he was impressed with Morrison's determination to understand all points of view, and he was instrumental in getting his party to agree to meet with Morrison and the unofficial American peacemakers in Belfast in 1993.

Martin McGuinness

McGuinness was a top Sinn Féin leader who later acknowledged that he had been an active IRA member. He became minister of education in the new Northern Ireland government in 1999 and later became deputy first minister in the government in which his political polar opposite, DUP firebrand Ian Paisley, was first minister. The two men wound up getting along so well that reporters called them the Chuckle Brothers.

David McKittrick

Seen by many as the greatest of the Northern Ireland journalists, McKittrick was an astute and brilliant observer and reporter on what was happening in Northern Ireland. He was a longtime writer for the *Independent* and author or co-author of several books on the Troubles and the peace process.

George Mitchell

The man from Maine presided over the peace talks that led to the Good Friday Agreement. He had been a majority leader of the US Senate, and, before that, a federal judge, so he knew how to be patient in the face of endless droning and bickering. He could also be extremely decisive. After Clinton appointed him economic envoy to Northern Ireland, Mitchell eventually won the trust of all sides, which led to his selection as chairman of the peace talks. He found ways through tangles and obstacles and helped lead the negotiators to the Good Friday Agreement in 1998.

Joe Moakley

Moakley was chairman of the Rules Committee of the House Representatives. When Morrison's 1990 comprehensive immigration reform bill was suddenly in mortal danger, Moakley and his staff helped rescue it.

Bruce Morrison

After a crushing defeat in the 1990 election for governor of Connecticut—for which he gave up his chance to stay in Congress, where he had been serving since 1983—Morrison became the first indispensable American politician in the Irish Peace Process. (Bill Clinton was the second and George Mitchell the third.) Morrison understood that the more extreme parties associated with those making war were also the key to making peace; he also knew that peace could only be accomplished by running the risk of engaging people who were widely (and often accurately) seen by those on the other side as terrorists. Morrison helped Bill Clinton make his campaign promises to change American policy on Northern Ireland, and when Clinton won the election, Morrison alternately praised him and held his feet to the fire, as needed. In Northern Ireland, he helped the United States be seen as a honest broker available to all sides.

Conor O'Clery

The veteran journalist was the *Irish Times*'s Washington correspondent in the years when Bill Clinton was changing American policy on Northern Ireland. O'Clery's fine eyewitness account of events large and small, released in 1996, was called *Daring Diplomacy* in the United States and *The Greening of the White House* in Ireland.

Niall O'Dowd

O'Dowd was an Irish immigrant, once illegal, who became the publisher of the influential *Irish Voice* newspaper and *Irish America* magazine. One of the most important figures in the Irish American push for peace, he was the impresario of the successful visit of the unofficial American peacemakers in 1993, and he selected Bruce Morrison as the group's political leader and spokesman. He also became an important and trusted intermediary between Gerry Adams and the White House, a crucial function that contributed greatly to the success of Clinton's new American policy on Northern Ireland.

Gerry O'Hara / Gearóid O hEára

O'Hara was a Sinn Féin official in Derry whose presence led the Royal Ulster Constabulary to stop the car he was driving and hold him and his American guests, including Congressman Morrison, at gunpoint in 1987. He later became a member of the board of the new Northern Ireland Policing Board.

Ian Paisley

Paisley, politically extreme and vehemently anti-Catholic, was a Presbyterian minister and leader of the breakaway Democratic Unionist Party. He was so relentless in his opposition to peace proposals that he became known as Dr. No. But in 2007, when DUP became the top unionist party, Paisley became first minister, with Sinn Féin's Martin McGuinness serving as deputy first minister. The two men would go on to govern effectively and with surprising conviviality; when Paisley died in 2014, McGuinness grieved the loss of a true friend.

Jonathan Powell

Powell was one of the British diplomats with whom Morrison met after Clinton's election to inform them of the new Northern Ireland policy Clinton had promised and urge them to regard it helpful, not intrusive. Later, in 1997, Powell became Tony Blair's chief of staff and was deeply involved in the peace process.

Dennis Prebensen

Prebensen was an Irish American activist who lived in Morrison's congressional district. In 1987, he invited his congressman to see the situation in Northern Ireland for himself, and when they were in Derry, he, his congressman, and Gerry O'Hara were held at gunpoint by the RUC for the better part of an hour.

Jackie Redpath

Redpath was a longtime unionist community worker and is the head of the Greater Shankill Partnership, a community-led organization in Belfast focusing on education, jobs, housing, and neighborhood renewal. He met with the American delegation headed by Morrison in 1993 and he helped them meet with a small group of loyalists who had been active in the paramilitary organization UVF.

Janet Reno

As Bill Clinton's Attorney General, she opposed issuance of a US visa to Gerry Adams.

Albert Reynolds

Reynolds, a successful businessman who was sure that there was always a way to negotiate a solution to a tough conflict, was prime minister of Ireland from 1992 to 1994. Advancing the peace process was a high priority for him when he took office, and he forged a bond with British prime minister John Major that led to the Downing Street Declaration in late 1993, in which the British and Irish agreed that the future of Northern Ireland would be determined by those who lived there. Reynolds played a pivotal role in the success of the peace process.

Mary Robinson

Irish president Mary Robinson served from 1990 to 1997. She was the head of state, which gave her no substantive governmental role, but she knew how to send a message through symbols: Pictures of her shaking hands with Gerry Adams in the summer of 1993 gave his legitimacy an important boost. Robinson later became U.N. Human Rights Commissioner.

George Schwab

Schwab was a CUNY professor and head of the American Committee on Foreign Policy. When Gerry Adams received a US visa to attend the peace conference that organization convened, he rode from JFK to Manhattan with Schwab, and they found they had plenty in common.

Jean Kennedy Smith

Not long after Smith became US ambassador to Ireland in 1993, she boldly and effectively pushed for a new American policy on Northern Ireland—to the considerable displeasure of the State Department. When change got closer, she pushed harder. She was the sister of a president and two senators, but on Northern Ireland, she was entirely her own woman.

Nancy Soderberg

Soderberg was Bill Clinton's campaign foreign policy advisor in 1992 and then deputy assistant to the president for National Security Affairs from 1993 to 1997. Although she initially had her doubts about the new policy Clinton had promised, in time she came to accept, as Bruce Morrison urged, that engaging with Sinn Féin was the way to move the IRA away from warfare. Soderberg was instrumental in the success of Clinton's new policy. She always said that she didn't care whether Northern Ireland joined the Republic or stayed British; she just wanted the killing to stop.

Gusty Spence

Spence was a UVF man who came to believe while in prison that loyalists should practice politics instead of warfare. He led the group that met in secret with Morrison and the other Americans in 1993, which changed their view of the loyalist community. In 1994, Spence led the way to the loyalist ceasefire.

John Taylor

He was an Ulster Unionist Party official who helped party leader David Trimble accept the final draft the Good Friday Agreement.

David Trimble

Trimble headed the UUP from 1995 to 2005 and was in office during the negotiations that led to the Good Friday Agreement. His decision to accept the agreement draft as it stood after the negotiations had run out the clock on Mitchell's deadline was the crucial last step to final agreement. Trimble won the Nobel Peace Prize in 1998 and was elected first minister in the new government a few months later.

Gerry Vinton

Vinton was a former UVF man who arranged and participated in the 1993 secret meeting between loyalists and Morrison and the other Americans, which changed the Americans' view of the loyalist community.

GLOSSARY

Northern Ireland Political and Paramilitary Terms and Organizations

Alliance Party

The small party that has attempted to appeal to both populations. It became the fifth-largest party in Northern Ireland, supported by less than 10 percent of the voters.

Democratic Unionist Party (DUP)

Now the leading unionist party supported by the Protestant majority, it began as a radical breakaway party led by Ian Paisley.

Irish Republican Army (IRA)

Its incarnation during the Troubles was the Provisional Irish Republican Army, and it carried out the armed republican cause. It was closely allied with Sinn Féin and ultimately accepted Gerry Adams's urging that it replace armed struggle with politics. Splinter groups claiming to be the only ones left who remain true believers, bestowing names like Real IRA upon themselves, carried out violent actions after Good Friday, including the Omagh bombing that killed twenty-nine people, but they have been consistently denounced by Sinn Féin and what remains of the IRA.

Loyalists

During the Troubles, they were the more extreme members of the Protestant majority, who were more willing to take to the streets and supply manpower to the loyalist paramilitary forces.

Nationalists

During the Troubles, they were the more moderate members of the Catholic minority. They had led the nonviolent opposition to the pervasive discrimination against Catholics. They typically supported the unification of Ireland, but they wanted it done through peaceful means.

Republicans

Those Catholics who were generally more willing to support the armed struggle for reunification of Ireland being waged by the IRA, or at least accepted that reunification might only be possible through military force.

Sinn Féin

Long led by Gerry Adams, during the Troubles it was the smaller and more pro-republican party supported by the Catholic community. It was closely allied with the IRA, but in the mid-eighties Adams began a strategy of seeking to achieve republican goals through politics and to persuade the IRA to turn to politics instead of warfare. Its mastery of grass roots politics has made it the leading party supported by the Catholic community.

Social Democratic and Labour Party (SDLP)

Long led by John Hume, it was the leading party supported by the Catholic community during the Troubles and was more moderate than Sinn Féin, which has now overtaken it within the Catholic community.

Ulster Defence Association (UDA)

It was the most vicious loyalist paramilitary force.

Ulster Unionist Party (UUP)

Throughout the Troubles, it was the largest party supported by the Protestant majority and was generally more moderate than the radical breakaway DUP, which is currently the leading Protestant party.

Ulster Volunteer Force (UVF)

It was the loyalist paramilitary force that the great David Ervine said was "returning the serve." Loyalist paramilitary men who turned to politics during the Troubles were typically UVF.

Unionists

The vast majority of unionists are Protestants and they want Northern Ireland to remain part of the UK. They have largely asserted their power through politics and control of civic institutions.

Irish American Organizations

Americans for a New Irish Agenda (ANIA)

This organization succeeded Irish Americans for Clinton-Gore. Headed by Bruce Morrison, ANIA had the express purpose of turning Clinton's campaign pledges on Northern Ireland into American policy.

Irish Northern Aid Committee (Noraid)

Noraid was for many years the strongest Irish American voice on Northern Ireland. Many of its members were sympathetic to and very supportive of the IRA. The group claimed their fundraising was in order to send money to widows and orphans of the fallen, but the authorities insisted that much of the money went to buying weapons for the IRA.

INDEX

A

Act of Union, 32–33

Adair, Johnny "Mad Dog," 121–122

Adams, Gerry

  ballot box strategy of, 38–39

  Bill Clinton's greeting of, 181–182

  contributions to peace process, 231

  and Good Friday Agreement, 219

  John Hume's meetings with, 21, 38–39, 52

  influence on IRA and Sinn Féin, 203–204, 226

  and IRA ceasefires, 107–108, 147–148, 194

  at Kashmir Road meeting, 182–184

  as local politician, 181–182, 242

  on Mitchell report, 192

  Bruce Morrison's impression of, 9

  at National Committee on American Foreign Policy conference, 142, 143

  New York visit of, 139–143

  Niall O'Dowd's meetings with, 67

  on Omagh bombing, 228

  Jean Kennedy Smith and, 113–114

  and "South California IRA," 137–138

  unofficial peacemakers' meetings with, 76, 92–93, 103

  US access for, 172–174

  US visa for, 48–50, 52, 54–55, 59, 64, 73, 75, 116–117, 121–145

Ad Hoc Committee on Irish Affairs, xiv, 6–9

adopted child syndrome, 80

AFL-CIO, 12

Ahern, Bertie, 119, 215, 217, 218, 229, 232

Alderdice, John, 142

Alliance Party, 142, 241

all-party talks, 209–222

  American, loyalist, and republican views of, 210–211

  American-quality of, 212–213

  Clinton administration's support for, 171–178

  and drafting of Good Friday Agreement, 215–221

  importance of Sinn Féin in, 197–199

  Bruce Morrison on, 214–215

  and new IRA ceasefire, 209–210

  preconditions for, 160–163, 168, 169, 195–196

twin-track approach to, 175–178

American government, 194–195, 199–203. *see also* Clinton, Bill, and administration; United States

Americans for a New Irish Agenda (ANIA), 57–62, 128, 129

Anglo-Irish Agreement, 38

Anglo-Irish Treaty (1921), 36

ANIA. *see* Americans for a New Irish Agenda

Annesley, Hugh, 203, 204

Apple, R. W., 187

Atlantic Philanthropies, 70

B

Baker, James, 26

Baldwin, Ted, 18

ballot box strategy, 38–39

Barry, Bill, 141

Begin, Menachem, 141

Begley, Thomas, 121, 122

Belfast, Northern Ireland
  Bill Clinton's trip to, 179–180, 184–186
  Jackie Redpath on, 93–94
  response to Good Friday Agreement in, 232–233
  during unofficial peacemakers' trip, 81–83
  view of IRA ceasefire in, 155

Belfast Telegraph, 84–85

Biaggi, Mario, 7

Blair, Cherie, 229

Blair, Tony, 164, 206–208, 210, 215, 217–220, 229, 232, 236

Bloody Sunday Massacre, 4, 37

Boyne, Battle of, 32, 43

Brabourne, Baroness, 37

British army, 30, 69, 82

British embassy, 60–62

British Foreign Office, 184

British government. *see also* Great Britain
  and Gerry Adams's access to US, 173–174
  "exploratory talks" of Sinn Féin and, 176
  importance of all-party talks to, 197–199
  and IRA ceasefire by, 157–170
  loyalist paramilitaries' response to ceasefire vs., 169–170
  meetings of IRA with, 130
  and Mitchell report by, 194
  opposition to Gerry Adams's visa by, 134–137, 139
  peace talks among approved parties by, 204–206
  and "permanent" ceasefire, 158–160
  preconditions for all-party talks from, 160–163, 168, 169
  previous involvement in Northern Ireland by, 166–167
  protection of Prime Minister's position in, 163–166
  resistance to Bill Clinton's visit from, 177–178
  during the Troubles, 29–30
  warfare between Irish and, 30–37

British Irish Association meeting, 111–120

Brown, Jerry, 26, 46–47, 51

Bruton, John, 113, 119–120, 174, 177–178

Bush, George H. W., 14, 26, 43, 45, 52, 53, 56

C

Cahill, Joseph, 153–154

Cameron, David, 241

Canada, Fenian Brotherhood's invasion of, 34

Canary Wharf attack (1995), 193–194, 197–199

Carey, Hugh, 91

Carson, Edward, 34

Carter, Jimmy, 49

Castlereagh Holding Centre, 3

Castro, Fidel, 104

Catholics, 2, 7, 29–31, 41

ceasefires
IRA (*see* IRA ceasefires)
loyalist, 169–170

Charles, Prince of Wales, 229

Charles I, 31

Christopher, Warren, 135, 136, 138

Cibes, William, 17

Clinton, Bill, and administration, 6
and Gerry Adams/Sinn Féin's access to US, 172–174
and Gerry Adams's visa, 64, 125–126, 135–136, 138–139, 144
on British response to IRA ceasefire, 165, 167
and Joe Cahill's visa, 154
contributions to peace process by, 232
economic conference sponsored by, 174–175
economic envoy to Northern Ireland, 172
and end of IRA ceasefire, 195, 199–200
and Ray Flynn's canceled trip, 65–67

follow through on campaign promises of, 57–67, 116–117, 125–126, 173
and Good Friday Agreement, 218–219, 222
and 1994 IRA mortar attacks, 146
and Irish American Round Table, 57–62
Irish-American support of, 44–45
Irish Americans' views of, 64–65
and John Major, 53–54, 174, 179
and Bruce Morrison, 39, 41, 48, 51, 84
new Northern Ireland policy, 25–27, 44–51, 53–56
Northern Ireland visit, 175–188
on Omagh bombing, 227, 229
presidential campaign of, xiii, 39, 41–56
Albert Reynolds's opposition to peace envoy of, 62–64
support for all-party talks by, 171–178
and unofficial peacemakers' trip, 80–81, 104–105, 106–108

Clinton, Hillary Rodham, 6, 25, 180, 229

Collins, Michael, 36

communication, 108–109

Connecticut gubernatorial campaign of 1990, 15–19

Connolly, James, 35

Conservative and Unionist Party, 163

Conway Mill event, 102–103

Corrigan, Mairéad, 38

Craig, James, 86

Creighton, Jimmy, 245
Cromwell, Oliver, 31
Crowe, William J., 135–136

D

Daring Diplomacy (O'Clery), 232
Dearie, John, xiii
de Chastelain, John, 189, 204, 215,
    216, 239
decommissioning, of weapons. *see*
    Weapons decommissioning
DeLauro, Rosa, 19
Democratic Unionist Party (DUP),
    76, 77, 217–218
Department of Justice, 134
Derry, Northern Ireland, 1–9
de Valera, Éamon, 35, 36
Dinkins, David, 124, 126
Dodd, Christopher, 136
Donaghy, Gerry, 4
Downey, Roma, 145
Downing Street Declaration, 45,
    130–131, 135, 147, 157, 166,
    167, 170
Dublin, Ireland, 71–72
Dukakis, Michael, 26
Dunlop, John, 116
DUP. *see* Democratic Unionist
    Party

E

Easter Rising, 35
economic change, 90, 91, 115,
    132–133
economic development, 49,
    174–175
economic envoy, 172
Edwards, Anne, 180, 184–185

Eire, 36
elections, in Northern Ireland,
    190–192, 196–197, 200–201
Elizabeth II, 229, 241
Empey, Reg, 220
Enniskillen bombing (1987), 70
Ervine, David, 97–101, 244–245
Europa Hotel, 186

F

Federal Bureau of Investigation
    (FBI), 56, 134, 135
Federal Housing Finance Board,
    175, 232–233
Feeney, Chuck, 70–71, 125, 145,
    152, 171, 172, 194, 195, 213
Fenian Brotherhood, 34
Flowers, Gennifer, 44, 46
Flynn, Ray, 44, 65–67, 71
Flynn, William "Bill," 110, 125, 130,
    132, 140, 142, 145, 152, 169,
    195, 213
Foley, Thomas, 7, 133, 134, 136,
    138, 145, 232
Friends of Ireland, xiv, 6–7
Frost, David, 194

G

Galvin, Martin, 50, 128–129
Galway, James, 145
Gearan, Mark, 184
Giuliani, Rudy, 172
Glencairn meeting, 42, 233
Good Friday Agreement, 223–233
    and Downing Street Declaration,
    131
    drafting of, 215–221
    international recognition of,
    230–232

and Omagh bombing, 227–230
ratification of, 223–226
response in Belfast to, 232–233
Gore, Al, 172
Grant, Hugh, 135
Grasso, Ella, 15
Great Britain
Gerry Adams's visa and political
events in, 126–127
political process of US vs., 212
US relationship with, xiii, 24–25,
136–137, 179
and US involvement in Northern
Ireland, 24
Great Hunger (Great Famine),
33–34
The Greening of the White House
(O'Clery), 232

H
Haass, Richard, 242
Hamill, Catherine, 180–181
Henry II, 30
Henry VIII, 30–31
Herndon, Joe, 85
Higgins, Michael, 241
Hispanic Congressional Caucus, 12
Hitchens, Peter, 172
Holkeri, Harri, 189, 204, 215, 216
Holy Cross demonstrations,
238–239
Home Rule Act, 34
Howell, Ted, 208, 209
Hume, John, 145–146, 167
Gerry Adams's meetings with,
21, 38–39, 52
American influence of, 52, 73,
127, 133

Bill Clinton's meeting with, 183,
186
at National Committee on American Foreign Policy conference,
142, 143
Nobel Peace Prize for, 230
at Northern Ireland Forum for
Political Dialogue, 205
and Gerry O'Hara, 4–5
on Omagh bombing, 229
on response to Mitchell report, 191
support for Gerry Adams's visa
from, 132–134, 230
support for elections from, 200
unofficial peacemakers' meeting
with, 90–92
Hussein, Saddam, 26
Hutchinson, Billy, 97–101, 213
Hyland, Christopher, 44–45, 58, 59

I
Ickes, Harold, 50
Immigration Act (1990), 11–15, 74
Immigration Subcommittee of the
House Judiciary Committee, 11
International Body on Decom-
missioning, 203–204. *see also*
Mitchell report
IRA. *see* Irish Republican Army
IRA ceasefires
of 1994, 145–155
Gerry Adams's ability to produce,
147–148
and all-party talks, 209–210
American work to reestablish,
199–203
announcement of, 154–155,
157–158

British response to, 157–170
end of, 193–208
for Ray Flynn's trip, 65, 67
Kashmir Road meeting on state
of, 182–184
and Mitchell report, 189
reestablishment of, 197
and unofficial American peacemakers, 71–72, 107–108, 120,
148–153
and visa for Gerry Adams, 135,
139, 144–145
and visa for Joe Cahill, 153–154
and White House St. Patrick's
Day party, 145–147
Irish, warfare of British and, 30–37
Irish America, 22
Irish American Forum, 47–51
Irish American Round Table, 57–62
Irish Americans
on Bill Clinton and administration, 27, 47–53, 64–65,
129–130
importance of Northern Ireland
to, xiii
interest in immigration reform
bill, 12
political power of, 34
self-image of, 24
support for Gerry Adams's visa
by, 125–129
support for new Northern Ireland policy by, 23–24, 44–45
Irish-Americans for Clinton-Gore,
xiv, 57
Irish Citizen Army, 35
Irish Civil War, 36
Irish Free State, 36
Irish News, 85

Irish Northern Aid Committee
(Noraid), 7, 128, 145, 153
Irish Peace Process, 39
Irish Republic, 35
Irish Republican Army (IRA)
and Ad Hoc Committee on Irish
Affairs, 7
British government's meetings
with, 130
British view of, 24
Bill Clinton's analysis of, 199–200
creation of, 30
decommissioning of, 228, 239, 240
Enniskillen bombing by, 70
in Irish War of Independence, 36
Ted Kennedy's relationship with,
132–133
loyalist paramilitaries vs., 95–97
John Major's understanding of,
203–204
mortar attacks on Heathrow
Airport by, 146
power of, 197–199
and RUC, 2
and Shankill bombing, 121–123
and Sinn Féin, 1–2, 92
Special Category Status in prison
for members of, 37
stand down of, 240
as terrorist organization, 105
during the Troubles, 37
Irish Voice, 22–23
Irish Volunteers, 34
Irish War of Independence, 36

J
James II, 32
James VI of Scotland (James I of
England), 31

Jamison, Joe, 150
Jefferson-Jackson-Bailey dinner, 19
John Paul II, pope, 76
Joint Declaration, 159

K
Kashmir Road meeting, 182–184
Keaton, Michael, 145
Kelly, Sean, 121
Kennedy, Edward "Ted," 14, 52, 73,
    78, 91, 132–134, 136, 145, 146,
    172, 194
Kennedy, John F., 15, 26
Kerry, Bob, 135
King, Peter, 140

L
Labour Party, 164, 206–207
Lake, Tony, 135, 145, 176
Larry King Live, 142
Larsen, Don, 110
Lawlor, Richard, 7–8
Lenahan, Bill, 150
Lieberman, Joe, 16
loyalist paramilitaries, 95–101,
    169–170, 206
loyalists
    on all-party talks, 210–211
    in Belfast, 82–83
    beliefs of, 29
    on Bill Clinton's Northern
        Ireland visit, 180–181
    decommissioning preconditions
        for, 161
    unofficial peacemakers' meetings
        with, 92–101
    views of British by, 43
Luther, Martin, 30

M
Mackie International, 180
Maginnis, Ken, 220
Major, John
    and Tony Blair, 206–207
    and Bill Clinton, 53–54, 174, 179
    and Bill Clinton's Northern
        Ireland trip, 189
    and Downing Street Declaration,
        130
    and end of IRA ceasefire,
        195–197
    and IRA ceasefire, 151
    and IRA ceasefires, 201–204
    and loyalist ceasefire, 169–170,
        173–174
    and loyalist paramilitaries, 206
    on Mitchell report, 191–192
    reception of Mitchell report by,
        190
    and Albert Reynolds, 39, 62, 72,
        245
    on twin-track approach, 177–178
    understanding of Sinn Féin and
        IRA by, 203–204
    unofficial peacemakers' influence
        on, 171
Making Peace (Mitchell), 205
Making Sense of the Troubles
    (McKittrick and McVea), 191
Man and Superman (Shaw), 33
Mary II, 32
Maskey, Alex, 211
Maxwell, Paul, 37
Mayhew, Sir Patrick, 86–88, 173
Mazzoli, Roman, 13
McBride Principles, 49, 50
McCormack, Inez, 112, 115–117,
    225

McCurry, Mike, 46, 49–50,
134–135
McGimpsey, Christopher, 42,
77–79, 89, 90
McGrory, Mary, 187–188
McGuinness, Martin, 85, 92, 228,
240, 242
team and friendship with Ian
Paisley, 240, 245
McKittrick, David, 109–110,
118–119, 191, 241
McMichael, Gary, 211
McVea, David, 191
media coverage
of Gerry Adams US visa, 134
of Bill Clinton's Northern Ireland
visit, 187–188
of unofficial peacemakers' trip,
84–88, 92–93
MI5, 83, 243
Mitchell, George, 101, 145
and Gerry Adams's influence on
IRA, 203–204
at all-party talks, 211–215
contributions to peace process
by, 232
as economic envoy to Northern
Ireland, 172
and end of IRA ceasefire, 194,
195
and Good Friday Agreement,
215–221
at peace talks among British-
approved parties, 204–206
and twin-track approach, 176,
177
Mitchell report, 189–192
Moakley, Joe, 13–14
Molyneaux, Jim, 77–78

Moore, Richard A., 43
Morrison, Bruce, 145. *see also*
unofficial peacemakers' trips
to Northern Ireland
on Gerry Adams, 140, 148, 226
and all-party talks, 209, 212,
214–215
on ANIA, 60
background of, 5–8
in Belfast after the peace,
232–233, 236, 244
at British Irish Association meeting, 111–120
on British response ceasefire,
160, 161, 163–165, 168
on change, 112
and Bill Clinton/Clinton administration, 39, 41, 48, 51–52, 65,
84, 175, 182, 187, 200
Connecticut gubernatorial campaign of, 15–19
on Downing Street Declaration,
131
on economic conference,
174–175
on elections, 201
on end of IRA ceasefire, 194, 196
on Chuck Feeney, 70
on Good Friday Agreement,
223–225
on John Hume, 90, 91, 134
immigration reform bill of,
11–15
and IRA ceasefires, 151,
154–155, 182–184, 201–204,
207–208
and Irish American activists,
64–65, 125–128
legacy of, 21–22

on 1992 New York Democratic
primary, 47
on Nobel Peace Prize, 230–232
Northern Ireland analysis by,
45–46
Northern Ireland visits of, 41–44
Niall O'Dowd's meetings with,
21–27
on Omagh bombing, 227–229
on paramilitary groups, 96–97
political projects of late 1980s, 9
on Albert Reynolds, 63–64
RUC stop of, 1–9
and Sinn Féin, 102–103, 197–199
and Nancy Soderberg, 52–53, 195
on Margaret Thatcher, 37
on the Troubles, 36–37
on US visa for Gerry Adams,
126–127, 139, 140, 143, 144
UVF meeting with, 98–100
on White House St. Patrick's Day
party, 146
Morrison, Drew, 208
Morrison, Nancy, 207–208, 235, 236
Morrison, Van, 185
Morrison visas, xiv, 23, 44, 48
Mountbatten, Louis "Dickie," 37, 229
Mountbatten, Nicholas, 37
Moynihan, Daniel Patrick, 91, 133,
146
My Life (Clinton), 181

N

National Committee on American
Foreign Policy, 130–132,
142–143
nationalists, 29, 82–83, 225
National Security Agency (NSA), 172

National Security Council (NSC),
138
new American Northern Ireland
policy, 39
at British Irish Association meeting, 117
Clinton's letter outlining, 54–55
in general election, 53–56
Irish American support for,
44–45
and 1992 New York Democratic
primary, 45–51
New Haven Legal Assistance, 6
Newman, Paul, 145, 146
New York Democratic primary
(1992), 45–51
New York Times, 134
Nixon, Richard, 17
Nobel Peace Prize, 230–232
Noraid. *see* Irish Northern Aid
Committee
northern Catholic rebellion (1641),
31
Northern Ireland
after Irish Civil War, 36
in British politics, 164
Bill Clinton's visit to, 175–188
creation of, 29
economic conference on invest-
ing in, 174–175
economic envoy to, 172
Ray Flynn's canceled trip to,
65–67
Bruce Morrison's visit to, 41–44
new elections in, 176
power of politicians in, 165–166
in 1980s, 2
violence during the Troubles in,
30

Northern Ireland Civil Rights Association, 29
Northern Ireland Forum for Political Dialogue, 205
Northern Ireland Policing Board, 226
NSC (National Security Council), 138, 172

O

O'Brien, Conan, 145
O'Cleireacain, Carol, 50
O'Cleireacain, Seamus, 50
O'Clery, Conor, 132, 133, 138, 167, 176, 232
O'Connell, Daniel, 33
O'Dowd, Niall, 37, 145, 213, 233. *see also* unofficial peacemakers' trips to Northern Ireland
    Gerry Adams's meeting with, 67
    and end of IRA ceasefire, 195
    and Ray Flynn's canceled trip, 65–67
    and Christopher Hyland, 44–45
    Christopher Hyland's meeting with, 58, 59
    and IRA ceasefire, 150
    and Irish American support for Bill Clinton, 52, 53
    at Kashmir Road meeting, 182–184
    Bruce Morrison's meeting with, 21–27
    and US involvement in Northern Ireland policy, 22–25
    and US visa for Gerry Adams, 125, 130, 137–138
O'Dwyer, Paul, 145
O'Hara, Gerry (Gearóid O hEára), 1–9, 226

O'Leary, Brenda, 229
Omagh bombing, 227–230
O'Neill, Bill, 15, 16, 19
O'Neill, Nikki, 19
O'Neill, Terrence, 30
O'Neill, Tip, 91
Orange Order, 32
O'Rourke, Kelvin, 229

P

Paisley, Ian, 76, 98, 118, 181, 186, 217–218, 231, 240, 245
    team and friendship with Martin McGuinness, 240, 245
Parades Commission, 238
parallel decommissioning, 190–192, 196
Parks, Rosa, 172
Parnell, Charles Stewart, 34
Patten, Christopher, 238
peace envoy, 59
    Bill Clinton's campaign promise of, 48–51, 54, 172
    lack of, 222
    Albert Reynolds's opposition to, 62–64
    in unofficial peacemakers' trip, 75, 88–90, 106–107
peace talks among British-approved parties (1996), 204–206
Peace Train, 77
peace walls, 82
Pearse, Padraig, 35
"permanent" ceasefire, 158–160, 171
Perot, Ross, 46, 53, 56
Pinochet, Augusto, 3
Plantation of Ulster, 31
political change, economic and, 90, 91, 115, 132–133

Potato Famine, 33–34
Powell, Johnathan, 61, 134–135, 220, 236
Prebensen, Dennis, 3, 4, 8
Presidential Medal of Freedom, 232
Proclamation of the Irish Republic, 35
Protestants, 31

Q

Qaddafi, Muammar el-, 153
Quayle, Dan, 43

R

Reagan Democrats, 12, 27, 44, 47
Real IRA, 227
Red Hand Commando, 95
Redpath, Jackie, 93–95, 122
referendum campaign, Good Friday Agreement, 223–225
religion, in warfare between British and Irish, 30–31
Reno, Janet, 138
republicans
    after Canary Wharf attack, 197–198
    on all-party talks, 210–211
    in Belfast, 82–83
    beliefs of, 29
    on Bill Clinton's Northern Ireland visit, 180–181
Republic of Ireland, 36
"revolutionary patience," of Sinn Féin, 198–199
Reynolds, Albert, 39, 108, 119, 145
    on Gerry Adams's visa, 132
    and American peace envoy, 62–64
    on Joseph Cahill's visa, 153–154
    on decommissioning precondition, 202–203
    and Downing Street Declaration, 130
    and John Major, 62, 72, 166, 167, 245
    resignation of, 174
    unofficial peacemakers' meeting with, 72–73, 151
Rising Sun Halloween shooting, 122
Robinson, Mary, 43, 72, 93, 103
Robinson, Peter, 183, 243
Rodell, Susannah, 134
Rowland, John, 16, 17
Royal Ulster Constabulary (RUC)
    and Gerry Adams's influence on IRA, 203, 204
    and Good Friday Agreement, 226
    Bruce Morrison and Gerry O'Hara's stop by, 1–9
    in the Troubles, 30
    and unofficial American peacemakers' trip, 69, 82
Roybal, Ed, 12–14
RUC. *see* Royal Ulster Constabulary

S

Salvadoran refugees, 12
Sandinistas, 104
Sands, Bobby, 37
Saville Commission, 240–241
Schwab, George, 140–142
SDLP. *see* Social Democratic and Labour Party
self-determination, 224–225
Shankill Road bombing, 121–125, 180–181
Shaw, George Bernard, 33

Simpson, Alan, 12–14

Sinn Féin
Gerry Adams's influence on, 226
at all-party talks, 210
and British Irish Association
meeting, 111
decommissioning preconditions
for, 161–162
and Downing Street Declaration,
147
in elections, 200–201
"exploratory talks" of British and,
176
and Ray Flynn's canceled trip to
Northern Ireland, 65–67
founding of, 35–36
and Friends of Ireland, 7
and Good Friday Agreement, 218
and IRA ceasefires, 150, 197,
207–208
and John Major, 159, 168–169, 203
in Bruce Morrison's analysis of
Northern Ireland, 45
on Omagh bombing, 228
and peace talks among British-
approved parties, 204
power of, 197–199
preconditions for, 195–196
protocol of, for RUC stops, 3
revolutionary patience of,
198–199
and SDLP, 133
as terrorist organization, 1–2, 105
unofficial peacemakers' meeting
with, 71–72, 76, 80, 87, 92, 93,
102–106, 149
US access for, 172–174

Smith, Jean Kennedy, 73–74,
112–115, 132, 153–154

Smith, John, 164

Social Democratic and Labour
Party (SDLP), 4–5, 133, 200,
201, 205

Soderberg, Nancy, 59, 145
and Gerry Adams's visa, 126–
129, 135–137, 139
on British response to IRA ceasefire, 167
on Joseph Cahill's visa, 154
in Clinton presidential campaign,
51–53
and Bill Clinton's Northern Ireland visit, 175, 176
on Chris Hyland's outreach
efforts, 58
and IRA ceasefire, 144, 149,
195
on preconditions for all-party
talks, 173

"South California IRA" bomb
threats, 137–138

special envoy to Northern Ireland,
xiv

Spence, Gusty, 97–101, 169

Spring, Dick, 151, 174

St. Andrews Agreement, 240

St. Patrick's Day Shamrock ceremony (1996), 199–200

State Department, 56, 117, 134,
135, 136–137

Steinberg, James, 209–210

Stephanopoulos, George, 135, 136

Stern Gang, 140–141

Sterrett, David, 180

Stormont Estate, 86

Strand Two, 216–217

Sullivan Principles, 49

surrender, 159, 168–169

T

Taoiseach, 36

Taylor, John, 76–77, 220

terrorists, 45, 105, 152, 159

Thatcher, Margaret, 37, 38, 166, 167

Toad's Place, 15–16

Trimble, David, 76, 89, 176,
    186–187, 191, 216–219,
    230–231

the Troubles, 2, 29–39
    Belfast during, 83
    interest in peaceful resolution of,
        38–39
    start of, 29–30
    violence during, 30, 37–38, 83
    and warfare between Irish and
        British, 30–37

Tsongas, Paul, 26

twin-track approach to all-party
    talks, 175–178

U

Ulster Freedom Fighters (UFF), 95

Ulster Unionist Party (UUP), 42,
    76–79, 84, 88–90, 120, 220

Ulster Volunteer Force (UVF), 34,
    95–101

unconditional ceasefire, 168

unionists
    in Belfast, 82–83
    beliefs of, 29
    decommissioning preconditions
        of, 162–163
    power of, 163–164, 165
    and ratification of Good Friday
        Agreement, 224–225
    unofficial peacemakers' meetings
        with, 92–101
    view of British by, 43

Union Jack controversy, 241–242

United Kingdom, 32–33, 175–188.
    see also Great Britain

United Nations, 174

United States. *see also* new Ameri-
    can Northern Ireland policy;
    US visas
    access of Sinn Féin and Gerry
        Adams to, 172–174
    Great Britain's relationship with,
        xiii, 24–25, 136–137, 179
    involvement in Northern Ireland
        policy, 22–25
    political process in Great Britain
        vs., 212
    support for IRA ceasefire from,
        150
    views of all-party talks in,
        210–211

United States Chamber of Com-
    merce, 12

unlimited ceasefire, 151–155,
    157–158

unofficial American peacemak-
    ers' trips to Northern Ireland,
    69–110
    to break stalemate after IRA
        ceasefire, 171
    Clinton administration's policy
        following, 106–107
    conditions in Belfast during,
        81–83
    Dublin meetings preceding,
        71–72
    Chuck Feeney and William J.
        Flynn on, 70–71
    focus/purpose of, 75–76, 80–81
    John Hume's meeting with,
        90–92

Sir Patrick Mayhew's meeting
  with, 86–88
media coverage of, 84–88,
  92–93
Bruce Morrison as spokesman
  for, 74
Bruce Morrison's confidence
  about, 79–80
prior to 1994 IRA ceasefire,
  148–153
Sinn Féin's meeting with,
  102–106
unionist and loyalist meetings
  with, 92–101
UUP meeting with, 76–79,
  88–90
US visas
  for Gerry Adams, 48–50, 52,
    54–55, 59, 64, 73, 75, 116–117,
    121–145
  for Joe Cahill, 153–154
  Morrison, xiv, 23, 44, 48
UUP. *see* Ulster Unionist Party
UVF (Ulster Volunteer Force), 34,
  95–101

V
Vinton, Gerry, 95, 97–101
violence, 30, 37–38, 83, 104–106
visas. *see* US visas

W
warfare, Irish and British, 30–37
Washington 3, 173, 174, 178
weapons decommissioning
  Irish government on, 174, 178
  Mitchell report on, 189–192
  as precondition for all-party
    talks, 161–163, 171, 173–174,
    176–178, 195–196, 202–203
Weicker, Lowell, 16–17
White House St. Patrick's Day par-
    ties, 145–147, 173
William III, 32
Williams, Betty, 38
Wilson, Jim, 76, 78–79, 88–89
Wolfe Tone, Theobald, 32
Woodward, Joanne, 146
World War I, 34

Y
Yeats, William Butler, 119

AUTHOR'S NOTE AND
ACKNOWLEDGMENTS

The story of the Irish Peace Process is ultimately a story of heroes—very human heroes chasing peace after thirty years of the Troubles and 800 years of conflict, much of it violent, between the British and the Irish. Many of those heroes appear in the pages of *Peacerunner,* but some do not because their stories didn't intersect with Bruce Morrison's in a way that brought them into this book. These come immediately to mind: Father Alec Reid, a tireless go-between who connected the republicans who wanted politics instead of war with the wider world and whose witnessing of the IRA decommissioning process greatly enhanced its credibility; the Rev. Harold Good, a Methodist who also witnessed and attested to the IRA decommissioning; and the Rev. Roy Magee, a Presbyterian who worked hard to help bring about the loyalist ceasefire. Hillary Clinton's work to encourage and empower women in Northern Ireland to make their own voices heard and take an even more active role in their land's future, especially in the months and years following Good Friday, was very important and helpful and deserves acknowledgment outside the overheated world of presidential campaigns.

The story of the peace process is also the story of politics practiced with bravery and determination to make things better. If this book seems like a valentine to the practice of politics, that's because it is. In societies more or less democratic, there are basically two ways to end wars: by one side defeating the other militarily, or through politics.

Diplomats, academics, religious leaders, NGOs, and media can help, but they can't do the political deal. Northern Ireland, in the words of the great Inez McCormack, ultimately chose dialogue and deal, and they, and the world, are better off for it.

————

Peacerunner had its earliest glimmerings in 2010 when Tim McMillin confronted me at a Gettysburg College reunion: "You said you were going to write the Great American Novel."

The absurdity struck me immediately: "What? Are you sure that's what I said? I don't have any idea how to do that."

But I was lucky: Tim's challenge got the wheels turning. I knew it wasn't going to be a novel, Great American or otherwise, but before the year was out, I was confident that the story in this book was worth telling.

I started interviewing Bruce Morrison and others and put together an outline and a first chapter. I reached out to David Kuhn and soon enough had a fine New York agent and, with the help of David and his associates Grant Ginder and Becky Sweren, a well-done proposal. Whether sending out the proposal on the eve of Hurricane Sandy had anything to do with it, I don't know, but we got dozens of rejections. Becky Sweren never said die, and by the summer of 2013, we had a nice publishing deal with BenBella. Publisher Glenn Yeffeth, who likes to think of himself as the swift mammal ready to grab what the dinosaurs drop, has been wise and wonderful throughout. Friends in the field tell me that the BenBella model is the future of book publishing.

In these improbable circumstances, the list of those to whom I'm indebted is long. It begins with Bruce Morrison, one of many heroes of the Irish Peace Process and the one I have been privileged to know and work with for more than forty years. Bill Clinton and Hillary Clinton have been enthusiastic about the project since its early days, and I am deeply grateful for their help and support. Niall O'Dowd and Nancy Soderberg were among the first I interviewed (and later peppered with endless follow-ups, random questions, and progress reports), and their generous availability and enthusiasm was a real boost early on. A further note about Niall O'Dowd, another wonderful peacerunner: He harnessed the idea of changing American policy on Northern Ireland to the idea of *Bill Clinton for President*, and he worked tirelessly to promote both causes. He made great connections on both sides of the Atlantic, and he chose Bruce Morrison to be the political leader and spokesman for the unofficial American peacemakers who journeyed to Northern Ireland in 1993. I don't know if Niall envisioned the brilliant political strategy—spanning years, never written down, only revealed piecemeal as needed—and the practice of politics at the highest and best level that are Morrison's Irish story, but he's the one who made the pick. And the rest is history—and *Peacerunner*.

Interviews long and short graciously given by Bruce Morrison, Bill Clinton, Tony Blair, George Mitchell, Richard Lawlor, Gerry O'Hara, Dennis Prebensen, Bill Flynn, Gerry Adams, Chris McGimpsey, Billy Hutchinson, Jackie Redpath, Gerry Vinton, Inez McCormack, Christopher Hyland, Nancy Morrison, Jonathan Powell, Paul Bew, George Schwab, Mike McCurry, Anne Edwards, and Carol O'Cleireacain have anchored *Peacerunner* in what really happened and given it the pulse of life.

Historians Joe Lee, director of Glucksman Ireland House at NYU, and Christine Kineally, director of the Great Hunger Museum at Quinnipiac University, were wonderful resources for this nonhistorian writing a true story. My own grappling with the job of writing a brief history of 800 years left me in awe, and very appreciative, of what real historians do. Chapter four of this book benefited enormously from their kind and generous help.

Others who helped along the way are a legion: Sheldon Messinger, my law office mate in the beginning stages of this frolic and detour, as lawyers call such things, was a wonderful sounding board and giver of good advice and great encouragement. Our secretary Concetta Ferrucci typed up hours of recorded interviews with great care and good cheer. Betsy Pittman and those working with her at the Dodd Center at the University of Connecticut, repository of Bruce Morrison's papers, were unfailingly helpful. The staffs at several Connecticut libraries—Yale's Sterling Memorial and the New Haven, Hamden, and Meriden public libraries—were equally helpful, especially Rebecca Starr at Meriden late on a Saturday afternoon. Whenever I called the Belfast public library or a newspaper in a smaller town, I found good people who really wanted to help me get the picture. The woman at police headquarters in Derry who giggled when I asked if the RUC kept records of encounters like the one at the beginning of the book gave me a special glimpse into those times. Joanne Murphy collected articles from Belfast newspapers that were unavailable in the United States and shipped them to me via Dropbox. When I went to Northern Ireland, Richard McAuley, at the wheel of his marvelously named Citroen *Picasso*, and his brother Martin gave me an extensive tour of Sinn Féin's Belfast, and Chris McGimpsey took me through his Belfast in his majestic right-hand-drive Chrysler 300. Chris and Jackie Redpath were especially helpful in helping me make contact with others I wanted to reach.

———

Daily newspapers and books providing relatively contemporaneous accounts of events leading up to, during, and after the peace process were invaluable. Standouts include *Endgame in Ireland and The Fight for Peace* by David McKittrick and Eamon Mallie, *Making Sense of the Troubles* by David McKittrick and David McVea, and Conor O'Clery's Washington-based while-it-was-happening account of Bill Clinton's entry into the peace process, called *Daring Diplomacy* in the United States and *The Greening of the White House* in Ireland. These men were there and paid careful attention. Their access and observations, backed by their extensive experience and wise and intimate knowledge of Northern Ireland and its history, were invaluable as I began writing the story told in this book. In addition, they encouraged me to make use, in the telling of this story, of what they had seen and the statements they had gathered in their own work. I am especially grateful for Conor's accounts of events and his wonderful vignettes from Washington and New York, including tales and writings of Mary McGrory. I am equally grateful for quotes David and his co-authors related from Albert Reynolds about why arms decommissioning should not have been a precondition to all-party talks, from Gary McMichael and Alex Maskey about why they were willing to participate in talks that had their mortal enemies at the table, and from Tony Blair, Bill Clinton, Reg Empey, and Ken Maginnis about the very last stages of the Good Friday negotiations. I am indebted to these professional eyewitnesses for their splendid work, grateful for their generosity to me, and so impressed by their professional mastery of the crucial events of their times. Plus, they are really good company at a hotel bar or a visit over breakfast. I hope to see each of them again and hear more great stories.

Niall O'Dowd's autobiography *An Irish Voice* contains many important recollections of events and great inside stories. George Mitchell's *Making Peace*, his account of his role in the peace process all the way through the Good Friday Agreement, is a splendid first-person account of how it was on the inside. I should also mention Morrison's lengthy interview conducted for the Atlantic Philanthropies Oral History Project by Amy Arlana Starecheski in 2007, as well the 1997 piece in the *Hartford Courant* by Andrew Marlatt called *Bruce's Truce*, a more compact account of Morrison's activities in the peace process. Morrison didn't keep a diary or take notes, so the accounts of those hearing from him closer in time to the events covered in this book were exceptionally valuable and were often a springboard for new recollections and insights from him.

––––––

Several good friends and relatives read the manuscript in various stages of development and contributed fine ideas and great enthusiasm that was more helpful than they know. Phil Allen and Walter Wagoner were the best enthusiasts for this project an author could hope for, from the beginning and throughout. My mother-in-law, Nancy Hodermarsky—poet, English teacher, and lawyer—was a wonderful reader and suggester of never-ending enthusiasm. She also agreed to ask our friend Roger Kuhn if he'd help me connect with David Kuhn, the agent I hoped would like the book I was starting. My brother Tony Rhodin, a great writer and editor; my soon-to-be son-in-law, Brian Spring; and my friends Steve Futterman, also a great writer, Ben Pesner, and Deirdre Rosenberg were helpful and encouraging readers, as was Tim McMillin, who got this whole thing started by calling me to account for what I hadn't written in the forty-five-year interval between our contacts.

My friend David Richards was a great fan of this project, and when he and Carol learned that there was a publishing deal at last, they gave my wife, Maria, and me champagne in the orchard in Stonington, Maine. It grieves me that *Peacerunner* wasn't in its final form before David died of ALS in 2015, but I'm grateful that I got to read him excerpts that covered the whole story pretty thoroughly during his last summer.

———

It was pure pleasure working with BenBella editors Oriana Leckert, Leah Wilson, and Vy Tran. Eric Wechter, whom I never met, was a fine copyeditor. Friends and relatives from the worlds of writing and editing, generous and enormously helpful in the never-ending quest for the right shape of things—and for just the right word in just the right way—were Sarah Flynn, Tony Rhodin, Joe Haberstroh, Liz Moore, Kent Jones, Terry Hawkins, Ben Pesner, and Steve Futterman.

I couldn't be happier with the look of this book outside and in. I loved working in a real partnership on design issues with Sarah Dombrowsky and Jessika Rieck at BenBella. I was able to hold up my end with the help of my friends and relatives from the worlds of art and design: Phil Allen, Cat Hnatov, Tom Strong, Sloan Wilson, and Lisa Hodermarsky were beyond true blue—over and over in the case of Phil and Cat.

As a publisher, BenBella has been wonderfully professional and supportive. Adrienne Lang and Alicia Kania—Glenn Yeffeth, too—always leave me feeling I'm in good hands. Friends and new acquaintances also helpful at various stages from the world of publishing were Tina Weiner, Steve Wasserman, John Ryden, and Roxanne Coady. As the writing comes to an end, I'm looking forward to working with BenBella's Jennifer Canzoneri on the marketing that they do so well.

Kent Jones, Paul Donnelly, Ruth Ben-Arzi, Josh Pesner, and Maya Hormadaly lent me invaluable and cheerful help as I went forth on the long blurb quest that has yielded such splendid results.

And I am so grateful to those accomplished men and women who were willing to publicly endorse this fledgling effort by an unknown author.

————

And now to family. My father died long before this project was ever imagined. He was a fine writer and I am grateful for that influence. He loved Ireland and maybe that added fuel to the fire. My mother lived with me in the last years of her life but died before I had a good first draft. She wasn't communicating so well at that time, but her concentration as I read her the first chapter of the book was extraordinary; when I finished she exclaimed, "That must have been frightening, having that gun aimed at his knee!" She didn't miss a thing and I'm sorry I didn't get to read the entire book to her.

My many siblings—our father had children in four different marriages—were inexhaustible in their enthusiasm, good wishes, and willingness to lend support of all kinds, as was my daughter-in-law, Nikki Rhodeen. So was my lifelong friend and long-ago blood brother, Phillip Morrow. And my cousins, nieces, and nephews, especially Ric Carey and Bill Gans. And so was Kassie Rhodeen.

Those to whom *Peacerunner* is dedicated—my wife, my sons and daughters, and my wife's sons—are the ones who lived with the book and its author, some all the time, others now and then. Each and every one of them was a wonderful source of enthusiasm, support, and understanding, with an abiding willingness to listen to an awful lot about this book on many occasions over a long time—everything from readings at the table to struggles with word choices.

Everybody has some good luck: I've learned that the trick is to know when you've been lucky. One of the glories of my life is that when I met Maria Hodermarska at that July Fourth party on Deer Isle off the coast of Maine, I knew I had been lucky and acted fast. Her help and support have been everything a lucky author could ever wish for. Plus, she insisted that I go see Northern Ireland for myself and bought me a ticket. My love and gratitude are boundless.

NEW HAVEN, CONNECTICUT
OCTOBER 2015

ABOUT THE AUTHOR

P enn Rhodeen has been a practicing lawyer in New Haven, Connecticut, since 1971, after graduating with honors from the University of Wisconsin Law School. He was a staff lawyer at the New Haven Legal Assistance Association for seven years and a member of the criminal law unit for about half of that time. His private practice has focused primarily on matters involving children and on medical malpractice cases. He served as department counsel for the New Haven Police Department and is a lecturer at the Yale Child Study Center. Prior to becoming a lawyer, he worked as a newspaper reporter and a school teacher. Since high school he has been involved in political campaigns ranging from local to presidential. He heard Martin Luther King speak of his dream during the March on Washington, watched the Kennedy funeral procession from the North Lawn of the White House, and went to Woodstock.

Penn lives in New Haven and in Brooklyn, New York. He has five adult children and is married to Maria Hodermarska, who teaches drama therapy at NYU. They get to spend part of each summer on Deer Isle, off the coast of Maine.

Peacerunner is his first book. He is already mapping out the next one.